Adobe AIR *in Action*

Tanvi,

Do lots and lots
more programming!.
and have fun with it!

Kathryn

Adobe AIR
in Action

JOSEPH LOTT
KATHRYN ROTONDO
SAMUEL AHN
ASHLEY ATKINS

MANNING

Greenwich
(74° w. long.)

For online information and ordering of this and other Manning books, please visit
www.manning.com. The publisher offers discounts on this book when ordered in quantity.
For more information, please contact:

> Special Sales Department
> Manning Publications Co.
> Sound View Court 3B   fax: (609) 877-8256
> Greenwich, CT 06830   email: orders@manning.com

⊗ Recognizing the importance of preserving what has been written, it is Manning's policy to have
the books we publish printed on acid-free paper, and we exert our best efforts to that end.
Recognizing also our responsibility to conserve the resources of our planet, Manning books are
printed on paper that is at least 15% recycled and processed without elemental chlorine.

Manning Publications Co.
Sound View Court 3B
Greenwich, CT 06830

Development editor: Nermina Miller
Copyeditor: Benjamin Berg
Typesetter: Dottie Marsico
Cover designer: Leslie Haimes

ISBN 1-933988-48-7

Printed in the United States of America

1 2 3 4 5 6 7 8 9 10 – MAL – 14 13 12 11 10 09 08

contents

preface

My friend Paul Newman (yes, that's really his name, and no, not *that* Paul Newman) called me a year ago to ask if I'd like to help write a book about Apollo, which was the codename for Adobe AIR at that time. I was already overworked, but I hesitantly agreed. Although I'd known of Apollo in a general way prior to that, it was only at that point that I started to seriously take a look at the technology. Paul later had to bow out of the project due to other demands on his time, but I continued to look at Apollo and prepare to write this book.

Previously, I'd held a few prejudices in regard to Apollo. I've worked with Flash and Flex for a decade, and the idea of using Flash or Flex to build desktop applications was hardly a new one. I'd been building executables from Flash for nearly as long as I'd worked with it. I've used programs such as FlashJester, Northcode SWF Studio, and Multidmedia Zinc with varying degrees of success to enable enhanced features for desktop applications built using Flash, and I'd previously seen Apollo as merely another alternative to these programs. Frankly, I felt a bit of resentment that Adobe, a huge corporation, would try to swoop in and crush these existing companies with a competing product. However, after working with Apollo, I saw that it was really quite different from these other products.

Soon after, Adobe changed the name from Apollo to Adobe AIR. AIR allows developers to use existing Flash and Flex skills to build desktop applications. In that regard, it's similar to the other products I previously mentioned. However, AIR doesn't create system-specific executables. Instead, AIR applications require the AIR runtime. In this regard, AIR has less in common with programs such as Zinc, and more in common with runtime environments such as Java or .NET. This understanding changed how I looked at AIR.

Nearly a year on and the manuscript is written, edited, and ready to go to print. During that time, the authors have learned a lot about AIR, and we've endeavored to share that with you in the pages of this book. We sincerely hope you find this book valuable and that we can provide you with useful understanding of how to work with AIR.

JOEY LOTT

acknowledgments

The authors of this book would like to thank all of the people who have contributed to the printed version you're reading. This includes a long list of people at Manning who helped shape the book. Michael Stephens had the initial vision to see the potential for an Adobe AIR title, and for that we thank him. Nermina Miller was the development editor for this book; without her, the book schedule and process would surely have deteriorated entirely. It's thanks to Nermina that you have a complete and coherent manuscript to read! We'd also like to thank Benjamin Berg for copyediting the manuscript when it was final.

We'd like to thank Karen Tegtmeyer for coordinating the reviews of the manuscript, which helped us to improve the content and writing in response to the comments of early access readers as well as of peer reviewers. Their feedback, as we continued to write and revise, was invaluable. Special thanks to our peer reviewers, Bernard Farrell, Ryan Stewart, Dusty Jewett, Christopher Haupt, Tim O'Hare, Robi Sen, Mike Clymer, Sean Moore, Clint Tredway, Jeremy Anderson, Patrick Peak, Oliver Goldman, Jack D. Herrington, Nathan Levesque, Bruno Lowagie, Daniel Todd, and Brendan Murray.

Robert Glover was the technical editor for this book, which means he went through every chapter and every line of code to ensure its technical accuracy. As you can imagine, this is a very important role, and we offer our sincere thanks to Robert for his fine work.

Thanks are also due to the following production staff who contributed to the book in various ways such as book design, cover design, typesetting, and proofreading:

Dottie Marsico, Tiffany Taylor, Anna Welles, Leslie Haimes, Gabriel Dobrescu, Ron Tomich, and Mary Piergies.

We'd also like to thank the AIR team at Adobe for building a great product, for providing excellent documentation, and for making themselves available to address our queries. Special thanks to Oliver Goldman, who not only reviewed several chapters in detail, but also took time to personally respond to emails regarding technical details of AIR and digital signing.

Without you, our readers, colleagues, and peers, there would be no need or demand for this book—so we'd like to thank you too for your interest and enthusiasm.

about this book

This is a book about Adobe AIR for Flash and Flex developers. Although it's entirely possible to create AIR applications using HTML and JavaScript, this book focuses exclusively on using Flash and Flex to build AIR applications. The AIR APIs are remarkably similar in ActionScript and JavaScript. However, we found that trying to address all the JavaScript nuances at the same time as the Flash and Flex nuances would have resulted in an unfocused book. We opted instead to hone in on just Flash and Flex.

It's possible that some readers will still feel that we've tried to cover too much territory by including both Flash and Flex coverage in one book. That is a fair critique. By including both, we necessarily had to compromise at certain points, opting to show code examples more suitable for Flash at some times and code examples more suitable for Flex at other times. Although this can be seen as a weakness, we also see it as a strength. We think this provides a greater context for understanding AIR, and it allows you to make better decisions about how best to solve a problem when building AIR applications. Ultimately, you'll make up your own mind about whether our approach works well or not, but we certainly encourage you to view the book from our perspective.

Audience

It's no surprise that this book is intended for Flash and Flex developers who want to use their existing skills to build AIR applications. There are tens, if not hundreds, of books in the market that provide detailed introductions to Flash, ActionScript, and

Flex development. We don't attempt to provide any such introductory material in this volume. Therefore, if you aren't already familiar with Flash, Flex, or common ActionScript APIs, you'll probably struggle with this book. We'd encourage you to first learn the basics of Flash and Flex before attempting to build AIR applications. Everything in this book builds upon what we assume is a preexisting foundation in Flash and/or Flex.

Organization

This book is remarkably straightforward. It's a relatively thin volume of only eight chapters. Therefore, we didn't think it necessary to break the book into parts thematically. Chapter 1 provides an introduction to what AIR is, as well as the necessary basics for getting started. Chapter 8 ties everything together by covering how to actually build, deploy, and update AIR applications. Each of the remaining six chapters focuses on one logical grouping of AIR APIs. For example, chapter 2 covers local file system access such as reading and writing files.

Code conventions

This book is rife with code, ranging from short snippets to full applications. You'll find that all code is shown in `monospaced font` to help it stand out from the rest of the text. Additionally, many of the longer blocks of code are presented in the form of numbered code listings with headers. These code listings are always referenced in the surrounding text, and are frequently annotated.

Code downloads

Almost all of the code listings in this book are available for download from the book's web site at www.manning.com/AdobeAIRinAction.

Author Online

The purchase of *Adobe AIR in Action* includes free access to a private forum run by Manning Publications where you can make comments about the book, ask technical questions, and receive help from the authors and other users. You can access and subscribe to the forum at www.manning.com/AdobeAIRinAction. This page provides information on how to get on the forum once you are registered, what kind of help is available, and the rules of conduct in the forum.

Manning's commitment to our readers is to provide a venue where a meaningful dialogue among individual readers and between readers and authors can take place. It's not a commitment to any specific amount of participation on the part of the authors, whose contribution to the book's forum remains voluntary (and unpaid). We suggest you try asking the authors some challenging questions, lest their interest stray!

The Author Online forum and the archives of previous discussions will be accessible from the publisher's web site as long as the book is in print.

About the authors

JOEY LOTT has extensive professional experience using Adobe technologies like Flex, Flash, and ActionScript. He is the author, or coauthor, of *ActionScript Cookbook, Programming Flash Communication Server, The Flash 8 Cookbook,* and several other related books. With Sam Ahn, he is a partner and founder of The Morphic Group.

KATHRYN ROTONDO is a software developer at Schematic. She received a graduate certificate in software engineering from the Harvard Extension School and a certificate in Flash from the Rhode Island School of Design.

SAM AHN has architected and built RIAs over the past several years for clients including Pfizer, Wyeth, MINIUSA, and Puma. Along with Joey Lott, he is a partner and founder of The Morphic Group, an interactive development company focusing on Flash/Flex application development.

ASHLEY ATKINS is a senior software developer at Six Red Marbles, and has over six years of experience developing in ActionScript. His range of work extends from creating simple educational interactions to architecting and developing applications in Flex and AIR.

About the title

By combining introductions, overviews, and how-to examples, the *In Action* books are designed to facilitate learning and remembering. According to research in cognitive science, the things people remember are things they discover during self-motivated exploration.

Although no one at Manning is a cognitive scientist, we are convinced that for learning to become permanent it must pass through stages of exploration, play, and, interestingly, retelling of what is being learned. People understand and remember new things, which is to say they master them, only after actively exploring them. Humans learn in action. An essential part of an *In Action* guide is that it is example-driven. It encourages the reader to try things out, to play with new code, and to explore new ideas.

There is another, more mundane, reason for the title of this book: our readers are busy. They use books to do a job or to solve a problem. They need books that allow them to jump in and jump out easily and learn just what they want just when they want it. They need books that aid them *in action*. The books in this series are designed for such readers.

About the cover illustration

The figure on the cover of *Adobe AIR in Action* is a "Backwoods Legislator, a Deputy from the Provinces." The illustration is taken from an early 19th century travel book, *L'Encyclopedie des Voyages,* published in France. Travel for pleasure was a relatively new phenomenon at the time and travel guides such as this one were popular, introducing both the tourist and the armchair traveler to the inhabitants of other regions of

France, to its soldiers, civil servants, and aristocracy—as well as to people from foreign lands.

The diversity of the drawings in the *Encyclopedie des Voyages* speaks vividly of the uniqueness and individuality of the world's towns and provinces just 200 years ago. This was a time when the dress codes of two regions separated by a few dozen miles identified people uniquely as belonging to one or the other. The travel guide brings to life a sense of isolation and distance of that period and of every other historic period except our own hyperkinetic present.

Dress codes have changed since then and the diversity by region, so rich at the time, has faded away. It is now often hard to tell the inhabitant of one continent from another. Perhaps, trying to view it optimistically, we have traded a cultural and visual diversity for a more varied personal life. Or a more varied and interesting intellectual and technical life.

We at Manning celebrate the inventiveness, the initiative, and the fun of the computer business with book covers based on the rich diversity of regional life two centuries ago brought back to life by the pictures from this travel guide.

Introducing Adobe AIR

1

This chapter covers

- Learning about the elements of Adobe AIR
- Understanding AIR application descriptors
- Creating new AIR projects
- Compiling AIR applications

Whether you're using HTML, Flash, Flex, or any of the other myriad technologies, there's one common thread among them: all these applications are built using technologies that are designed for the Web. That's fantastic if your goal is to build a web application, but it's a real bummer if you want to build a desktop application. Adobe integrated runtime (AIR) solves this problem for you. Using Adobe AIR, you can leverage your existing web application skills with Flash and Flex (and HTML and JavaScript) to create desktop applications. This is an exciting prospect.

Every flight starts with a preparation for takeoff. Your journey through Adobe AIR is no different. We'll start you off with a review of AIR and then delve into how you can use Flex and Flash to build AIR applications. Specifically, we'll look at necessary introductory concepts for creating a solid foundation with AIR, such as these:

- The different parts of Adobe AIR—including the runtime environment, installers, and AIR applications—and the relationships among all these parts.
- Application security and authenticity issues, including digital signing. You'll learn what digital signing is, different types of digital signing, and why and when to choose which.
- Basic steps for creating AIR applications using Flex Builder, Flash CS3, or the Flex 3 SDK.

Without any further ado, let's go ahead and jump to understanding what this whole AIR thing is about.

1.1   Anatomy of Adobe AIR

Adobe AIR allows web application developers to use their existing skill sets to build desktop applications. You can use your HTML, JavaScript, Flash, and Flex skills to create applications that can run on desktop systems with runtime environment without the need to compile them for running natively on specific operating systems.

In this section, we'll define runtime environment and talk about why you might want to build desktop applications. On top of that, we'll tell you why you'd want to use your existing skills to do that.

1.1.1   Developing for a runtime environment

If you use a Windows computer, you've undoubtedly run many .exe files. An .exe file is a compiled application that's capable of issuing commands directly to the system on which it's running. That means that an .exe file (or the equivalent) has the advantage of being relatively self-contained. However, there's a setback as well, because this approach requires that you compile the application to a platform-specific format. That means that you must create a Windows-only or an OS X–only version of an application using this approach. The steps for the traditional approach to building applications are as follows:

1 Write the code in a preferred language.
2 Compile the code to a format that can be run natively on a specific operating system.
3 Run the compiled application.

A more flexible way is to use a runtime environment rather than targeting a specific operating system. This runtime environment approach is used by many popular application platforms, including Java and .NET, and it's the approach used by Adobe AIR as well. When using a runtime environment, the application creation process is as follows:

1 Write the code in a preferred language.
2 Compile the code to an intermediate format.
3 Run the compiled intermediate format in a runtime environment.

Runtime environments give developers the freedom to write code once and run it from any computer regardless of the operating system, as long as the runtime environment is installed. A runtime environment is itself a library that runs natively on an operating system. The runtime environment is responsible for acting as a proxy for the programs that it runs. Because the runtime environment provides this level of abstraction between the programs that it runs and the system on which it's running, it's theoretically possible to create runtime environments on many different types of computer systems that can all run the exact same application files without any differences among the platforms.

What does all this have to do with Adobe AIR? As we mentioned earlier, AIR is a runtime environment. When you create an AIR application, you compile it and then package it to an intermediate format called an .air file. An .air file and its contents won't install or run on a computer unless the user has previously installed the AIR runtime environment. If the AIR runtime is installed, the .air file enables running the application on both a Windows machine and an OS X machine. That is a huge boon to you as an application developer.

Web applications have advantages over traditional desktop applications, to be certain. So why would you even want to create desktop applications in the first place? Presumably, if you're reading this book, you already have a few reasons, but it's worth discussing some of the important motivations.

1.1.2 *Why build desktop applications?*

A web-based email client allows you to read your email from any computer connected to the internet. This illustrates one of the primary advantages of web applications, which is that they aren't restricted to one machine. Consider that web applications

- Allow you to easily deploy updates and new versions of your software.
- Generally provide a level of security for users because they're subject to the security limitations of the browser and player (Flash Player, for example) used.
- Allow you to distribute computing by running some behaviors on the client machine and some behaviors on the server.

However, web applications aren't without disadvantages. The two really big ones are that they

- Don't have access to operating system–level features and functionality like desktop applications do.
- Require that the computer be connected to the internet to work. This is disadvantageous if you want to use the application when you're not online, such as when you're on an airplane or in the park.

AIR applications bring together the best of both web applications and desktop applications. Because AIR applications are based on web application technologies, you (as the developer) have extraordinarily easy ways to access web resources and integrate existing web applications in part or whole. However, because AIR applications run on the desktop, they have access to system resources normally not accessible to web applications. That means you can do things such as drag-and-drop between AIR applications and the file system, access local databases, and, perhaps most importantly, create effective sometimes-connected user experiences that allow the user to work with the application both online and off. AIR applications also have features that allow you to enable seamless updates, so that users can always be assured they're working with the latest version of the application (a topic discussed in chapter 8).

The other question we'd like to answer is why you'd want to create desktop applications using web technologies. The most obvious reason for this is that you have existing skills with web technologies that you'd like to leverage in different ways. If you can create desktop applications using skills you already have, that's an advantage over having to learn a new language and new technologies just to create an application for the desktop. But there are more reasons why you might want to create desktop applications using web technologies. Web technologies are uniquely suited for creating applications that connect to and use web resources. In a world that increasingly demands online and networked experiences in desktop software, it's advantageous to create those desktop applications using languages that are designed specifically for online experiences. Yet another reason to use HTML, JavaScript, Flash, and Flex to create desktop applications is that these languages tend to be vastly superior to other, more traditional desktop application languages when you want to create compelling, engaging, and interesting user interfaces.

1.1.3   *Exploring AIR possibilities*

AIR represents all sorts of exciting possibilities for web application developers to create desktop applications. But what exactly can you expect? Here we'll give you the basics of what you can do with AIR. Throughout the book, you'll learn all the details.

Everything you can do when building web applications you can do when building AIR applications. That's because AIR includes the WebKit engine (the same engine used in the Safari browser) and Flash Player. Therefore, you can still use the same core ActionScript and JavaScript features that you would use when deploying to the Web. In addition, you have access to an AIR-specific API. This includes the features outlined in table 1.1.

Table 1.1   Understanding AIR-specific API feature categories

Feature	Description
File system integration	AIR enables reading, writing, deleting, and all basic file system operations.
Drag-and-drop	Users can drag-and-drop files and directories from the operating system to the AIR application.
Copy-and-paste	Users can use operating system–level copy-and-paste features to copy data between AIR applications and the operating system.
Local databases	AIR applications have the ability to create and connect to local databases.

Table 1.1 Understanding AIR-specific API feature categories *(continued)*

Feature	Description
Audio	HTML-based AIR applications can utilize audio easily.
Embedded HTML	Flex- and Flash-based AIR applications can render HTML and JavaScript within display objects.

You have access to all these behaviors in AIR applications. In order to use them, however, AIR applications need to run in a runtime environment that supports them. In the next section, we'll look at how to run AIR applications.

1.2 *Running AIR applications*

When you create an AIR application, you use the AIR toolset, whether Flex Builder 3, the AIR SDK, or whatever other AIR tool is appropriate, and package up the files for your application in an .air file. You'll learn more about the specifics of how to package the files in an .air file later in this chapter, in section 1.4. For now, you only need to know that an .air file is the one file you distribute when you want someone to install your application. You'll likely hear the term *installer file* used interchangeably with the term *.air file*.

Once you have an .air file, you can distribute that file to anyone who already has the AIR environment installed on her computer, and she will be able to easily install it. If that user already has AIR installed, all she'll have to do to install your application is double-click on the .air file you've sent her or that she's downloaded.

On the other hand, if a user doesn't already have AIR installed on her computer, she'll have to install it before she can install your application. There are two ways that users can install AIR:

- *Manual install*—A manual install is achieved by downloading the platform-specific (Windows or OS X) installer from Adobe and running that.
- *Seamless install*—The seamless install feature requires that you publish an .swf file (called a badge) to the Web, and users must click on that .swf in order to install your application. If they already have AIR installed, they'll immediately be able to install your application. On the other hand, if they don't have AIR installed, they'll be able to install it first.

NOTE *Cross-reference*—You can learn more about distributing AIR applications, including the seamless install feature, in chapter 8.

However a user goes about installing an AIR application, whether by double-clicking an .air file you've emailed him or by clicking on an install badge in a web page, once he's started the installation, he'll be prompted through several standard install wizard steps. Figure 1.1 shows an example of what the first step looks like.

After an AIR application is installed on a user's system, he can run it at any time just as he can any other application: by double-clicking on a desktop icon or selecting the application from a menu.

Figure 1.1   Installing an AIR application brings up the AIR install screen with information about the publisher and application.

Now that you know how to run AIR applications, we're ready to look at how you can begin building applications.

1.3   *AIR application security and authenticity*

Our introduction to Adobe AIR would be remiss without a discussion of two related issues: security and authenticity. These two issues are important for you to consider as an application developer, because any breaches or violations would reflect poorly on you. Therefore it's important that you have a good understanding of what AIR does and doesn't enforce in the way of application security and authenticity, and what steps you need to take to protect users of your applications.

1.3.1   *Understanding AIR application security*

One of Adobe's flagship products is Flash Player, a product that has been so successful, in part, because of the extraordinary measures taken by Adobe (and previously Macromedia) to ensure that Flash developers can't intentionally or unintentionally harm a user's computer system. Flash Player has a lot of security features to protect users. This gives them peace of mind when viewing Flash content on the Web. Users know that the Flash content won't cause problems for their computer systems.

AIR applications are desktop applications, and as such it's essential that they have greater access to the user's computer system than web-based Flash applications. Even though AIR applications can run Flash content, that Flash content has more opportunities to harm the user's system than web-based Flash content. It's a trade-off: a vastly greater feature set, but increased risk as well.

AIR applications still run through a mediator—the runtime environment itself. Therefore, Adobe has a great deal of control over what an AIR application can and can't do. However, while many risks are mitigated by the runtime environment, AIR still allows applications many more privileges than their web counterparts might have.

The first thing that you as an AIR developer must be aware of is that it's incumbent on you to treat the users of your application with great respect by taking security matters seriously. For example, it's important that you closely manage all parameters to code that might run in your application. Don't allow users to arbitrarily enter values, and don't use dynamic, network-originating values as parameters for code that can do things such as access the file system. You can read a more detailed security whitepaper from Adobe at download.macromedia.com/pub/labs/air/air_security.pdf.

1.3.2 *Ensuring application authenticity*

In order to give users of your application peace of mind, Adobe requires that all AIR applications be digitally signed. (Note that signing is only necessary to build the installer, and you can still build and test your AIR applications without a signature of any sort.) A digital signature helps to potentially verify two things to the user: authenticity and integrity. A digital signature is meant to mimic a traditional handwritten signature of ink on paper in that it verifies the publisher of the application (authenticity) and that it hasn't been altered since it was published (integrity).

You can prove that AIR enforces integrity if you'd like with a simple test. What you can do is verify that the AIR runtime will refuse to install a modified .air file. All that you need is an .air file and zip utility. The .air format is an archive format that any zip utility can read. Do the following:

1 Run the .air file to verify that the AIR runtime will initially prompt you to run the installation. You don't need to actually click the Install button on the wizard once it appears. All you need to verify is that the AIR runtime will give you the option to install.

2 Click the Cancel button to exit the install wizard.

3 Use a zip utility to add a file to the archive. Any file will work. For the purposes of this exercise, you can create a new blank text file and add it to the archive. If you're on a Windows computer, the simplest way to achieve this is to change the .air file extension to .zip, drag the text file into the .zip archive, and then change the file extension back to .air.

4 Run the .air file. This time you'll receive an error message saying that the .air file is damaged and can't be installed.

For AIR applications, digital signatures appear together with digital certificates. There are two basic types of certificates: self-signed certificates and those issued by certification authorities. There are advantages and disadvantages to each.

Self-signed certificates are advantageous in that they're the easiest to procure. The Flash CS3 AIR update and the Flex 3 SDK (and subsequently Flex Builder 3) provide mechanisms for creating self-signed certificates for your AIR applications. You can read the details of how to create these types of certificates later in this chapter.

Self-signed certificates provide a level of security to users, in that they verify the integrity of the application. However, they do little or nothing to assure users about the authenticity of the publisher. It's a bit like acting as a notary for your own documents. As a result, Adobe displays the publisher identity as unknown in the installation wizard for self-signed certificates. This is clearly disadvantageous, because it doesn't create a feeling of security for users, and they're less likely to opt to install an application from an unknown publisher than they would be if the identity of the publisher could be verified.

A certification authority is an organization that issues certificates and acts as a third party to verify your identity. A certification authority issues certificates only after it has verified your identity, usually by requesting documents such as government-issued IDs. The advantage of a certificate issued by a certification authority is that it gives more assurance of your actual identity than a self-signed certificate. When a certificate is issued by a certification authority, Adobe displays the identity listed in the certificate as the publisher identity in the installation wizard. On the other hand, some of the disadvantages might be obvious: obtaining a certificate from a certification authority is more difficult and requires more time than a self-signed certificate. Also, be aware that most certification authorities charge a fee for certificates. (At the time of this writing, the largest issuer charges $299 USD for a code-signing certificate for an AIR application.)

Two of the best-known certificate issuers are VeriSign (www.verisign.com) and thawte (www.thawte.com), though technically thawte is now owned by VeriSign. If you want to provide the highest level of certification for your AIR application, you'll need to purchase a certificate from one of these issuers. You'll need what's called a *code-signing certificate*. You can find more information about purchasing a certificate from the web sites of the issuers.

NOTE There are certification authorities other than VeriSign and thawte, and there are even noncommercial certification authorities such as CAcert.org that grant code-signing certificates. You should do your research before purchasing or otherwise acquiring a certificate (CAcert.org still requires that you do a fair amount of legwork to obtain a code-signing certificate) to make sure that the certificate will be trusted on the majority of computers. If the certificate isn't trusted, the publisher of the AIR application will still show up as unknown. Speak to someone at the organization that grants the certificates and ask questions if you're in doubt.

When getting started building AIR applications, you'll probably be hesitant to invest in purchasing a certificate just to put together a few examples and send the installers to your friends. Again, remember that the certificate is only necessary when you want to create the installer. You can always test AIR applications without a certificate.

However, when you're ready to create an .air file for your application, you'll need to give careful consideration to how you want to digitally sign the application. You can only associate a certificate with an application once. That means you can't use a self-signed certificate initially and change to a certificate from a certification author-ity later on. If you re-sign with a different certificate, users of earlier versions of the application won't be able to upgrade.

1.4   *Building AIR applications*

Now that you've learned about what AIR is, the various pieces of AIR, how to run AIR applications, and AIR security and authenticity issues, you're almost ready to learn how to build an AIR application. In fact, in the next few sections of this chapter, that's exactly what you'll learn. You'll even have a chance to build a few simple AIR applica-tions to wet your feet in preparation for the rest of the book. Before rushing into uncharted territory, we'll take a few moments to map the terrain so that you can get a sense of what's in store.

There are many ways you can create AIR applications. Table 1.2 provides a quick guide to the toolsets.

We've included HTML/JavaScript toolsets for creating AIR applications in table 1.2 in order to provide a complete picture of AIR toolsets. However, in this book we focus exclusively on using Flex and Flash to create AIR applications. In sections 1.6, 1.7, and 1.8, you can read more about how to build AIR applications using Flex Builder, Flash, and the Flex SDK, respectively.

NOTE   All the AIR toolsets are available from the Adobe web site (www.adobe.com/go/air).

Table 1.2   The Adobe AIR toolsets

Name	AIR application source type	Free	Description
Flex Builder 3	Flex/ActionScript	No	Commercial tool for building Flex-based web and AIR applications. The tool itself is built on Eclipse. Flex Builder 3 automates and simpli-fies building AIR applications.
Flex 3 SDK	Flex/ActionScript	Yes	The Flex 3 SDK is the free SDK that includes all the compilers and tools that power Flex Builder 3, but doesn't include the automation and graphic user interface of Flex Builder.
Flash CS3 with AIR update	Flash/ActionScript	No	Flash CS3 doesn't ship with AIR capabilities. However, with the free update for Flash CS3, you can build AIR applications directly from Flash authoring.
Dreamweaver CS3 with AIR extension	HTML/JavaScript	No	A commercial HTML editor with an AIR exten-sion that automates much of the building of an AIR application.
AIR SDK	HTML/JavaScript	Yes	The free SDK that includes all the necessary command-line tools for building HTML/JavaScript-based AIR applications.

In section 1.5, you'll first learn about application descriptors. An understanding of application descriptors is essential to a full picture of how to create AIR applications. Even though many of the AIR tools (Flex Builder and Flash CS3 with the AIR update) will automatically create the descriptor file for a project, it's still a good idea to familiarize yourself with what a descriptor looks like and what data it contains. You're encouraged to read all of section 1.5 before jumping to 1.6, 1.7, or 1.8. However, if you're anxious to start building an application and you do jump ahead, we won't tell on you.

We'll next continue with application descriptors. Once you've read the next section, go ahead and jump to the section that discusses the toolset you'll be using to build AIR applications.

1.5   *Introducing AIR application descriptors*

Regardless of which toolset you use to create an AIR application, you'll need to create an application descriptor. Some of the toolsets will autogenerate a basic application descriptor for you, but it's important to understand what an application descriptor is and how you can use it.

AIR application descriptors are XML files, which describe AIR applications. When you package an AIR application to distribute, you'll need the descriptor to provide some information that the AIR toolset can use to correctly assemble the application for distribution. This information includes, but is not limited to, a unique identifier for the application, a version, and information that gets displayed during install.

To give you an idea of what a basic descriptor file looks like, here's an example. Note that all descriptor files should begin with an XML declaration (`<?xml version="1.0" encoding="utf-8" ?>`).

```
<?xml version="1.0" encoding="utf-8" ?>
<application xmlns="http://ns.adobe.com/air/application/1.0.M4">

    <id>com.manning.books.airinaction.Example</id>

    <version>1.0</version>

    <filename>ExampleApplication</filename>

    <initialWindow>
       <content>ExampleMain.swf</content>
    </initialWindow>

</application>
```

If you want to jump ahead to get started building AIR applications, you can do so. The preceding example descriptor file provides what you'll need in a descriptor file for a basic AIR application. If you do choose to jump ahead, you'll want to revisit this section later to learn more about descriptors in greater depth.

In the following sections, you'll learn the details of the elements of a descriptor file.

1.5.1   *The application element*

The application element is always required, and it's the root element of the descriptor file. The application element requires an xmlns attribute. The xmlns attribute defines the namespace for the descriptor. The namespace value is always predefined, and, for every application you build for a version of AIR, the namespace value will always be the same. For AIR 1.0, the value should be http://ns.adobe.com/air/ application/1.0.M4. The namespace indicates which version of AIR is required to run the application. Each new version of AIR will use a new namespace.

Additionally, you can specify a minimumPatchLevel attribute. Use the minimum-PatchLevel attribute if you want to require the user to have an AIR (the runtime) patch applied in order to run the application. This attribute is optional. You should only use it if you know that your application requires a particular patch to run correctly.

Because the application element is the root element of the descriptor file, all the elements that follow are nested as children within the application element. The next four elements (id, version, filename, and initialWindow) are the only required elements.

1.5.2   *The id element*

The id element should be a unique identifier for the application. Only one application with a given identifier can be installed on a system at a time. The application identifier is a combination of the publisher identifier (gathered from the certificate used to publish the .air file) and the value of the id element. That means that, strictly speaking, the value of the id element needs to be unique only within the scope of all applications for the publisher. Although it's not absolutely necessary, we find it convenient to create a globally unique id by using the existing convention of reverse domain names. The example used in the earlier simple descriptor example is com.manning.books.air.Example. This uses com.manning, which is the reverse of manning.com, to ensure global uniqueness. The id value must be between 1 and 212 characters, and only alphanumeric characters plus dots and hyphens are permitted.

1.5.3   *The version element*

The version element is a way you can specify the version number of your application. AIR won't interpret the version value in any way, but you can use the value to programmatically test that the user has the latest version of your application. Because AIR doesn't try to interpret the version value in a particular way, you can use any string value. Versions are typically numeric, such as 1.0 or 2.5.1, or they might include alphabetical characters denoting revisions, such as 4.0a.

1.5.4   *The filename element*

The filename element is how you specify the name of the .air file. The filename value is also used for the application name (in the installer) if no name element is specified.

A `filename` value must include only valid filename characters, and it shouldn't include a file extension. Furthermore, a `filename` value may not end with a dot.

1.5.5 *The initialWindow element*

The `initialWindow` element provides information about the actual content (either an .swf or .html file) that should be used to build the application. The `initialWindow` element is a container for additional elements. The only required child element is the `content` element, which specifies the .swf (or .html) file to use. The following illustrates a basic `initialWindow` element:

```
<initialWindow>
    <content>ExampleMain.swf</content>
</initialWindow>
```

Additionally, the `initialWindow` element allows for the following optional elements:

- `systemChrome`—This value indicates whether the window containing the application should use the chrome (frame and title bar) provided by the operating system. If you set this to `standard`, the standard operating system chrome is applied. If you set the attribute to `none`, the system chrome is not applied. For Flex-based AIR applications, the Flex components apply a custom chrome when the `systemChrome` attribute is set to `none`.
- `transparent`—This Boolean value indicates whether the application window should support alpha blending with the rest of the desktop (meaning you can see through the application). If you set this to `true`, you can create alpha effects, but be aware that setting `transparent` to `true` requires more system resources and can cause the application to render more slowly. Additionally, you must set `systemChrome` to `none` if you want to set `transparent` to `true`.
- `visible`—This Boolean value indicates whether or not the application window should be visible initially. Typically you set this attribute to `false` only when you want to hide the window until you can programmatically position and resize it from within the application code itself. You can then use code within the application to toggle the visibility of the application window.
- `height`—The height of the application window in pixels.
- `width`—The width of the application window in pixels.
- `minimizable`, `maximizable`, `resizable`—These elements allow you to specify Boolean values indicating whether or not the application is minimizable, maximizable, or resizable when running. The default values are all `true`.
- x, y—The x and y coordinates of the initial placement of the application.
- `minSize`, `maxSize`—The minimum and maximum sizes of the window when resized.

The following is an example of an `initialWindow` element with most of these values set:

```
<initialWindow>
    <content>ExampleMain.swf</content>
    <systemChrome>none</systemChrome>
    <transparent>true</transparent>
    <height>500</height>
    <width>500</width>
    <minimizable>false</minimizable>
    <maximizable>false</maximizable>
    <resizable>false</resizable>
    <x>0</x>
    <y>0</y>
</initialWindow>
```

As you saw earlier in this section, the only required value for initialWindow is the content value. If you omit the others, the default values are used.

1.5.6 *The name element*

The name element is a sibling of initialWindow, meaning it should be nested as a child of the application tag. The name value is used to determine the default installation directory. The name value is also displayed in the title bar when the application is running. Additionally, the name appears on the first screen of the installer, as seen in figure 1.1. If no name value is specified, the value of filename is used instead.

1.5.7 *The title and description elements*

The title and description elements are all siblings of initialWindow, meaning they should be nested as children of the application tag. Each of these elements is optional, and these elements control what values are displayed in the installer.

The title element determines what appears in the headers in the installer, as shown in figures 1.1 and 1.2. The description is shown on the second screen of the installer, as shown in figure 1.2.

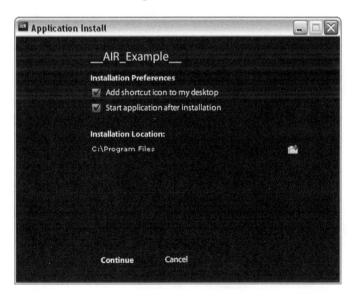

Figure 1.2   The second screen of the installer for an AIR application, allowing the user to specify installation settings

The title and description are only used during the installation, and they never appear while the application itself is running.

1.5.8 *The installFolder element*

The `installFolder` element is an optional element that determines the name of the subdirectory used as the default install directory. The user always has the option to change the install directory during installation of the AIR application. However, using the `installFolder` element, you can specify a subdirectory that should appear as part of the default value as seen in figure 1.2.

NOTE You cannot change the main directory of the default installation directory used by AIR applications.

On Windows, that directory is always the Program Files directory of the primary disk; on OS X, that directory is always /Applications. However, using the `installFolder` element, you can change the subdirectory. For example, if you use an `installFolder` value of `ExampleInc/ExampleApplication`, on a Windows machine the application will be installed in `Program Files\ExampleInc\ExampleApplication`, and on an OS X machine the application will be installed to /Applications/ExampleInc/ExampleApplication.app.

The `installFolder` element should be a child of the `application` tag. It's an optional element. If you omit the element, the application is installed in a subdirectory based on the `name` or `filename` element value.

1.5.9 *The programMenuFolder element*

The `programMenuFolder` element is used only by Windows and ignored by other operating systems. This element allows you to specify a folder name from which the shortcut should be accessible within the All Programs menu in the Start menu.

1.5.10 *The icon element*

By default, AIR applications use the standard AIR icons for use on the desktop, in the Start menu, on the task bar, and so forth. However, you can customize the icons by using the `icon` element in the application descriptor XML file. The `icon` element should have four child elements called `image16x16`, `image32x32`, `image48x48`, and `image128x128`. Each of these child elements should have values of paths to image files. The images specified must be in .png format, and are compiled into the AIR application. The following is an example of a value `icon` element:

```
<icon>
    <image16x16>icon16.png</image16x16>
    <image32x32>icon32.png</image32x32>
    <image48x48>icon48.png</image48x48>
    <image128x128>icon128.png</image128x128>
</icon>
```

Remember to save .png files with transparency if you're using nonrectangular shapes.

1.5.11 *The customUpdateUI element*

If present in the descriptor file, `customUpdateUI` configures the application to be capable of handling updating itself programmatically. (See chapter 8 for more information on how to do this.) The value should be `true` if you want the application to programmatically update itself. Otherwise, if `false` or omitted, the standard AIR update dialogs are used.

1.5.12 *The fileTypes element*

The `fileTypes` element is an optional element that allows you to register file types with the application. When you register a file type with an application, double-clicking on a file of that type will automatically launch the AIR application if it isn't yet running. An event is then sent to the running AIR application, providing information about the file that was just double-clicked, and the AIR application can determine how to handle the event. You can learn more about handling this event in chapter 3.

If you use a `fileTypes` element, it should contain one or more `fileType` elements nested within it. Each `fileType` element should contain `name` and `extension` elements. Optionally, a `fileType` element can also contain `description` and `contentType` elements. The `contentType` value can be a MIME type. (You can read more about MIME types at en.wikipedia.org/wiki/MIME.) The following is an example of a `fileTypes` element that registers just one file type:

```
<fileTypes>
   <fileType>
      <name>com.manning.ExampleApplicationSavedSettings</name>
      <extension>exp</extension>
      <description>A saved settings file for Example Application
➥</description>
      <contentType>text/xml</contentType>
   </fileType>
</fileTypes>
```

You'll notice that the `name` element uses reverse domain names in this example in order to ensure global uniqueness for this arbitrary name. You'll also notice that the extension value doesn't include the preceding dot.

1.6 *Building AIR applications using Flex Builder*

Flex Builder 3 has built-in AIR application development features, and it includes all necessary AIR tools. If you intend to build Flex-based AIR applications, Flex Builder 3 is an excellent choice.

In the next few sections, you'll learn the basics of working with Flex Builder 3 to create AIR applications. Specifically, you'll learn about configuring a new AIR project, creating the MXML and other file(s) for the project, testing/debugging the project, and creating an installer for the application.

1.6.1   Configuring a new AIR project

When you want to start a new AIR application using Flex Builder 3, the first thing you should do is create an AIR project. You can create an AIR project by selecting File > New > Flex Project from the Flex Builder 3 menus. Doing so will open the New Flex Project dialog, as shown in figure 1.3.

Figure 1.3   The first step of the New Adobe AIR Project dialog in Flex Builder 3 asks for a project name and an application type. Set the application type to desktop application for AIR applications.

The wizard is the same you'd use to create a new Flex project in Flex Builder 3, and you can consult your Flex Builder reference if you're uncertain about any of the details of those steps. The only thing you'll do differently is select Desktop application as the application type from the first screen of the wizard. In figure 1.3, this option is selected.

Once you've created the project, the Flex Builder automatically creates two files in the src directory: a main MXML file and a default application descriptor XML file. Figure 1.4 shows the Navigator pane from Flex Builder listing these files for a new project.

Figure 1.4   The Navigator pane listing the files for a new AIR project lists the source files for the AIR application as well as the descriptor XML file.

Of course, you can edit the descriptor file in the way that you learned earlier in this chapter. You can also edit the main MXML file and add additional files as described in the next section.

1.6.2   Creating AIR project files

Once you've created an AIR Project in Flex Builder, you'll undoubtedly want to edit the main MXML file, and you'll likely want to add additional MXML, ActionScript, CSS, and other types of files. For the most part, you can use the same file types, MXML and ActionScript code, CSS, and structure you'd use for a standard Flex application. The primary difference between an AIR application and a Flex application is that the root tag for an AIR application is `WindowedApplication` rather than `Application`. The following is the default code placed in the main MXML file when Flex Builder creates a new AIR project:

```
<?xml version="1.0" encoding="utf-8"?>
<mx:WindowedApplication xmlns:mx="http://www.adobe.com/2006/mxml"
  ➥layout="absolute">

</mx:WindowedApplication>
```

The `WindowedApplication` component is a subclass of the `Application` component, meaning that all the functionality of a standard Flex application is included in an AIR application. However, `WindowedApplication` instances have additional functionality for AIR-specific behaviors. For example, `WindowedApplication` has a `title` property you can use to change the title shown in the title bar and taskbar for the application. You can learn more about using `WindowedApplication` in chapter 2.

1.6.3   Testing the AIR application

As you're building an AIR application, you'll undoubtedly want to test along the way. As with any other type of application, it's important to be able to see the progress incrementally as you build an AIR application. Flex Builder 3 makes it easy to test your application along the way. You

Figure 1.5   The Flex Builder toolbar has options to run, debug, and profile an AIR application.

can do this by way of the run, debug, or profile options in Flex Builder. You can access these options from the Run menu or by clicking on the corresponding buttons in the Flex Builder toolbar, as shown in figure 1.5.

The run option allows you to test the AIR application in the standard fashion without any additional information, as is provided by the debug and profile options. When you select the debug option, Flex Builder launches your AIR application in debug mode, which outputs `trace()` statements to the console and allows you to step through the code using breakpoints. The profile option launches the application in a profile mode that allows you to see memory usage details in real time as the application runs.

When you test an AIR application using the run, debug, or profile options, you don't need to digitally sign the application. That's only necessary when you publish the .air file.

1.6.4   *Creating an installer*

When you're ready to distribute your AIR application, you'll need to create an .air file to use as an installer. As you'll recall from the discussion earlier in this chapter, an .air file packages up all the necessary files for your AIR application and allows a user to double-click on the one file in order to install the application.

Creating an .air file in Flex Builder 3 is simple. All you need to do is the following:

1   Select the File > Export > Release Build or Project > Export Release Build option from the Flex Builder menus. This will open the Export Release Build dialog, as shown in figure 1.6. There are two steps to the wizard: selecting the project, application, and .air file to export; and digitally signing the application.

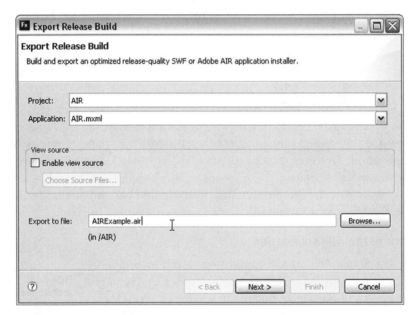

Figure 1.6   The first screen of the Export Release Build dialog prompts you to select the type of export.

2   Fill out the form, selecting the project and application you want to export and then specifying an .air file to save, as shown in the figure. Once you've completed this first step, click Next.

3   Digitally sign the application, as shown in figure 1.7. This is done by applying a certificate. (You read about certificates in the application authenticity section, earlier in this chapter.) If you have a certificate that you obtained from a certification authority or you have a preexisting self-signed certificate, you can simply browse to select that certificate. In that case, you can jump ahead to step 5. Otherwise, create a new self-signed certificate by clicking the Create button and continue to step 4.

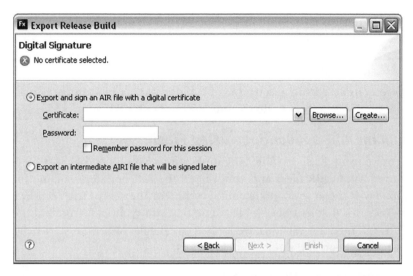

Figure 1.7 The second screen of the Export Release Build dialog asks you to digitally sign the application.

4 Click the Create button to see the Create Self-Signed Digital Certificate dialog, as shown in figure 1.8. Fill out the form and click OK. If you've filled out valid information, you'll get a message telling you the certificate was created successfully, and then you'll be returned to the Export Release Build dialog.

5 Browse to the keystore for the certificate you'd like to apply. (If you just created a self-signed certificate, you should select the .pfx file that was created in the previous step.) Once you've selected a keystore, whether a preexisting one or a

Figure 1.8 Creating a self-signed certificate

new one, specify the password for that certificate in the Password field of the Export Release Build dialog.

6   Click the Finish button, and Flex Builder will create the .air file. That is all that's necessary to create the distributable installer for an AIR application using Flex Builder 3.

We've completed our discussion of building AIR applications using Flex Builder 3. Next we'll look at how to do the same using Flash CS3.

1.7   *Building AIR applications using Flash*

If you're using Flash to build AIR applications, you'll need Flash CS3 (earlier editions cannot output AIR files) and you'll need the AIR update, available for free from the Adobe web site at www.adobe.com/go/air. For the rest of this section (and the rest of the book for that matter), we'll assume that you've already installed the free update.

In the next few sections, we look at the details of how to start new AIR projects in Flash, test them, and then create installers.

1.7.1   *Configuring a new AIR project*

In order to create a new AIR project using Flash, you must use the Flash welcome screen. If you've disabled the display of the welcome screen, you need to select Edit > Preferences from the Flash CS3 menus, and in the General category you need to select Welcome Screen from the On launch menu option.

From the welcome screen, you'll see an option called Flash File (Adobe AIR) under the Create New column, as shown in figure 1.9. (If you don't see that option, chances are you either haven't yet installed the AIR update as described in the previous section, or the update didn't install correctly.) Click on the Flash File (Adobe AIR) option in the Create New column to start a new AIR project. It's just that simple.

In order to test the application, Flash and AIR need to locate the descriptor file, so it's important that you save the .fla file before you try to test it. Until you save the .fla file, Flash won't be able to automatically create the accompanying descriptor file. Once you've saved the file, a descriptor XML file is saved in the same directory. In section 1.7.4, you'll see how to modify that descriptor file. However, the default values in the file will be enough to allow you to test the application.

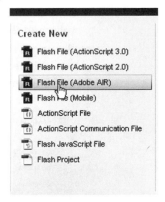

Figure 1.9   Select the Flash File (Adobe AIR) option from the welcome screen to start a new AIR project.

1.7.2 Creating AIR project files

Flash-based AIR projects are similar to standard Flash projects intended for the Web in terms of necessary project files. You don't have to do anything differently in terms of the types of files you create or where you create them. You can still add assets to the library, work with timelines, use the drawing tools, and write ActionScript code in the same way you would for any Flash project. It's worth noting that AIR requires Action-Script 3 for any ActionScript that you might write.

NOTE   AIR applications are capable of playing back Flash content that uses ActionScript 1.0 and ActionScript 2.0 if you load that content into the AIR application at runtime. However, if you want to create a new AIR application, you must use ActionScript 3 for the ActionScript contained within the main .swf file of that application.

1.7.3 Testing the AIR application

Testing an AIR application is also exactly the same as testing a standard Flash application. You can simply select Control > Test Movie or use the keyboard shortcut that you're used to. The only difference is that an AIR application will run in an AIR window rather than in the standard Flash player.

If you'd like to debug an AIR application, you'll find that too is exactly the same process you'd use to debug a standard Flash application. You can simply select Debug > Debug Movie or use the keyboard shortcut, and you can debug the AIR application just the same as a regular Flash application.

1.7.4 Creating an installer

Flash has a few commands that allow you to create the .air file for your application without having to run anything from a command line or edit anything by hand. In the Commands menu are two options for AIR: AIR—Application & Installer Settings and AIR—Create AIR File.

The AIR—Application & Installer Settings command allows you to modify the descriptor file from a form rather than having to edit the XML by hand. Figure 1.10 shows what the form looks like by default for a project called Example.fla. You can see that the file name, name, and ID are all based on the name of the .fla file. Furthermore, the default ID uses `com.adobe.example` to precede the name based on the .fla file name. The version defaults to 1.0. You can modify any and all of the elements of the form, and those changes will be reflected in the descriptor file.

The form requires that you specify a digital signature. As you read in section 1.3.2, all AIR applications must have a digital signature. When building an AIR application using Flash, you specify the certificate using this option in the form. Complete the following steps to apply a certificate:

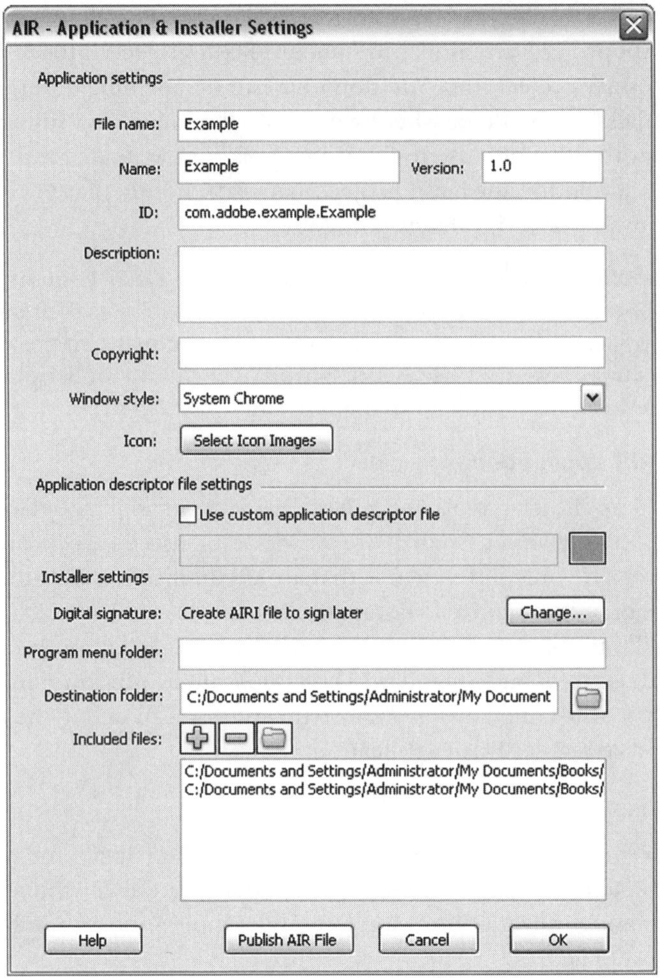

Figure 1.10   Editing the Application & Installer Settings for an AIR application in Flash

1   Click the Change button to open the Digital Signature dialog, as shown in figure 1.11.

2   Select the Sign the AIR file with a digital certificate option, then select a certificate to use. If you're using a certificate from a certification authority or an existing self-signed certificate you already created, you can immediately browse to find that certificate file. In that case, you can skip ahead to step 6. Otherwise, if you need to create a new self-signed certificate, continue to step 3.

3   Click the Create button to open the Create Self-Signed Digital Certificate dialog, as shown in figure 1.12.

Figure 1.11   Use the Digital Signature dialog to specify the certificate for the AIR application.

4 Fill in all the fields in the Digital Signature dialog, including the password, which you need to remember because you'll use it to apply the certificate to your AIR application.

5 Save the certificate somewhere on your system by clicking OK. This returns you to the previous dialog.

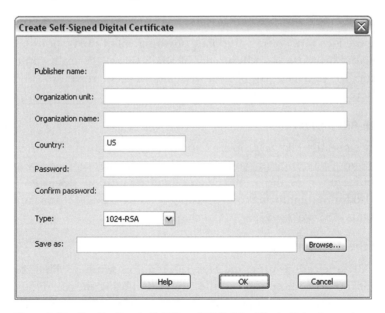

Figure 1.12   Use the Create Self-Signed Digital Certificate dialog to create a new certificate for your AIR application.

6   Browse to find and select the keystore for the certificate that you'd like to apply.

7   Specify the password for the certificate, once you've selected a certificate to use. Click OK in the Digital Signature dialog and you'll be returned to the AIR—Application & Installer Settings dialog.

8   Create an .air file from this dialog by clicking the Publish AIR File button. If you aren't ready to publish the .air file yet, simply click OK.

You can return to the AIR—Application & Installer Settings dialog to publish the .air file at any time. Or, having already applied the certificate, you can now simply select the Commands > AIR—Create AIR File menu option in Flash.

We've now completed our discussion of building AIR applications using Flash CS3. We'll next look at how to do the same using the Flex SDK.

1.8   Building AIR applications using the Flex SDK

If you build Flex applications using the Flex SDK, you can use the Flex 3 SDK to create AIR applications as well. The Flex 3 SDK is free, yet isn't limited in terms of the features you can build into your AIR applications. You can build the same AIR applications using the Flex 3 SDK as you could using Flex Builder 3. The differences are that the Flex SDK doesn't automate tasks (such as creating main application MXML files and default application descriptor XML files), and the Flex SDK doesn't include the same graphical user interface as Flex Builder. With that said, the next few sections describe how to create AIR applications using the Flex SDK.

1.8.1   Configuring a new AIR project

Because the Flex SDK doesn't automate anything, all of the responsibility for creating the directory structure and AIR project files falls to you. Typically you'll want to create a directory for your new AIR project. You should then create two subdirectories, one for the source files and one for the output (the .swf files and the .air file).

1.8.2   Creating AIR project files

Again, because the Flex SDK doesn't automatically create project files, that responsibility is yours. At a minimum, you always need to have at least one MXML file with `WindowedApplication` as the root tag and one application descriptor XML file. See section 1.6 for more information regarding `WindowedApplication`. You can also learn more about `WindowedApplication` in chapter 2.

1.8.3   Testing the AIR application

Testing AIR applications using the Flex SDK requires two steps. First you must compile the application. Then you can run the application using the AIR debug launcher.

You can compile an AIR application using the `mxmlc` compiler, much as you'd compile a standard Flex application. The difference is that you must add a compiler option when calling `mxmlc` in order to use the AIR-specific configuration file included in the SDK. The compiler option is +configname=air. Here's an example of the command that compiles Main.mxml as an AIR application:

```
mxmlc +configname=air Main.mxml
```

To simplify things, the Flex SDK also includes amxmlc, which merely calls mxmlc with the +configname=air option. Therefore, you can omit that compiler option if you call amxmlc instead of mxmlc:

```
amxmlc Main.mxml
```

When you compile the application, you have an .swf file. You then need to launch that .swf using the AIR debug launcher, an executable called adl. The adl executable is in the same directory as the compilers, meaning that if the compilers are in your system path then so too is adl. When you want to launch the application, you merely specify the descriptor file that you want to test as an argument to adl:

```
adl Main-descriptor.xml
```

Running the preceding command will launch the application described by Main.descriptor.xml.

1.8.4 Creating an installer

In order to create an AIR installer (an .air file) using the Flex SDK, you need to use the AIR packaging tool, an executable called adt. You'll find adt in the same directory as the Flex compilers and the AIR debug launcher.

CREATING A CERTIFICATE

The first thing you need to do is make sure you have a certificate for your AIR application. If you have a certificate from a certification authority or if you've already created a self-signed certificate, you're done with that step. However, if you need to create a self-signed certificate, you must use adt to accomplish that. Use the following syntax to create a self-signed certificate:

```
adt -certificate -cn name key_type pfx_file password
```

Substitute the name, key_type, pfx_file, and password for values you want to use in the certificate. The name is the common name of the certificate, and it can be an arbitrary string that you choose. The key_type value should be either 1024-RSA or 2048-RSA. The pfx_file value should be the path to which you want to save the certificate (which should use a .pfx file extension). The password is a value that you'll need to remember when you apply the certificate to an AIR application. The following example creates a new certificate:

```
adt -certificate -cn ExampleCertificate 1024-RSA certificate.pfx 2u4fs8
```

PACKAGING THE AIR APPLICATION

Once you have a certificate, you can create an AIR installer using the following syntax:

```
adt -package SIGNING_OPTIONS air_file descriptor FILES_TO_INCLUDE
```

In this syntax, the *air_file* and *descriptor* should be replaced by the actual values you want to use. The *air_file* value should be the path to which you want to save the .air file. The descriptor should be the path to the descriptor .xml file for the application. The *SIGNING_OPTIONS* and *FILES_TO_INCLUDE* are complex groups of arguments that we'll discuss in more detail next.

The *SIGNING_OPTIONS* group of arguments varies significantly depending on how you digitally sign the application. There are a variety of signing option arguments that are all described in detail in Adobe AIR documentation. Rather than repeat that here, we'll instead talk about the most common signing scenarios and how you would go about achieving each using adt.

- Signing with a PKCS#12 certificate (includes using a .pfx file such as you might generate when creating a self-signed certificate). If you have a PKCS#12 certificate, you need only specify two arguments: storetype and keystore. The storetype argument value should be pkcs12, and the keystore value should be the path to the keystore file that holds the certificate (for example, the .pfx file). The following is an example of a call to adt that uses a self-signed certificate stored in a .pfx file:

```
adt –package –storetype pkcs12 –keystore selfsigned.pfx installer.air
➥descriptor.xml Main.swf
```

- Signing with a Java keystore. A Java keystore is of type JKS. The simplest way to work with a Java keystore is if the keystore contains only one certificate and you want to use the default Java keystore. In such a case, you need only to specify the storetype argument using the value jks, as in the following example:

```
adt –package –storetype jks installer.air descriptor.xml Main.swf
```

If the keystore has more than one certificate, you can specify the alias of the certificate to use with the alias argument, as shown in the following example:

```
adt –package –alias sampleCertificateAlias –storetype jks installer.air
➥descriptor.xml Main.swf
```

And if you want to use a nondefault keystore, you can do that simply by specifying a value for the keystore argument, as in the following example:

```
adt –package –storetype jks –keystore codeSigningCertificates.keystore
➥installer.air descriptor.xml Main.swf
```

When using adt, you can also use other keystore types, including PKCS#11 (hardware-based keystore), KeychainStore (OS X Keychain store), and Windows-MY and Windows-ROOT.

Certificates issued by certification authorities expire after a certain amount of time (normally one year). When you create an AIR application using a certificate, normally that application installer will expire when the certificate expires. (Note that installed instances of the application will be unaffected, but the installer itself will no longer work after the certificate expires.) However, if you can verify that the certificate is valid at the time you sign the application (when you create the .air file), the AIR application installer will not expire. In order to verify that the certificate is valid, you must point adt to a time stamp server (must be RFC3161-compliant) using the tsa argument. The following is an example that time stamps the application using http://ns.szik-szi.hu:8080/tsa as the time stamp server:

```
adt -package -storetype pkcs12 -keystore certificates.pfx -tsa
➥http://ns.szikszi.hu:8080/tsa installer.air descriptor.xml Main.swf
```

The *FILES_TO_INCLUDE* group allows you to specify all the files to include in the .air file. Remember that the .air format is an archive format. Any files you specify in the *FILES_TO_INCLUDE* group will be packaged in the archive, and when the application is installed, those files will be extracted.

You must always include the initial window content file (.swf) in your installer. The following is an example that creates an .air file including just the initial window content (which we assume in this example is Main.swf):

```
adt -package -storetype pkcs12 -keystore selfsigned.pfx installer.air
➥descriptor.xml Main.swf
```

However, you may want to include additional files in your installer—images, audio files, video files, text files, and so on. You can simply list these files along with the initial window content:

```
adt -package -storetype pkcs12 -keystore selfsigned.pfx installer.air
➥descriptor.xml Main.swf image.jpg video.flv data.txt
```

You can also specify entire directories. The following example simply includes all the files in the current directory:

```
adt -package -storetype pkcs12 -keystore selfsigned.pfx installer.air
➥descriptor.xml
```

You can also use the -C flag to change directories, and everything that follows will be assumed to be relative to that directory. For example, the following includes Main.swf from the current directory and several images from the assets/images subdirectory:

```
adt -package -storetype pkcs12 -keystore selfsigned.pfx installer.air
➥descriptor.xml Main.swf assets/images/image1.jpg
➥assets/images/image2.jpg assets/images/image3.jpg
➥assets/images/image4.jpg
```

When you package the application this way, the directory structure is preserved exactly as you've specified in the list of files. That means that, once the application is installed on a system, the image files will all exist in an assets/images directory relative to Main.swf. If that's how your application expects the files to be organized, there's no problem. However, if you want to add files from disparate locations, but you want them organized differently in the .air file (and subsequently when the application is installed), you'll want to use the -C flag. Consider the following command:

```
adt -package -storetype pkcs12 -keystore selfsigned.pfx installer.air
➥descriptor.xml Main.swf -C assets/images image1.jpg image2.jpg
➥image3.jpg image4.jpg
```

In this example, the images are added to the archive in the same directory as Main.swf. That means that, if Main.swf looks for image files in the same directory as itself, this way of adding files to the archive is correct.

NOTE   There are additional options when running `adt` to create an installer. We've outlined the necessary steps for creating an .air file. Consult the official documentation for more information.

Once you run `adt`, you'll have an .air file you can then distribute.

We've now completed the discussion of building AIR applications using the Flex SDK. Next we'll look at a few quick-start applications. These quick-start applications will allow you to use what you've learned so far to build simple, working AIR applications.

1.9   *Quick-start AIR application for Flex*

In this section, you'll build a quick-start application using Flex Builder. This application is simple, and not very practical. The point in this exercise is not to build a really useful application, but to walk through the steps of building an AIR application using Flex. This application simply uses a tree component to list the contents of a user's file system, and allows the user to select image files and display them.

The first step is to create a new Flex project, selecting Desktop application as the Application type. Give this project a name of QuickStartAIRApplication. When you create this project, Flex Builder automatically creates QuickStartAIRApplication.mxml and the descriptor file.

Add the code shown in listing 1.1 to QuickStartAIRApplication.mxml.

Listing 1.1   The MXML document for the Flex quick-start

```xml
<?xml version="1.0" encoding="utf-8"?>
<mx:WindowedApplication xmlns:mx="http://www.adobe.com/2006/mxml">

    <mx:Script>
        <![CDATA[

            private function changeHandler(event:Event):void {
                var ext:String = event.target.selectedItem.extension;

                if(ext == "jpg" || ext == "png") {
                    image.source = event.target.selectedItem.nativePath;
                }
            }

        ]]>
    </mx:Script>
    <mx:HBox width="100%" height="100%">
        <mx:FileSystemTree width="50%" height="100%"
            change="changeHandler(event);"/>
        <mx:Image id="image" width="50%" height="100%"
            scaleContent="true" />
    </mx:HBox>
</mx:WindowedApplication>
```

Annotations:
- Root element is WindowedApplication **①**
- Get file extension **②**
- Is jpg or png
- **③** Display file system contents

The overall structure of this code should be familiar to you if you have worked with Flex before. However, there are a few items that are probably new to you since they are AIR-specific. Don't worry. We'll explain many of these items in more detail throughout this book. For now, we'll just briefly explain each of these unfamiliar pieces. The first thing you'll note is that the root tag is `WindowedApplication` ❶ instead of `Application`. This is a requirement for Flex-based AIR applications. You'll notice that we are using an AIR-specific component called `FileSystemTree` ❸ that displays the contents of the local file system. When the user clicks on an item in that component, the `selectedItem` of that component is a `File` object with an extension property ❷ that will return the file extension of the selected file.

That's all there is to the quick-start application for Flex. Go ahead and run the application. Figure 1.13 shows the result.

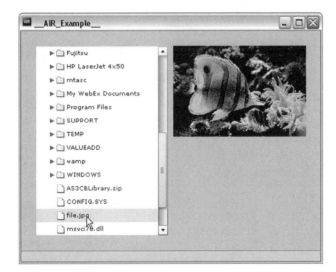

Figure 1.13 The quick-start application allows you to browse your local disk for image files.

As you can see, Flex Builder makes building AIR applications simple. Although this example probably has a few things that are new to you, much of it is likely to be familiar. You already know MXML and most of the components used in this example. Those components that are new to you follow the same rules as other components you already know.

Next we'll build a different quick-start application using Flash CS3.

1.10 Quick-start AIR application for Flash

In this section, you'll build a quick-start application using Flash. This application is necessarily simple and fairly impractical. However, the point is not to make a really useful AIR application, but to walk through the steps and build a real, working AIR application using Flash. The application uses a List component to display a file system directory listing from the user's desktop. Double-clicking on directories allows the user to navigate through the file system.

The first thing you want to do is create a new AIR project in Flash by selecting Flash File (Adobe AIR) from the Create New column of the welcome screen. This opens a new Flash file configured for AIR. You should save this file right away as QuickStart-AIRApplication.fla.

Now that you've saved the file, create a new directory structure of com/manning/books/airinaction in the same directory to which you've just saved the Flash file. Then create a new ActionScript file from Flash, and save the file in com/manning/books/airinaction using the filename QuickStartAIRApplication.as.

In the Flash file, open the components panel and the library panel. Then drag the List component from the components panel into the library panel. This adds the List component to the project, and we can now create instances of it using ActionScript code. Go ahead and save the Flash file again.

Return to the ActionScript file, and add the code in listing 1.2. We'll use this class file as the document class for the Flash application.

Listing 1.2 The code for the document class for the Flash quick-start

```
package com.manning.books.airinaction {

    import flash.display.MovieClip;
    import flash.events.MouseEvent;
    import fl.controls.List;
    import fl.data.DataProvider;          ❶ Import the
    import flash.filesystem.File;            File class

    public class QuickStartAIRApplication extends MovieClip {

        private var _list:List;

        public function QuickStartAIRApplication() {

            _list = new List();
            addChild(_list);

            _list.addEventListener(MouseEvent.DOUBLE_CLICK, clickHandler);

            _list.width = 550;
            _list.height = 400;                   ❷ Display file/
                                                     directory name
            _list.labelField = "name";

                                                          ❸ Display
            _list.dataProvider = new                         user's
                                                             desktop
    DataProvider(File.desktopDirectory.getDirectoryListing());
        }
                                                      ❹ Test if
        private function clickHandler(event:MouseEvent):void {   selected is
            if(_list.selectedItem.isDirectory) {                 directory
                _list.dataProvider = new
    DataProvider(_list.selectedItem.getDirectoryListing());
            }
        }                                         Update list ❺
    }

}
```

Some of this code may be new to you since it is AIR-specific. We'll talk about all of the new code in more detail throughout the book. For now we'll quickly mention what some of the unfamiliar code is and what it does. First you might notice that we import the File class ❶. This class is used to represent files and directories on the local file system, and you'll learn about this in chapter 2. Next you can see that we're setting the list to display the value of the name property of each element in its data provider ❷. The data provider we'll use is a collection of File objects, and File objects have name properties. The File.desktopDirectory property is a reference to the user's desktop directory, and calling getDirectoryListing() returns an array of the contents of that directory. We then place that in a DataProvider instance ❸ and assign that to the list. The isDirectory property will tell us if a File object represents a directory or not. We only want to change the directory listing if the user double-clicks on a directory. Therefore we test for the value of isDirectory ❹. And only in that case do we update the list's data provider, this time calling getDirectoryListing() ❺ for the selected item.

Save the ActionScript file and return to the Flash file. In the Flash file, set the document class to com.manning.books.airinaction.QuickStartAIRApplication. Save the Flash file, and test the application. You should see a listing of the desktop files and directories. If you double-click on an item in the list, it'll refresh with the contents of the new directory if you've double-clicked on a directory. Figure 1.14 shows what the application looks like.

You've just written your first (albeit simple) AIR application using Flash. This is just the starting point. Now that you've seen how easy it can be to create an AIR application, you'll build more complex, sophisticated, and useful applications throughout the book.

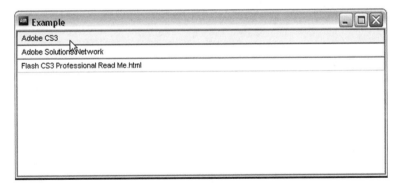

Figure 1.14 The Flash quick-start application allows the user to navigate the local file system.

1.11 *Summary*

In this chapter, we started from the premise that you didn't know anything about AIR, and by the end of the chapter you built your first AIR application(s) using Flex and/or Flash. You learned what AIR is, what toolsets to use, and how to get started. Specifically, you learned that you can use Flex Builder 3, Flex 3 SDK, or Flash CS3 with the AIR extension to build Flash- or Flex-based AIR applications. Because AIR applications run within a runtime environment other than Flash Player, they have access to a greater scope of behavior than their web-based counterparts. AIR applications can access the local file system; create, read, and write to local databases; and participate in system-level drag-and-drop features among other behaviors that are above and beyond what is available to a web-based Flash or Flex application.

In the next chapter you'll learn more about how to use and manage windows, menus, and AIR applications. You'll learn how to create new windows, and the different types of windows you can create. You'll also learn how to correctly work with windows once they've been opened. Then you'll learn about the different ways to work with menus in AIR applications, from application and window menus to context menus.

Applications, windows, and menus

2

This chapter covers
- Creating new windows
- Managing open windows
- Running application-level commands
- Adding system-level menus to applications

In chapter 1, you learned a lot of important foundational information that should provide context for understanding what AIR is and the general process for building and deploying AIR applications. Now we're ready to start looking at all the details of building AIR applications. We're going to start from the ground up. In this chapter, we'll cover the following:

- *Applications*—The first thing we'll look at is how to work with and understand an AIR application programmatically. In the first part of this chapter, you'll learn everything you need to know about programmatically creating AIR applications.

- *Windows*—Every AIR application, no matter how simple or complex, contains at least one window, and many contain more than one. Windows are fundamental but fairly sophisticated at the same time. AIR gives you a lot of control over windows, including window style, shape, behavior, and more. All of these topics are covered in this chapter.
- *Menus*—AIR applications allow you to create a variety of different types of menus, including system menus, application menus, context menus, and icon menus. We'll talk about all these types of menus in this chapter.

With what you learn in this chapter, you'll have much of what you need for the building of all sorts of amazing AIR applications. In fact, in this chapter you'll start work on an application that uses the YouTube service to allow users to search YouTube videos and play them back from their desktop. You'll be able to accomplish all of that using just the material contained in this chapter.

We'll get started by looking at the metaphor that AIR uses for how it organizes an application into an application object and window objects. In the next section, you'll learn how to work an application object and window objects using both Flash and Flex.

2.1   *Understanding applications and windows*

This may seem a bit obvious, but it's worth explicitly pointing out that AIR applications have programmatic constructs for everything that's represented visually or behaviorally in the application. That's true not only of things that you may already be familiar with from your Flex and Flash background (movie clips, buttons, UI controls) but also of AIR-specific concepts such as the concept of an application or a window.

There is just one application, and there are one or more windows per AIR application. Therefore, it follows that every Flex- or Flash-based AIR application has just one ActionScript object representing that application, providing access to application-level information (application descriptor data, user idle timeout) and behavior (registering file types, exiting the application). Furthermore, every window in a Flex- or Flash-based AIR application has an ActionScript object representing it. Those window objects provide access to window-specific information (width, height, screen placement) and behavior (minimize, restore).

Every AIR application has at least one window, the window specified as the content for the initial window in the application descriptor file. That window is what you see when you run the application. However, you can open more than one window per application. You can think of each window as a new thread of the application, much like new instances of a web browser, or you can think of each window as a panel in your application. Both are perfectly valid ways to think of and treat windows in an AIR application. It depends on what you're trying to accomplish. What's true in any case is that there's just one application ActionScript object per AIR application, and that object keeps track of all the windows in your application (see figure 2.1). We'll look at how to work with these objects and their relationships to one another throughout this chapter.

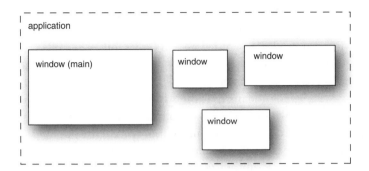

Figure 2.1 Every AIR application has one application object and one or more window objects.

The ways in which you work with an application and its windows are related, yet slightly different, depending on whether you're using Flash or Flex to build your AIR application. However, the core ActionScript principles used when building Flash-based AIR applications are fundamental both for Flash-based and Flex-based AIR application development. Therefore, if you use Flex to build AIR applications, you'll want to learn the underlying ActionScript principles as well as the Flex-specific concepts. In the following sections, we'll talk about these foundational concepts. If you use only Flash to build AIR applications, you need only read section 2.1.2. If you use Flex, read both that section and section 2.1.3.

2.1.1 *ActionScript application and windows*

When you're working with the intrinsic AIR ActionScript API for applications and windows, you need to understand two primary classes: `flash.desktop.Native-Application` and `flash.display.NativeWindow`. If you're building Flash-based AIR applications, these are the only two application and window classes you'll need to work with.

CREATING AN APPLICATION

Every AIR application automatically has one instance of `NativeApplication`. You can't create more than one `NativeApplication` instance. In fact, you can't create a `NativeApplication` instance at all. The one instance is created for you when the application starts, and is accessible as a static property of the `NativeApplication` class as `NativeApplication.nativeApplication`. We'll see lots of ways you can use this `NativeApplication` instance later in the chapter.

CREATING WINDOWS

Every window in an AIR application is fundamentally a `NativeWindow` object. While the initial window is automatically created when the application starts, it's your responsibility as the application developer to programmatically create any additional windows your application requires. You can create new windows by constructing new `NativeWindow` objects and then opening them.

Before you can create a `NativeWindow` object, you first must create a `flash.display.NativeWindowInitOptions` object that the `NativeWindow` constructor uses to determine a handful of initial parameters such as the type of window, the chrome the window should use, and so forth. Arguably the most important properties of a `NativeWindowInitOptions` object are the `type`, `systemChrome`, and `transparent` properties. These properties have dependencies on one another as well.

The `type` property has three possible values defined by three constants of the `flash.display.NativeWindowType` class: `STANDARD`, `UTILITY`, and `LIGHTWEIGHT`. The default `type` is `standard`, which means that the window uses full system chrome and shows up as a unique system window. (It shows up in the task bar for Windows or window menu for OS X.) Standard windows are most appropriate for opening things that are conceptually new instances, such as a new photo for editing in a photo-editing program. Utility windows have a thinner version of system chrome. Unlike standard windows, utility windows don't show up in the task bar or window menu. That makes utility windows best suited for content that's conceptually linked with the main window, such as tool palettes. Lightweight windows have no system chrome. Like utility windows, they don't show up in the task bar or window menu. Because lightweight windows don't have any system chrome, you must set the `systemChrome` property to `none` as well.

The `systemChrome` property determines the chrome that appears around the window. The possible values are defined by two constants of the `flash.display.NativeWindowSystemChrome` class: `STANDARD` and `NONE`. The standard chrome uses the system chrome for the operating system. That means that AIR windows using standard chrome will look just like other native applications running on the same computer. Setting the `systemChrome` property to `none` will remove any chrome from the window. (Note that the initial window is an exception to this rule, because it uses AIR chrome if the system chrome is configured to `none` in the descriptor file.) That means that windows initialized with `systemChrome` set to `none` won't have built-in mechanisms for maximizing, minimizing, restoring, closing, resizing, or moving. If you want to enable those behaviors on such a window, it's up to you to do that programmatically. (These topics are covered later in this chapter.)

The `transparent` property is a Boolean property that indicates whether or not the window can use alpha blending to allow transparency such that other windows can be seen beneath it. The default value for this property is `false`. Setting it to `true` enables alpha blending. Be aware that enabling transparency will use more system resources than would be used with a nontransparent window. Also be aware that, if you set `transparent` to `true`, you must also set the `systemChrome` to `none`. Unlike standard windows, a transparent window allows you to create nonrectangular shapes and fading effects.

NOTE   By default, windows have a background color. Setting `transparent` to `true` will remove the background color, allowing for alpha blending. It also allows you to create irregularly shaped windows. See the section titled "Creating irregularly shaped windows" later in this chapter for more details.

You can also use the `minimizable`, `maximizable`, and `resizable` properties of a `NativeWindowInitOptions` object to specify whether or not the window will allow for minimizing, maximizing, and resizing of the window. The default value for all these properties is true.

Once you've created a NativeWindowInitOptions object, you can construct a NativeWindow object by calling the constructor and passing the NativeWindowInit-Options object to the constructor, as shown in listing 2.1.

Listing 2.1   Creating a NativeWindow object

```
package {

    import flash.display.MovieClip;
    import flash.display.NativeWindow;
    import flash.display.NativeWindowInitOptions;
    import flash.display.NativeWindowType;

    public class Example extends MovieClip {

        public function Example() {
            var options:NativeWindowInitOptions =
            ➥new NativeWindowInitOptions();          ❶ Create the
            options.type = NativeWindowType.UTILITY;      window options

            var window:NativeWindow = new NativeWindow(options);   ◁┐
                                                   Construct the
            window.width = 200;    ┌ ❸ Set the initial   new window ❷
            window.height = 200;   │    width and height

        }

    }

}
```

In this example, we first create the window options and set the type and chrome values on that options object ❶. Next we create the window itself, passing it the options ❷. We also set the initial width and height to 200-by-200 ❸. See the "Adding content to windows" section for more information on how setting the width and height works.

We've successfully created a window, set options on the window, and even set the size of the window. However, the code up to this point won't actually display the window. We'll look at how to do that next.

OPENING WINDOWS

If you were to run the code in listing 2.1, you wouldn't see a new window appear. The reason is that, although you've constructed a new window, you haven't yet told the application to open it. You can open a window by calling the activate() method. Adding one line of code (see bold text in listing 2.2) to the code from listing 2.1 will launch a new 200-by-200 utility window.

Listing 2.2   Opening the new window

```
package {

    import flash.display.MovieClip;
    import flash.display.NativeWindow;
    import flash.display.NativeWindowInitOptions;
```

```
import flash.display.NativeWindowType;

public class Example extends MovieClip {

    public function Example() {

        var options:NativeWindowInitOptions =
        ➥new NativeWindowInitOptions();
        options.type = NativeWindowType.UTILITY;

        var window:NativeWindow = new NativeWindow(options);
        window.width = 200;
        window.height = 200;

        window.activate();

    }

  }

}
```

The new window that's created in this example is 200-by-200 pixels with a white background. But it doesn't have any other content yet. Most windows have some sort of content, and it's your responsibility to add it, as you'll see in the next section.

ADDING CONTENT TO WINDOWS

When you create a new window, it doesn't have any content other than a background (and even the background is absent if you've created a transparent window). It's your responsibility to add content to the window using the window's `stage` property.

You may be surprised to learn that `NativeWindow`, despite being in the `flash.display` package, isn't actually a display object. It doesn't inherit from `DisplayObject`, the base display type in ActionScript. Instead, windows *manage* display objects. A `NativeWindow` object has a `stage` property of type `flash.display.Stage`. The stage is a reference to the display object used as the container for the contents of the window. Because a `Stage` object is a display object container, it allows you to add and remove and manage content just as with any other display object container via the `addChild()`, `removeChild()`, and related methods.

Listing 2.3 uses the code from listing 2.2 as a starting point, and then adds a text field to the window. The new code is shown in bold.

Listing 2.3   Adding content to the window

```
package {

    import flash.display.MovieClip;
    import flash.display.NativeWindow;
    import flash.display.NativeWindowInitOptions;
    import flash.display.NativeWindowType;
    import flash.text.TextField;
    import flash.text.TextFieldAutoSize;

    public class Example extends MovieClip {

        public function Example() {
```

```
var options:NativeWindowInitOptions =
➥new NativeWindowInitOptions();
options.type = NativeWindowType.UTILITY;

var window:NativeWindow = new NativeWindow(options);
window.width = 200;
window.height = 200;

var textField:TextField = new TextField();
textField.autoSize = TextFieldAutoSize.LEFT;
textField.text = "New Window Content";

window.stage.addChild(textField);

window.activate();

        }

    }

}
```

❶ Create new display object

❷ Add content to the window

We change two things in this example. First we add a text field with the text New Window Content ❶. In this example, we're using a text field, but you could also use any other type of display object. Then we add the text field to the window via its stage ❷. We use the addChild() method to add the text field to the stage, which is the standard way to add content to a display object container. Figure 2.2 shows what the result of this code looks like (on Windows).

You'll probably notice that the text appears differently than you would have expected. That's because (perhaps unexpectedly) the stage of the new window is set to scale by default. That means that when you set the width and height of the window (as we have in this example), the content scales accordingly based on a default initial size for the window. In this case, the stage scaled larger considerably, and that causes the text to be larger than you might have expected

Figure 2.2   The new window with text scales its content, causing the text to appear differently than you might expect.

Using the scaleMode property of the stage, you can adjust that setting if appropriate. In this particular example, it would be better if the content didn't scale. As such, we can set the scaleMode property to the StageScaleMode.NO_SCALE constant, and it'll no longer scale. As soon as we do that and test the application, it's apparent that the align property of the stage needs to be set as well. In this case, it's best if the stage is always aligned to the top left. Listing 2.4 shows these additions in bold.

Listing 2.4   Adjusting the scale and alignment of the contents of a new window

```
package {

    import flash.display.MovieClip;
    import flash.display.NativeWindow;
```

```
import flash.display.NativeWindowInitOptions;
import flash.display.NativeWindowType;
import flash.text.TextField;
import flash.text.TextFieldAutoSize;
import flash.display.StageScaleMode;
import flash.display.StageAlign;

public class Example extends MovieClip {

    public function Example() {

        var options:NativeWindowInitOptions =
        ➥new NativeWindowInitOptions();
        options.type = NativeWindowType.UTILITY;

        var window:NativeWindow = new NativeWindow(options);
        window.width = 200;
        window.height = 200;

        var textField:TextField = new TextField();
        textField.autoSize = TextFieldAutoSize.LEFT;
        textField.text = "New Window Content";

        window.stage.scaleMode = StageScaleMode.NO_SCALE;
        window.stage.align = StageAlign.TOP_LEFT;

        window.stage.addChild(textField);

        window.activate();

    }

  }

}
```

Figure 2.3 shows what this new window looks like.

NOTE If you test any of the preceding examples, you may discover that utility windows don't automatically close when you close the main application window. Even though the utility window isn't accessible from the task bar or window menu, it remains open until you close it. As long as the window is open, it may prevent you from testing your application again. Make sure to close the utility windows each time you close your main application window. For more information regarding how to manage utility windows, consult section 2.2.3.

Figure 2.3 By setting the stage's `scaleMode` and `align` properties, the content appears correctly in the new window.

Now that you've had a chance to see how to create and work with windows using ActionScript in a basic manner, we can look at how to create ActionScript classes for windows.

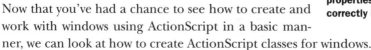

CREATING ACTIONSCRIPT CLASS–BASED WINDOWS

Thus far we've seen how to create new windows using the basic ActionScript concepts. As you create more and more sophisticated windows, it's generally advantageous to encapsulate the window code into ActionScript classes. Each window class should inherit from `NativeWindow`. The class can then contain all the code to add content, manage scale and alignment issues, and so on. Listing 2.5 shows an example of a simple window class.

Listing 2.5 Creating a basic window class

```
package {

    import flash.display.NativeWindow;
    import flash.display.NativeWindowType;
    import flash.display.NativeWindowInitOptions;

    public class ExampleWindow extends NativeWindow {

        public function ExampleWindow() {
            var options:NativeWindowInitOptions =
            ➥new NativeWindowInitOptions();

            options.type = NativeWindowType.UTILITY;

            super(options);

            width = 200;
            height = 200;

        }

    }

}
```

You can see that this window is responsible for setting its own chrome and type as well as its width and height. Note that the first thing it does is create a `NativeWindowInitOptions` object and then pass that in to the super constructor.

You can create an instance of this sort of window in much the same way you would any other `NativeWindow` instance: construct an instance and then call `activate()` to open it. Listing 2.6 shows what that code looks like.

Listing 2.6 Creating and opening an instance of ExampleWindow

```
package {

    import flash.display.MovieClip;

    public class Example extends MovieClip {

        public function Example() {
            var window:ExampleWindow = new ExampleWindow();
            window.width = 200;
            window.height = 200;
```

```
                window.activate();

            }

        }

    }
```

We have just one more basic concept to discuss before moving on to new topics. So far you've seen how to create rectangular windows. Next we'll look at how to create irregularly shaped windows.

CREATING IRREGULARLY SHAPED WINDOWS

The ability to easily create irregularly shaped windows is a nice feature of AIR applications. Creating an irregularly shaped window is the same as creating a rectangular window except that you must turn off system chrome and set the window to be transparent. Then you can add a nonrectangular background to the window using the window's `stage` property. Listing 2.7 shows an example of this by modifying the code from listing 2.5.

Listing 2.7 Creating a nonrectangular window

```
package {

    import flash.display.NativeWindow;
    import flash.display.NativeWindowSystemChrome;
    import flash.display.NativeWindowType;
    import flash.display.NativeWindowInitOptions;
    import flash.display.Sprite;
    import flash.display.Stage;
    import flash.display.StageAlign;
    import flash.display.StageScaleMode;

    public class ExampleWindow extends NativeWindow {

        private var _background:Sprite;

        public function ExampleWindow() {
            var options:NativeWindowInitOptions =            Set systemChrome ❶
            ➥new NativeWindowInitOptions();                         to none

            options.systemChrome = NativeWindowSystemChrome.NONE;  ◁
            options.type = NativeWindowType.LIGHTWEIGHT;

            options.transparent = true;   ◁   Make window
                                           ❷  transparent
            super(options);

            _background = new Sprite();          ❸  Create
            drawBackground(200, 200);               background
            stage.addChild(_background);

            width = 200;
            height = 200;

            stage.align = StageAlign.TOP_LEFT;
            stage.scaleMode = StageScaleMode.NO_SCALE;
```

```
        }

        private function drawBackground(newWidth:Number, newHeight:Number):
        ➥void {
            _background.graphics.clear();
            _background.graphics.lineStyle(0, 0, 0);
            _background.graphics.beginFill(0x0000FF, .5);
            _background.graphics.drawRoundRectComplex(0, 0, newWidth,
                                  newHeight, 20, 20, 20, 1);
            _background.graphics.beginFill(0xFFFFFF, .9);
            _background.graphics.drawRoundRectComplex(5, 5, newWidth - 10,
                                  newHeight - 10, 20, 20, 20, 1);
            _background.graphics.endFill();

        }

    }

}
```

There's a lot of code in this example, but it's not difficult to understand when we break it down. The first thing we do is make sure we set the systemChrome property of the options object to none ❶. This removes any chrome from the window, which would otherwise force a rectangular border. Next we set the window to use transparent mode ❷. This is important because normally the window has a solid rectangular background. To create a nonrectangular shape, we need to hide the background. Then we create a background display object, draw a nonrectangular shape in it, and add it to the stage ❸. In this example, we're drawing a rounded-corner rectangle that is a subtle variation on the standard, square-cornered rectangular background.

Figure 2.4 shows what the result of this example looks like.

If you create irregularly shaped windows, it's your responsibility to add the necessary user interface elements and code for the behaviors that are usually provided automatically by the system chrome: closing, minimizing, maximizing, and moving. See section 2.2 for more information on how to do this.

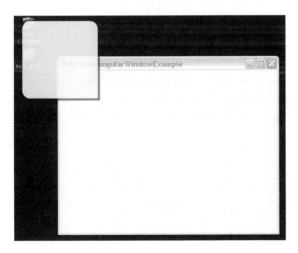

Figure 2.4 An irregularly shaped window with transparency overlaps desktop icons and the main application window.

2.1.2 *Flex application and windows*

When you create AIR applications using Flex, the workflow is a little different when it comes to creating and managing windows. But the underlying essentials are the same as those used by Flash-based AIR applications using `NativeApplication` and `NativeWindow`. The difference is that, when using Flex, there are two Flex components that simplify the process of working with an application or windows programmatically. The `WindowedApplication` component is how you work with applications, and the `Window` component is how you work with windows.

CREATING AN APPLICATION

All Flex-based AIR applications must be compiled from application MXML documents that use `WindowedApplication` as the root element. That's why, when you create a new MXML application document in an AIR project in Flex Builder, you see the following stub code:

```
<?xml version="1.0" encoding="utf-8"?>
<mx:WindowedApplication xmlns:mx="http://www.adobe.com/2006/mxml"
    layout="absolute">

</mx:WindowedApplication>
```

Because you can only have one MXML application document per Flex project, it follows that you can only have one `WindowedApplication` object per application. The `WindowedApplication` component extends the `Application` component normally used by web-based Flex applications. Therefore, the properties and methods of `Application` are accessible to `WindowedApplication` as well. However, static properties aren't inherited by subclasses. Therefore the `Application.application` property, which references the main application object, isn't inherited. If you want to reference the one `WindowedApplication` instance (outside of the MXML document itself, within which you can simply reference it using `this`), you must use `Application.application`. The `Application.application` object is typed as `Application` rather than `WindowedApplication`. Therefore you must cast the object if you intend to reference it as a `WindowedApplication`:

```
var windowedApplication:WindowedApplication =
➥Application.application as WindowedApplication;
```

`WindowedApplication` instances have a bunch of properties and methods, many of which we'll look at in more detail later in this chapter. However, for the most part, the principal property that you need to know about to access core underlying values and behaviors is the `nativeApplication` property, which is a reference to the underlying `NativeApplication` object.

CREATING WINDOWS

When creating Flex-based AIR applications, all windows should be based on the `Window` component. Although it's possible to create windows directly using `NativeWindow` (and although `NativeWindow` is still used behind the scenes), the Flex-specific `Window` component integrates well with the rest of the Flex framework and simplifies aspects of creating windows, as you'll see in the "Adding content to windows" section that follows shortly.

Creating a window using Flex is even simpler and more direct than creating a window using Flash. When working directly with `NativeWindow` objects, as you've learned, you have to first create a `NativeWindowInitOptions` object. The `Window` component in Flex hides that from you. You only need to create a new `Window` object (or an object from a subclass of `Window`), then set a few properties directly on that object if appropriate. For example, the code in listing 2.8 creates a new utility window.

Listing 2.8   Creating a new window using Flex

```
<?xml version="1.0" encoding="utf-8"?>
<mx:WindowedApplication xmlns:mx="http://www.adobe.com/2006/mxml"
  layout="absolute" creationComplete="creationCompleteHandler();">
  <mx:Script>
    <![CDATA[
      import mx.core.Window;

      private function creationCompleteHandler():void {
        var window:Window = new Window();        ◁┐ Construct new
                                                    │ window
        window.width = 200;        │ Set initial
                                   │ dimensions
        window.height = 200;       │

        window.type = NativeWindowType.UTILITY;   ◁┐ Make it a
      }                                             │ utility window

    ]]>
  </mx:Script>
</mx:WindowedApplication>
```

NOTE   Just as `WindowedApplication` objects have `nativeApplication` properties that reference the underlying `NativeApplication` object, `Window` objects have `nativeWindow` properties that reference the underlying `NativeWindow`. It's worth noting as well that `WindowedApplication` objects also have a `nativeWindow` property that references the underlying `NativeWindow` object for the main window.

You may have noticed, assuming you tested the preceding code, that no window appears when running the code. As when working with `NativeWindow` objects directly, you need to explicitly open the window once you've created it.

OPENING WINDOWS

As we just saw, you still need to programmatically open a window once you've created it. For `Window` objects, you need to call the `open()` method to open the window. Listing 2.9 modifies the code from listing 2.8 by simply adding a call to `open()` in order to open a new window.

Listing 2.9 Opening a window is as simple as calling the `open()` method

```
<?xml version="1.0" encoding="utf-8"?>
<mx:WindowedApplication xmlns:mx="http://www.adobe.com/2006/mxml"
 layout="absolute" creationComplete="creationCompleteHandler();">
   <mx:Script>
      <![CDATA[
         import mx.core.Window;

         private function creationCompleteHandler():void {
            var window:Window = new Window();

            window.width = 200;
            window.height = 200;

            window.type = NativeWindowType.UTILITY;

            window.open();
         }

      ]]>
   </mx:Script>
</mx:WindowedApplication>
```

In this example, the new window that appears is a 200-by-200 pixel window with the (Flex) default gray background and no other content. Next we'll look at how to add content to windows using Flex.

ADDING CONTENT TO WINDOWS

Adding content to windows in Flex is typically different from adding content to `NativeWindow` objects in Flash. When working with the latter, you must programmatically add content to the stage of the `NativeWindow` object after you've created it. When working with Flex-based windows, it's more common to simply create new MXML components based on `Window`, place the content in those components, and then open instances of those components as windows. Let's look at an example of this.

In the section on working with windows using `NativeWindow`, you saw an example in which you created a new window and then added text content to it. We'll now achieve a similar result, but this time using the Flex approach. Start by creating a new MXML component and call it SimpleTextWindow.mxml. The code for that component is shown in listing 2.10.

Listing 2.10 Creating a simple window component

```
<?xml version="1.0" encoding="utf-8"?>
<mx:Window xmlns:mx="http://www.adobe.com/2006/mxml" width="200"
  height="200" type="utility">
   <mx:Label text="New Window Content" />
</mx:Window>
```

Note that this component uses `Window` as the root element. This is important. All components that you want to use as windows must extend `Window`. Also note that we're setting the `width` and `height` as well as the `type` of the component in the MXML document itself. You *could* set those properties in the ActionScript instead, but in this case it's more sensible to set them in the window component itself if they should be consistent across all instances of the window.

Next we create an instance of the window in the main application MXML document, as shown in listing 2.11.

Listing 2.11 Creating an instance of the window component

```
<?xml version="1.0" encoding="utf-8"?>
<mx:WindowedApplication xmlns:mx="http://www.adobe.com/2006/mxml"
  layout="absolute" creationComplete="creationCompleteHandler();">
  <mx:Script>
    <![CDATA[

      private function creationCompleteHandler():void {
        var window:SimpleTextWindow = new SimpleTextWindow();
        window.open();
      }

    ]]>
  </mx:Script>
</mx:WindowedApplication>
```

Note that in this code we construct a new instance of the `SimpleTextWindow` component instead of creating a generic `Window` object. Note also that, because we set the `width`, `height`, and `type` properties in the MXML component itself, we don't need to set them when instantiating it. Figure 2.5 shows what the window looks like.

That wraps up our discussion of basic, rectangular windows in Flex. Before we move on to an entirely different topic, we'll discuss how to create irregularly shaped windows using Flex.

Figure 2.5 A simple text window created in Flex

CREATING IRREGULARLY SHAPED WINDOWS

You've already learned how to create irregularly shaped windows using ActionScript, and therefore it seems only fair to discuss how to do it using Flex. The basic concept is the same in ActionScript and Flex: create a window that has a transparent background and no system chrome. The steps to achieve this (set `systemChrome` to `none` and `transparent` to `true`) are similar in both cases. However, with Flex windows, there's a small wrench thrown in the works. Listing 2.12 shows a window component MXML document. The code sets the `systemChrome` property to `none` and the `transparent` property to `true`. It then uses ActionScript to draw a circle and add it to the display list.

Listing 2.12 Creating a transparent window in Flex with `systemChrome` set to none

```
<?xml version="1.0" encoding="utf-8"?>
<mx:Window xmlns:mx="http://www.adobe.com/2006/mxml" systemChrome="none"
  type="lightweight" transparent="true" width="200" height="200"
  creationComplete="creationCompleteHandler();">
```

```
<mx:Script>
    <![CDATA[

        private function creationCompleteHandler():void {

            var shape:Shape = new Shape();
            shape.graphics.lineStyle(0, 0, 0);
            shape.graphics.beginFill(0xFFFFFF, 1);
            shape.graphics.drawCircle(100, 100, 100);
            shape.graphics.endFill();

            rawChildren.addChild(shape);

        }

    ]]>
    </mx:Script>
</mx:Window>
```

If you create an instance of this window, you'll discover that there's still chrome applied to the window. You can see what this looks like in figure 2.6.

By default, Flex applies Flex chrome when `systemChrome` is set to none. If you want to remove all chrome, as is the goal in this example, you must take one additional step and set the `showFlexChrome` property of the window to `false`. All the other properties we've looked at for Flex windows thus far can be set on the instance using ActionScript or in the MXML using attributes. The `showFlexChrome` property can only be set using MXML, because it must be set before the window instantiates. The code in

Figure 2.6 Flex window with `systemChrome` set to none

listing 2.13 shows this change to the code. With the addition of setting this one property, the Flex chrome is also removed and the window is now shaped like a circle.

Listing 2.13   Setting `showFlexChrome` to `false` to hide the Flex window chrome

```
<?xml version="1.0" encoding="utf-8"?>
<mx:Window xmlns:mx="http://www.adobe.com/2006/mxml" showFlexChrome="false"
  systemChrome="none" type="lightweight" transparent="true" width="200"
  height="200" creationComplete="creationCompleteHandler();">
    <mx:Script>
        <![CDATA[

            private function creationCompleteHandler():void {

                var shape:Shape = new Shape();
                shape.graphics.lineStyle(0, 0, 0);
                shape.graphics.beginFill(0xFFFFFF, 1);
                shape.graphics.drawCircle(100, 100, 100);
                shape.graphics.endFill();

                rawChildren.addChild(shape);

            }

        ]]>
```

```
    </mx:Script>
  </mx:Window>
```

Now that you've had a chance to learn how to create windows using lower-level Action-Script and Flex-specific techniques, we'll look at how to manage those windows.

2.2 *Managing windows*

Creating and opening windows is only the first step in effectively using windows. There are a handful of core skills that you must master to be proficient at working with windows. In the next few sections, we'll look at how to position, order, move, resize, and close windows.

2.2.1 *Retrieving window references*

Generally it's useful to be able to retrieve references to open windows for an application. Retrieving references is important for a variety of purposes, including (though not limited to) positioning windows, ordering windows, and communicating between windows.

The `NativeApplication` object for an AIR application keeps track of all the windows open for that application. The `mainWindow` property references the main application window (the initial window). The `openedWindows` property holds an array of all the windows currently opened in the application. You can also retrieve a reference to a `NativeWindow` object that corresponds to a `Stage` object by using a `Stage` object's `nativeWindow` property. We'll see how to use these properties in a variety of ways throughout the next few sections.

2.2.2 *Positioning windows*

Positioning windows is such an essential task that you must understand the basics before working with windows extensively. Otherwise, you're likely to open windows at seemingly random locations, sometimes hidden by other windows and sometimes overlapping existing windows in unintended ways.

POSITIONING NATIVEWINDOW OBJECTS

You can set the x and y properties of a `NativeWindow` object to set the x and y coordinates of the window in the desktop. When you position `NativeWindow` objects directly, this feat is achieved simply. You can merely set the x and y properties immediately after creating the object or at any time after that. However, when you create a `Window` component using Flex, you need to be aware that the underlying `NativeWindow` object for a `Window` component doesn't get created immediately when you construct a new `Window` object. We'll look at how to address this issue in the next section.

POSITIONING WINDOW OBJECTS

As already mentioned, the `NativeWindow` object that's associated with a `Window` component doesn't get instantiated immediately when you construct a `Window` component. Instead, you need to wait for that `Window` object to dispatch a `windowComplete` event before you can access the underlying `NativeWindow` object and set the x and y properties. There are two common ways you can go about setting the x and y coordinates of a window: from the window that instantiates the new window or from within the new window itself.

When positioning the new window from the window that instantiates it, you want to register an event listener to listen for the `windowComplete` event, and then set the `x` and `y` properties of the new window's `nativeWindow` object when that event occurs. Listing 2.14 illustrates this. Listing 2.14 is a modification to listing 2.9, and changes are shown in bold.

Listing 2.14   Positioning a new window from the window that instantiates it

```
<?xml version="1.0" encoding="utf-8"?>
<mx:WindowedApplication xmlns:mx="http://www.adobe.com/2006/mxml"
  layout="absolute" creationComplete="creationCompleteHandler();">
    <mx:Script>
       <![CDATA[
          import mx.events.AIREvent;

          private function creationCompleteHandler():void {
             var window:SimpleTextWindow = new SimpleTextWindow();

             window.addEventListener(
                   AIREvent.WINDOW_COMPLETE,
                   windowCompleteHandler);          ◁─┐  Register
             window.open();                          ❶ listener
          }


          private function windowCompleteHandler(event:AIREvent):void {
             event.target.stage.nativeWindow.x = 0;      Set window  ❷
             event.target.stage.nativeWindow.y = 0;      coordinates
          }

       ]]>
    </mx:Script>
</mx:WindowedApplication>
```

In this example, you can see that, right after we create the window instance, we register a method as a listener for the `windowComplete` event ❶. The event handler method itself ❷ sets the x and y properties of the window.

In the preceding example, you saw how to position a window from the window that opened it. If you prefer to position a window from within that new window itself, you can do that by simply listening for the `windowComplete` event within that component instead. We'll next look at an example of that. Listing 2.15 shows the `SimpleTextWindow` from listing 2.8 with a few changes in bold. In this example, you can assume that the application document still looks just as it did in listing 2.11.

Listing 2.15   Positioning a window from within the window component

```
<?xml version="1.0" encoding="utf-8"?>
<mx:Window xmlns:mx="http://www.adobe.com/2006/mxml" width="200"
  height="200" type="utility"
```

```
windowComplete="windowCompleteHandler();">
  <mx:Script>
    <![CDATA[

      private function windowCompleteHandler():void {
        nativeWindow.x = 0;
        nativeWindow.y = 0;
      }

    ]]>
  </mx:Script>
  <mx:Label text="New Window Content" />
</mx:Window>
```

In these examples, we've looked at how to position windows when they first open. Of course, you can also use the same x and y properties of the nativeWindow object to position a window at any time, not just when it initially opens. Furthermore, you can use these same techniques to position the main application window when it initializes. Listing 2.16 shows one way to center the application on the screen.

> **Listing 2.16   Centering the application on the screen**
>
> ```
> <?xml version="1.0" encoding="utf-8"?>
> <mx:WindowedApplication xmlns:mx="http://www.adobe.com/2006/mxml"
>     layout="absolute"
>     windowComplete="windowCompleteHandler();"      ◁────┐    Listen for
>     creationComplete="creationCompleteHandler();">       ❶  windowComplete
>
>   <mx:Script>
>     <![CDATA[
>       import mx.events.AIREvent;
>
>       private function creationCompleteHandler():void {
>         var window:SimpleTextWindow = new SimpleTextWindow();
>         window.open();
>       }
>
>       private function windowCompleteHandler():void {
>         nativeWindow.x = (Capabilities.screenResolutionX - width) / 2;
>         nativeWindow.y = (Capabilities.screenResolutionY - height) / 2;
>       }
>                                                         Center
>     ]]>                                                 window  ❷
>   </mx:Script>
> </mx:WindowedApplication>
> ```

In this example, the first thing we do is tell the window how to handle the windowComplete event ❶. In this case, we tell the window to call a method named windowCompleteHandler() ❷ that we've defined in the script block. The event handler method uses the screen resolution that it retrieves from the intrinsic Capabilities object in order to move the window to the center of the screen.

Next we'll look at how to do a slightly more sophisticated version of this same thing by working with a virtual desktop.

WORKING WITH A VIRTUAL DESKTOP

It's not uncommon for systems to have more than one monitor these days. If a user of your application has more than one monitor, it's a good idea for you to allow her to take advantage of the extra screen space when using your application. AIR applications allow users to drag windows anywhere on the desktop, including additional monitors. However, you should also consider extra monitors when programmatically placing windows. Frequently, users opt to place the main application window on their main monitor while utility windows go on a second monitor. But a user might just as well choose to move the main application window onto her second monitor. In any case, it's courteous for your AIR application to remember where a user has placed windows previously and put them there again when restarting the application. You can store user preferences such as window placement in a shared object (this is a basic ActionScript skill), in a local database (see chapter 5), or even in a text file (see chapter 3). The actual storage of the values is not particularly relevant to this chapter. What *is* relevant is how you can determine the correct values and how you can figure out whether a window is on one screen or another.

AIR applications treat the entire space of any and all monitors as one virtual desktop. Figure 2.7 illustrates this idea.

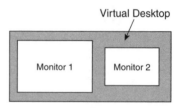

Figure 2.7 **AIR applications treat all monitors as one virtual desktop.**

In programmatic terms, each of these monitors has a representation as a flash.display.Screen object. A Screen object provides information about the size of the screen by way of a bounds property and a visibleBounds property. Because AIR applications can't change the resolution of monitors, the bounds and visibleBounds properties are read-only. Both these properties are flash. geom.Rectangle values with x and y values relative to the upper-left corner of the virtual desktop.

The Screen class also has two static properties that allow you to retrieve references to the Screen objects available to an AIR application. The Screen.mainScreen property returns a reference to the primary screen for the computer. The Screen.screens property returns an array of all the screens, the first of which is the same as the mainScreen reference.

The Screen class also has a static method called getScreensForRectangle(). This method allows you to retrieve an array of Screen objects over which a given Rectangle (relative to the virtual desktop) overlaps. The practical significance of this is that you can find out if a particular region (perhaps a window) exists on one screen or another, or both, or none.

The example in listing 2.17 illustrates a few of the virtual desktop and screen concepts by way of a crudely implemented window-snapping algorithm. In this example, the window snaps to the edge of the screen it's on if it's within 100 pixels of the edge. Much of this example is the same as listing 2.2. The changes are shown in bold.

Listing 2.17   Snapping a window to the edge of the screen

```
package {

    import flash.display.MovieClip;
    import flash.display.NativeWindow;
    import flash.display.NativeWindowInitOptions;
    import flash.display.NativeWindowType;
    import flash.display.NativeWindowSystemChrome;
    import flash.events.NativeWindowBoundsEvent;
    import flash.display.Screen;

    public class Example extends MovieClip {

        public function Example() {

            var options:NativeWindowInitOptions =
            ➥new NativeWindowInitOptions();
            options.type = NativeWindowType.UTILITY;

            var window:NativeWindow = new NativeWindow(options);
            window.width = 200;
            window.height = 200;

            window.activate();                                    Listen for ❶
                                                                  move event

            window.addEventListener(NativeWindowBoundsEvent.MOVE,
                                          moveHandler);

        }

        private function moveHandler(event:NativeWindowBoundsEvent):void {

            var window:NativeWindow = event.target as NativeWindow;

            var screens:Array =                                   Determine
            ➥Screen.getScreensForRectangle(window.bounds);     ❷ screen overlap
            var screen:Screen;

            if(screens.length == 1) {
                screen = screens[0];                  ❸ Select screen for
            }                                            snapping
            else if(screens.length == 2) {
                screen = screens[1];
            }

            if(window.x < screen.bounds.x + 100) {        ◁─┐ Snap to edges
                window.x = screen.bounds.x;               ❹   within 100 pixels
            }
            else if(window.x > screen.bounds.x + screen.bounds.width -
            ➥window.width - 100) {
                window.x = screen.bounds.x + screen.bounds.width -
                ➥window.width;
            }
            if(window.y < screen.bounds.y + 100) {
                window.y = screen.bounds.y;
            }
            else if(window.y > screen.bounds.y + screen.bounds.height -
            ➥window.height - 100) {
                window.y = screen.bounds.y + screen.bounds.height -
                ➥window.height;
```

```
            }
        }
    }
}
```

The first thing that's necessary in this example is to listen for the move event ❶ that the window dispatches when the user drags it. When the move event is handled, we tell the window to take action. The first thing it needs to do is retrieve an array of all the screens that the window currently overlaps using the `Screen.getScreensFor-Rectangle()` method ❷. We then make a judgment: if the window overlaps just one screen, get a reference to that screen; otherwise use the second screen of the two that the window overlaps ❸. The remaining logic ❹ tests which edges of the screen the window is nearest and then snaps to them if it's within 100 pixels.

You can see that this example illustrates several key skills in working with screens, including determining which screen a window resides on and getting the bounds of a screen. Next we'll look at the important concept of closing windows.

2.2.3 *Closing windows*

Closing windows may seem like a simple task, but it's an important one with nuances you need to consider. In the next few sections, we'll examine how to deal with several window-closing issues, including reopening closed windows, closing all windows on application exit, and closing windows with no chrome.

REOPENING CLOSED WINDOWS

As we've been working through the concepts in this chapter, you've likely followed along with the example code and created quite a few windows. In doing so, you've probably noticed that, when chrome is applied to a window, the close button automatically gets wired up to allow the user to close the window. As convenient as that is, it's also potentially problematic because, in an AIR application, a window can't be reopened once it's been closed. While that may be the intended behavior in some cases, in many cases you intend to allow a user to reopen a window after he's closed it. Consider an example of a utility window that shows a color palette for a drawing program. The user should be able to show and hide the window. If you use the default close behavior for a window in such a case, AIR would prevent you from showing the window once the user closed it. Listing 2.18 shows an example that illustrates the problem.

Listing 2.18 You can't reopen a window that has been closed

```
package {

    import flash.display.NativeWindowType;
    import flash.display.NativeWindowInitOptions;
    import flash.display.NativeWindow;
    import flash.display.MovieClip;
    import flash.events.MouseEvent;

    public class WindowExample extends MovieClip {
```

```
        private var _window:NativeWindow;

        public function WindowExample() {

            var options:NativeWindowInitOptions =
            ➡new NativeWindowInitOptions();
            options.type = NativeWindowType.UTILITY;

            _window = new NativeWindow(options);
            _window.width = 200;
            _window.height = 200;

            _window.activate();

            stage.addEventListener(MouseEvent.CLICK, openWindow);
        }

        private function openWindow(event:MouseEvent):void {
            _window.activate();
        }

    }

}
```

In this example, the intent is that, any time the user clicks on the main window, the application should open the utility window by calling the activate() method. However, if you were to test this example, you'd discover that, once you've closed the utility window, any attempt to reopen it results in a runtime error stating that you can't open a window that's been closed.

What's the solution to this dilemma? The answer is simpler than you might think: rather than closing the window when the user clicks on the close button, you should instead set its visibility to false. That hides the window but allows it to be reopened. In order to achieve this, you must catch the window after the user clicks on the close button but before AIR has had a chance to take the default action and really close the window. You can do that by listening for a closing event. All windows dispatch an event of type Event.CLOSING an instant after the user clicks on the close button but just before the window actually closes. When handling the closing event, you must then do two things: set the visible property to false and cancel the default behavior. Canceling the default behavior is critical because otherwise AIR will still close the window. You can cancel the default behavior for cancelable events in ActionScript (of which the closing event is one) by calling the preventDefault() method on the event object. Listing 2.19 shows how you can listen for the closing event, toggle the visibility, and prevent the default behavior.

Listing 2.19 Allowing a user to hide and show a window

```
package {

    import flash.display.NativeWindowType;
    import flash.display.NativeWindowInitOptions;
    import flash.display.NativeWindow;
    import flash.display.MovieClip;
    import flash.events.MouseEvent;
```

```
import flash.events.Event;

public class WindowExample extends MovieClip {

    private var _window:NativeWindow;

    public function WindowExample() {

        var options:NativeWindowInitOptions =
        ➥new NativeWindowInitOptions();
        options.type = NativeWindowType.UTILITY;

        _window = new NativeWindow(options);
        _window.width = 200;
        _window.height = 200;

        _window.activate();

        stage.addEventListener(MouseEvent.CLICK, openWindow);

        _window.addEventListener(Event.CLOSING, closingHandler);
    }

    private function closingHandler(event:Event):void {
        _window.visible = false;
        event.preventDefault();
    }

    private function openWindow(event:MouseEvent):void {
        _window.activate();
    }

}

}
```

You can see that basic closing of windows is something you must consider when building applications if users need to be able to reopen windows that they've hidden.

CLOSING ALL WINDOWS ON APPLICATION EXIT

As you may have noticed throughout earlier examples in this chapter, windows you open from the initial application window don't automatically close when the initial application window closes. That is expected behavior if the additional windows are standard windows that show up in the task bar or window menu. However, if the additional windows are utility or lightweight windows, you likely want them to close when the main application window with which they're associated closes.

You can use the openedWindows property of a NativeApplication object to retrieve an array of references to all the NativeWindow objects for the application. By looping through the openedWinodows array, you can programmatically close all the utility and lightweight windows. Typically you'll want to do this when closing the application. You can detect when an application is closing by listening for the exiting event that the NativeApplication object dispatches. You can programmatically close a window by calling the close() method on the NativeWindow object. Listing 2.20 shows an example that programmatically closes all other windows when the main application window is closed.

Listing 2.20 Closing windows on application exit

```
package {

    import flash.display.MovieClip;
    import flash.display.NativeWindow;
    import flash.display.NativeWindowInitOptions;
    import flash.display.NativeWindowType;
    import flash.desktop.NativeApplication;
    import flash.events.Event;

    public class Example extends MovieClip {

        public function Example() {

            var options:NativeWindowInitOptions =
            ➥new NativeWindowInitOptions();
            options.type = NativeWindowType.UTILITY;

            var window:NativeWindow = new NativeWindow(options);
            window.width = 200;
            window.height = 200;

            window.activate();

            this.stage.nativeWindow.addEventListener(          Listen for
            ➥Event.CLOSING, closingHandler);                ❶ exiting event
        }

        private function closingHandler(event:Event):void {
            var windows:Array =
            ➥NativeApplication.nativeApplication.openedWindows;
            for(var i:Number = 0; i < windows.length; i++) {   Close all
                windows[i].close();                            open
            }                                               ❷ windows
        }

    }

}
```

In order to know when to close all the windows, we need to listen for the closing event that the NativeApplication instance dispatches ❶. Then, when handling that event ❷, we loop through the openedWindows array of the NativeApplication instance and call the close() method for all the windows.

We've looked at closing all open windows when the closing event occurs for the main window. If you don't close all the windows when you close an application, you can potentially cause problems for users. If a window is hidden but still technically open, the user won't have any way to close the window once she's exited the application. That would unnecessarily tie up system resources.

ADDING CUSTOM CLOSE MECHANISMS FOR WINDOWS

As you learned in the preceding section, you can close a window using the close() method. You can use that same method to close a window via a custom user interface element designed to allow the user to close a window. This is an important consideration when building windows that have no chrome (such as an irregularly shaped window) because such windows have no default close button.

2.2.4 *Ordering windows*

You can change the z-axis values of windows in a variety of ways. Typically, the window with focus appears in front of all other windows, and users generally expect to have control over the stacking order of windows on their desktop. However, there are legitimate reasons to control the order of windows programmatically, some of which are as follows:

- When creating new windows, you might want to intentionally open them in front of or behind existing windows.
- You might want to create a window that always stays in front of all other windows, even if it doesn't have focus. This is useful for windows that require user attention or that contain information that should always be available to the user even if he is using other applications.
- You might want to make sure utility windows are brought to the front of other applications when the corresponding AIR application receives focus.

There are a handful of methods and a property that control ordering. All of these methods and the property are available for `NativeWindow` objects in ActionScript as well as `Window` components in Flex. These methods and the property are as follows:

- `orderToFront()`—Move the window in front of all other windows in the same AIR application.
- `orderToBack()`—Move the window behind all other windows in the same AIR application.
- `orderInFrontOf(window:IWindow)`—Move the window in front of another window.
- `orderInBackOf(window:IWindow)`—Move the window behind another window.
- `alwaysInFront`—This window should always appear in front of all other windows on the desktop.

As you may have noticed in earlier examples, when you have a utility window running for an application and another application gets focus on your system, returning focus to the AIR application with the utility window doesn't return the utility window to the front of other running application windows on your system. That makes it easy to "lose" utility windows behind other applications. A useful feature to build into AIR applications with utility windows is automatically bringing those utility windows to the front along with the application's main window when it receives focus. When an application loses focus, the `NativeApplication` object dispatches a deactivate event; when the application receives focus, it dispatches an activate event. Therefore, if you listen for the activate event, cycle through all the opened windows, and move each opened window to the front, you'll make sure no utility windows get lost behind other applications. Listing 2.21 shows a simple example of this.

Listing 2.21 Moving utility windows to the front along with the main window

```
package {

    import flash.display.MovieClip;
    import flash.display.NativeWindow;
    import flash.display.NativeWindowInitOptions;
    import flash.display.NativeWindowType;
    import flash.desktop.NativeApplication;
    import flash.events.Event;
    import flash.text.TextField;
    import flash.text.TextFieldAutoSize;
    import flash.display.StageScaleMode;
    import flash.display.StageAlign;

    public class Example extends MovieClip {

        public function Example() {

            var options:NativeWindowInitOptions =
            ➥new NativeWindowInitOptions();
            options.type = NativeWindowType.UTILITY;

            var window:NativeWindow = new NativeWindow(options);
            window.width = 200;
            window.height = 200;

            var textField:TextField = new TextField();
            textField.autoSize = TextFieldAutoSize.LEFT;
            textField.text = "New Window Content";

            window.stage.scaleMode = StageScaleMode.NO_SCALE;
            window.stage.align = StageAlign.TOP_LEFT;

            window.stage.addChild(textField);

            window.activate();

            this.stage.nativeWindow.addEventListener(Event.ACTIVATE,
                                        activateHandler);

        }

        private function activateHandler(event:Event):void {
            var windows:Array =
            ➥NativeApplication.nativeApplication.openedWindows;
            for(var i:Number = 0; i < windows.length; i++) {
                windows[i].orderToFront();
            }
        }

    }

}
```

If you were to test the preceding code, you'd see that, every time you bring the application window to the foreground, all of the utility windows also move to the foreground.

2.2.5   *Moving and resizing windows*

When a window has chrome around it, the user is able to move and resize the window through the standard user interface elements (dragging the title bar to move the window and dragging the borders to resize the window). When you don't display any system chrome for a window, the user won't have those options. Instead, if you want the user to be able to move or resize the window, you need to programmatically add that behavior. The good news is that AIR makes it simple to do so.

All `NativeWindow` objects have `startMove()` and `startResize()` methods. When you call these methods from an event handler for a `mouseDown` event, a `mouseUp` event will automatically stop the move or resize behavior—exactly the way a user would expect the feature to work.

The `startMove()` method doesn't require any parameters. You can simply call `startMove()` on the window when the user clicks on an object. The window will then move with the mouse until the user releases the mouse button. Listing 2.22 shows an example of this by modifying the `ExampleWindow` code from listing 2.7.

> **Listing 2.22   Enable dragging on a window using `startMove()`**

```
package {

    import flash.display.NativeWindow;
    import flash.display.NativeWindowSystemChrome;
    import flash.display.NativeWindowType;
    import flash.display.NativeWindowInitOptions;
    import flash.display.Sprite;
    import flash.display.Stage;
    import flash.display.StageAlign;
    import flash.display.StageScaleMode;
    import flash.events.MouseEvent;
    import flash.events.Event;

    public class ExampleWindow extends NativeWindow {

        private var _background:Sprite;

        public function ExampleWindow() {
            var options:NativeWindowInitOptions =
            ➥new NativeWindowInitOptions();

            options.systemChrome = NativeWindowSystemChrome.NONE;
            options.type = NativeWindowType.LIGHTWEIGHT;
            options.transparent = true;

            super(options);
            _background = new Sprite();
            drawBackground(200, 200);
            stage.addChild(_background);

            width = 200;
            height = 200;

            stage.align = StageAlign.TOP_LEFT;
            stage.scaleMode = StageScaleMode.NO_SCALE;
```

```
    _background.addEventListener(MouseEvent.MOUSE_DOWN,
                                  startMoveWindow);

    }

    private function drawBackground(newWidth:Number, newHeight:Number):
    void {
      _background.graphics.clear();
      _background.graphics.lineStyle(0, 0, 0);
      _background.graphics.beginFill(0x0000FF, .5);
      _background.graphics.drawRoundRectComplex(0, 0, newWidth,
                             newHeight, 20, 20, 20, 1);
      _background.graphics.beginFill(0xFFFFFF, .9);
      _background.graphics.drawRoundRectComplex(5, 5, newWidth - 10,
                           newHeight - 10, 20, 20, 20, 1);
      _background.graphics.endFill();

    }

    private function startMoveWindow(event:MouseEvent):void {
      startMove();
    }

  }

}
```

The startResize() method requires that you specify the side or corner of the window from which to resize. Valid values are constants of the flash.display.NativeWindowResize class: TOP, BOTTOM, LEFT, RIGHT, TOP_LEFT, TOP_RIGHT, BOTTOM_LEFT, and BOTTOM_RIGHT. For example, if you call startResize() with a value of NativeWindowResize.BOTTOM_RIGHT, the bottom-right corner of the window will move along with the mouse while the top-left corner stays fixed. You can call startResize() when the user clicks on an object. The window will start to resize along with the mouse movement until the user releases the mouse button. Listing 2.23 shows an example of resizing a window. The code is based on the window from listing 2.22.

Listing 2.23   Resizing a window

```
package {

    import flash.display.NativeWindow;
    import flash.display.NativeWindowSystemChrome;
    import flash.display.NativeWindowType;
    import flash.display.NativeWindowInitOptions;
    import flash.display.Sprite;
    import flash.display.Stage;
    import flash.display.StageAlign;
    import flash.display.StageScaleMode;
    import flash.events.MouseEvent;
    import flash.events.Event;
    import flash.display.NativeWindowResize;

    public class ExampleWindow extends NativeWindow {

        private var _background:Sprite;
```

```
private var _resizer:Sprite;

public function ExampleWindow() {
   var options:NativeWindowInitOptions =
   ➥new NativeWindowInitOptions();

   options.systemChrome = NativeWindowSystemChrome.NONE;
   options.type = NativeWindowType.LIGHTWEIGHT;
   options.transparent = true;

   super(options);
   _background = new Sprite();
   drawBackground(200, 200);
   stage.addChild(_background);

   width = 200;
   height = 200;

   stage.align = StageAlign.TOP_LEFT;
   stage.scaleMode = StageScaleMode.NO_SCALE;

   _background.addEventListener(MouseEvent.MOUSE_DOWN,
                                   startMoveWindow);

   _resizer = new Sprite();
   _resizer.graphics.lineStyle(0, 0, 0);
   _resizer.graphics.beginFill(0xCCCCCC, 1);
   _resizer.graphics.drawRect(0, 0, 10, 10);
   _resizer.graphics.endFill();
   _resizer.x = 180;
   _resizer.y = 180;
   stage.addChild(_resizer);

   _resizer.addEventListener(MouseEvent.MOUSE_DOWN,
                                   startResizeWindow);

   addEventListener("resizing", resizingHandler);
}

private function drawBackground(newWidth:Number, newHeight:Number):
➥void {
   _background.graphics.clear();
   _background.graphics.lineStyle(0, 0, 0);
   _background.graphics.beginFill(0x0000FF, .5);
   _background.graphics.drawRoundRectComplex(0, 0, newWidth,
                       newHeight, 20, 20, 20, 1);
   _background.graphics.beginFill(0xFFFFFF, .9);
   _background.graphics.drawRoundRectComplex(5, 5, newWidth - 10,
                       newHeight - 10, 20, 20, 20, 1);
   _background.graphics.endFill();
}

private function startMoveWindow(event:MouseEvent):void {
   startMove();
}

private function resizingHandler(event:Event):void {
   drawBackground(width, height);
   _resizer.x = width - 20;
```

```
        _resizer.y = height - 20;
    }

    private function startResizeWindow(event:MouseEvent):void {
        startResize(NativeWindowResize.BOTTOM_RIGHT);
    }

  }

}
```

You'll likely notice in this example that the window dispatches a resizing event as it resizes. You can use that event to redraw or rearrange the contents of the window appropriately.

We've now covered all the topics related to window behavior, and we're ready to move on to a more macroscopic view by looking at application-wide behavior. In the next section, we'll look at a variety of these topics, including detecting idleness and running an application in full-screen mode.

2.3 *Managing applications*

You've now learned all the basic window-specific information for building AIR applications. Next we'll look at application-level issues related to managing the application. We'll look at the following topics:

- Detecting idle users
- Launching AIR applications when the system starts
- Creating file associations
- Alerting the user
- Running applications in full-screen mode

AIR makes each of these tasks simple, as we'll see in the next few sections.

2.3.1 *Detecting idleness*

Often it's useful or important to detect when a user is no longer interacting with an application. For example, an instant messenger application can automatically set a user's status to away or idle if the user has stepped away from the computer. AIR applications automatically detect when a user hasn't interacted with the application for a specified amount of time. Once that threshold has been reached, the NativeApplication object dispatches a userIdle event. When the user returns to the application, the NativeApplication object dispatches a userPresent event. Both events are of type flash.events.Event, and the Event.USER_IDLE and Event.USER_PRESENT constants define the event names.

Default timeout value is 300 seconds. You can adjust this value by setting the idleThreshold property of the NativeApplication object. The value must be an integer representing the number of seconds without any detected activity before the NativeApplication object should dispatch a userIdle event.

In addition, you can request the amount of time since user interaction was last detected. The `timeSinceLastUserInput` property of the `NativeApplication` object will tell you how many seconds have elapsed since any mouse or keyboard input was received by the application.

2.3.2   *Launching applications on startup*

Typically, an AIR application runs only when the user double-clicks the application or a file of a type that's associated with it. However, you can also flag an AIR application to automatically launch when the user logs on to her computer system. Simply set the `startAtLogin` property of the `NativeApplication` object to `true`.

Note that, if `startAtLogin` is `true`, the application must be installed on the system. If you simply test this setting by testing your application from Flash or from Flex Builder, you'll receive a runtime error.

2.3.3   *Setting file associations*

By setting a file association, you allow the user to automatically launch the AIR application when he double-clicks a file of that type. In chapter 1, you learned how to define file types for an AIR application using the descriptor file. When you list file types in the descriptor, there are two possible options: if the file type isn't already associated with another application on the system, it's automatically registered with the AIR application; if the file type is registered with another application, no new association is made. In the second case, what happens is that the file type is then available for you to programmatically override the existing association. You can only do so at runtime using the methods listed in table 2.1.

When you want to create associations with file types that are commonly used by other applications, it's generally a best practice to request the user's permission to make the association. Consider, for example, if you associated .mp3 files with your AIR application using the descriptor file (hence not asking the user's permission). Because many users already have a preferred association for .mp3 files, you'd be likely to upset users if you changed that automatically without ever asking them. Therefore, although you can programmatically create associations for file types without first asking the user's permission, it's advisable that you do ask first.

Table 2.1   Methods for working with file associations

Method name	Description
`setAsDefaultApplication()`	Set the current AIR application as the default application for a particular file type.
`removeAsDefaultApplication()`	Remove the association between the current AIR application and a file type.
`isSetAsDefaultApplication()`	Find out if the current AIR application is already the default application for a file type.
`getDefaultApplication()`	Get the name of the default application for a file type.

To create associations for file types at runtime, use the `setAsDefaultApplica-tion()` method of the `NativeApplication` object. The method requires that you pass it one parameter specifying the file extension for the type of file you want to associate with the AIR application. The parameter value should include just the file extension as a string, not including an initial dot. For example, the following code associates .mp3 files with the application that is currently running:

```
NativeApplication.nativeApplication.setAsDefaultApplication("mp3");
```

If you'd like to remove an association, you can simply call the `removeAsDefaultAp-plication()` method, passing it the extension of the file type for which you'd like to remove the association:

```
NativeApplication.nativeApplication.removeAsDefaultApplication("mp3");
```

The `isSetAsDefaultApplication()` method returns a Boolean value indicating whether the AIR application is the default application for a specified file extension:

```
var isDefault:Boolean = NativeApplication.nativeApplication.
isSetAsDefaultApplication("mp3");
```

You can also use the `getDefaultApplication()` method to retrieve the name of the application with which a file type is associated. The method requires one parameter specifying the file extension as a string:

```
var defaultApplication:String = NativeApplication.nativeApplication.
getDefaultApplication("mp3");
```

All of these methods will only work for file types that have been included in the descriptor file in the `fileTypes` section. Also note that these methods will only work for an AIR application once it's been installed. That means these methods won't work correctly when testing the application in Flash or Flex Builder.

2.3.4 Alerting the user

Occasionally an AIR application needs to notify the user that something has occurred requiring the user's attention, even though the application may be minimized or not have focus. Operating systems have standard ways of alerting users about these sorts of things. For example, on Windows the corresponding item in the task bar flashes, and on OS X the item bounces in the application dock. AIR allows you to alert the user in these standard ways with a `notifyUser()` method on a `NativeWindow` object.

The `notifyUser()` method requires that you pass it a parameter with one of the two constants of the `flash.desktop.NotificationType` class: `NotificationType.INFOR-MATIONAL` or `NotificationType.CRITICAL`. These two types correspond to the two types of notifications that are allowed by the operating system.

The following example (listing 2.24) illustrates notification. Every five seconds, the application tests to see if the main window is active (has focus). If not, it notifies the user.

Listing 2.24 Alerting the user if the main window isn't active

```
package {

    import flash.display.MovieClip;
    import flash.display.NativeWindow;
    import flash.desktop.NativeApplication;
    import flash.utils.Timer;
    import flash.events.TimerEvent;
    import flash.desktop.NotificationType;

    public class Example extends MovieClip {

        private var _timer:Timer;

        public function Example() {

            _timer = new Timer(5000);

            _timer.addEventListener(TimerEvent.TIMER, timerHandler);
            _timer.start();

        }

        private function timerHandler(event:TimerEvent):void {
            var mainWindow:NativeWindow =
➥NativeApplication.nativeApplication.openedWindows[0] as NativeWindow;
            if(!mainWindow.active) {
                mainWindow.notifyUser(NotificationType.INFORMATIONAL);
            }
        }

    }

}
```

As you can see, alerting or notifying a user that a window requires her attention is simple.

One sure-fire way to get a user's attention is to launch an application in full-screen mode. Continue to the next section, where we'll learn how to do just that.

2.3.5 *Full-screen mode*

You can launch application windows in full-screen mode using the displayState property of a window's Stage object. Set the displayState property to StageDisplayState.FULL_SCREEN as in this example in listing 2.25. Note that because these applications run in full-screen mode without the standard mechanisms to close the applications, you must close the application using the standard keyboard shortcuts for your operating system.

Listing 2.25 Opening a window in full-screen mode

```
package {

    import flash.display.MovieClip;
    import flash.text.TextField;
    import flash.display.StageDisplayState;
```

```
public class Example extends MovieClip {

    public function Example() {

        stage.displayState = StageDisplayState.FULL_SCREEN;

        var textField:TextField = new TextField();
        textField.text = "Full screen example";
        addChild(textField);

    }

  }

}
```

This example uses a text field to illustrate a point. The default settings for a `Stage` object specify that the object should scale. Unless you want the content to scale, you should set the `scaleMode` property. In many cases, you'll also want to modify the `align` property. In this example, the text scales noticeably in most cases (depending on the starting dimensions of the window and the screen resolution). Listing 2.26 makes adjustments to the code, telling it not to scale the contents and to align them to the upper left.

Listing 2.26 Adjusting the scale mode and alignment of a full-screen window

```
package {

    import flash.display.MovieClip;
    import flash.text.TextField;
    import flash.display.StageDisplayState;
    import flash.display.StageScaleMode;
    import flash.display.StageAlign;

    public class Example extends MovieClip {

        public function Example() {

            stage.displayState = StageDisplayState.FULL_SCREEN;

            stage.scaleMode = StageScaleMode.NO_SCALE;
            stage.align = StageAlign.TOP_LEFT;

            var textField:TextField = new TextField();
            textField.text = "Full screen example";
            addChild(textField);

        }

    }

}
```

We've now covered all the basic application-level management topics. Next we'll move on to a new subject altogether: working with menus.

2.4   *Menus*

AIR applications can use menus in a variety of ways. Menus can appear at the application or window level, they can appear on application icons, they can appear as context menus, and they can appear as pop-up menus. In the following sections, we'll look at how to create menus and then apply them in each of these ways.

2.4.1   *Creating menus*

All menus in AIR applications are of type `flash.display.NativeMenu`. You can create a new menu by constructing a new `NativeMenu` object. The constructor doesn't require any parameters:

```
var exampleMenu:NativeMenu = new NativeMenu();
```

That's all there is to creating menus. Next we'll look at adding elements to menus.

2.4.2   *Adding elements to menus*

Once you've created a menu, you can add elements to it. Elements can generally be one of two types: menu items or other menus (submenus).

Menu items are of type `flash.display.NativeMenuItem`. You can create a new `NativeMenuItem` using the constructor and passing it the label for the item. The label is what gets displayed in the menu:

```
var item:NativeMenuItem = new NativeMenuItem("Example Item");
```

Add a menu item to a menu using the `addItem()` method (or the `addItemAt()` method if you want to insert the item at an index other than last):

```
exampleMenu.addItem(item);
```

As already mentioned, you can add other menus to menus in order to create submenus. To do this, use the `addSubmenu()` (or `addSubmenuAt()`) method, passing it the menu to add:

```
exampleMenu.addItem(submenu);
```

You've now seen how to create menus and add elements to them. In order for a menu to be functional, though, you have to be able to detect when the user has selected an option. Read on and we'll discuss how to do that in the next section.

2.4.3   *Listening for menu selections*

When a user selects an item in a menu, that item (a `NativeMenuItem` object) dispatches a select event. It's up to you to add listeners to items such that your application can respond when the user selects the item.

The select event is of type `flash.events.Event`. The `target` property of the event object references the `NativeMenuItem` object that dispatched the event. Sometimes menu items need to have data associated with them in order for the application to take meaningful or contextual action when the user selects the item. To do that, you can assign data of any type to the data property of the NativeMenuItem object. You can see examples of this in the example that follows later in listing 2.27.

There's just one more topic we need to cover before we start making menus appear in your application: special menu items such as checked items or separator lines. We'll cover that next.

2.4.4 *Creating special menu items*

Normal menu items appear simply as text. However, there are a few special types of menu items you can also use: checked items and separator items.

Checked items are useful when you have menu items that allow the user to toggle options on or off or to select among a list of items. You can display checks next to items by setting the checked property of the NativeMenuItem object.

Separator items are special types of menu items that serve simply to divide sections of a menu logically. Separator items are standard NativeMenuItem objects for which the isSeparator property is set to true. If the isSeparator property is true for an item, the item will appear as a line, and it won't be selectable.

We've covered enough theory. Now we need to see some practical examples of menus in use. In the next section, you'll learn how to use menus in a variety of ways.

2.4.5 *Using menus*

You can use menus in a handful of ways in AIR applications: application or window menus, dock application or system tray icon menus, context menus, and pop-up menus. In all cases the menus are instances of NativeMenu. The difference in each case is simply the way in which the menu is applied.

USING APPLICATION OR WINDOW MENUS

Application and window menus serve the same general purpose. Application menus are available only on OS X, and window menus are only available on Windows. Figure 2.8 shows an example of a window menu.

To apply a window menu, set the menu property of the NativeWindow object to which you want to apply the menu. To apply an application menu, set the menu property of the NativeApplication object. To determine whether the operating system supports one or the other, you can use the static supportsMenu property of the NativeWindow and NativeApplication classes. If NativeWindow.supportsMenu is true, you know that you can set the menu property of a Native-

Figure 2.8 Window menus appear at the top of a window in the manner that's familiar to most computer users.

Window object. If the NativeApplication.supportsMenu property is true, you can set the menu property of the NativeApplication object for the application. Because application menus and window menus typically are intended to accomplish the same thing, you'll usually want to use code such as the following after you've created the NativeMenu object. In the following code, you can assume that customMenu is a NativeMenu object you've already created:

```
if(NativeApplication.supportsMenu) {
   NativeApplication.nativeApplication.menu = customMenu;
}
else if(NativeWindow.supportsMenu) {
   NativeApplication.nativeApplication.openedWindows[0].menu = customMenu;
}
```

Listing 2.27 shows a complete, working example of a window or application menu that uses many of the concepts discussed through this section. This example creates a menu that allows the user to save (nonfunctional) or close the application, open a new window, and then toggle focus between opened windows.

Listing 2.27   Creating application or window menus

```
package {

    import flash.display.MovieClip;
    import flash.display.NativeWindow;
    import flash.display.NativeWindowInitOptions;
    import flash.display.NativeWindowType;
    import flash.desktop.NativeApplication;
    import flash.display.NativeMenu;
    import flash.display.NativeMenuItem;
    import flash.events.Event;

    public class Example extends MovieClip {

        private var _windowsMenu:NativeMenu;                   ❶ Create main menu

        public function Example() {

            var mainMenu:NativeMenu = new NativeMenu();   ◁──┘    ❷ Create
                                                                     applications
            var applicationMenu:NativeMenu = new NativeMenu();       menu

            var save:NativeMenuItem = new NativeMenuItem("save");
            var close:NativeMenuItem = new NativeMenuItem("close");

            close.addEventListener(Event.SELECT, selectHandler);  ◁──  ❸ Listen for
                                                                          select
            applicationMenu.addItem(save);     ❹ Add menu               event
            applicationMenu.addItem(close);       items

            _windowsMenu = new NativeMenu();      ❺ Create
                                                     windows      ❻ Listen for
            var newWindow:NativeMenuItem =           menu            select events
            ➥new NativeMenuItem("new window");
                newWindow.addEventListener(Event.SELECT, selectHandler);  ◁

                var line:NativeMenuItem = new NativeMenuItem("", true);  ◁──┐
                                                                  ❼ Create
            _windowsMenu.addItem(newWindow);                         separator
            _windowsMenu.addItem(line);                              item

            mainMenu.addSubmenu(applicationMenu, "Application");  ┐  ❽ Add
            mainMenu.addSubmenu(_windowsMenu, "Windows");         ┘     submenus

            var mainWindow:NativeWindow =
        NativeApplication.nativeApplication.openedWindows[0] as NativeWindow;  ◁
                                                        ❾ Reference main window

                if(NativeApplication.supportsMenu) {
```

```
            NativeApplication.nativeApplication.menu = mainMenu;
        }
        else if(NativeWindow.supportsMenu) {
            mainWindow.menu = mainMenu;
        }

        mainWindow.addEventListener(Event.CLOSE, closeAll);
    }
    private function closeAll(event:Event = null):void {
        var windows:Array =
        ➥NativeApplication.nativeApplication.openedWindows;
        for(var i:Number = 0; i < windows.length; i++) {
            windows[i].removeEventListener(Event.CLOSE, closeHandler);
            windows[i].close();
        }
    }
    private function selectHandler(event:Event):void {
        if(event.target.label == "close") {
            closeAll();
        }
        else if(event.target.label == "new window") {
            var windowTitle:String = "Window " +
NativeApplication.nativeApplication.openedWindows.length;

            var options:NativeWindowInitOptions =
new NativeWindowInitOptions();
            options.type = NativeWindowType.UTILITY;
            var window:NativeWindow = new NativeWindow(options);
            window.width = 200;
            window.height = 200;
            window.title = windowTitle;

            window.addEventListener(Event.ACTIVATE, activateHandler);
            window.addEventListener(Event.CLOSE, closeHandler);

            var menuItem:NativeMenuItem = new NativeMenuItem();
            menuItem.label = windowTitle;
            menuItem.data = window;
            menuItem.addEventListener(Event.SELECT,
                                    selectWindowHandler);

            _windowsMenu.addItem(menuItem);

            window.activate();
        }
    }
    private function selectWindowHandler(event:Event):void {
        event.target.data.activate();
    }
    private function activateHandler(event:Event):void {
        var item:NativeMenuItem;
        for(var i:Number = _windowsMenu.numItems - 1; i >= 0; i--) {
            item = _windowsMenu.getItemAt(i);
            item.checked = (item.data == event.target);
```

Apply menu ⑩

Listen for close ⑪

Close all opened windows ⑫

Remove listener to prevent error ⑬

Close all windows ⑭

Open new window ⑮

Create unique window title ⑯

Create new utility window ⑰

Handle events ⑱

Create window menu item ⑲

Add item to menu ⑳

Activate corresponding window ㉑

Update checked state in menu ㉒

```
        }
    }
    private function closeHandler(event:Event):void {    ◁┐
        var item:NativeMenuItem;
        for(var i:Number = 0; i < _windowsMenu.numItems; i++) {
            item = _windowsMenu.getItemAt(i);
            if(item.data == event.target) {
                _windowsMenu.removeItem(item);
                break;
            }
        }
    }
}
```

㉓ **Remove corresponding menu item**

The preceding is a long example. We'll break it down and look at each piece. The first thing we do is create a new menu ❶, because that's essential to everything that follows. We'll call this the main menu, because it's the container for all the rest of the menus that we'll add to it. Next we create another menu and two items ❷. This menu will be a submenu of the main menu. We add an event listener to one of the items ❸ in order to be able to respond when the user selects that menu item. We've created the menu items, but we haven't yet added them to the menu. We do that next ❹ using the addItem() method. Our main menu is going to have one more submenu, and we create that next ❺ along with a menu option. As with the application menu's close option, we add a listener to the new window option ❻. The windows menu is a dynamic menu because, as the application runs, we'll add more options to it each time the user opens a window. In order to differentiate between the static and dynamic items in the windows menu, we want a separator line. We can create that line by creating a new item with the second parameter set to true ❼. With the two submenus created, we can add them to the main menu ❽. Now that we've created the menu, we need only to apply it either as a window or an application menu. We get a reference to the main window ❾, then test what type of menu the system supports and assign the menu accordingly ❿. We also listen for a close event in order to close all the open windows when the main window closes ⓫.

The closeAll() method ⓬ is a typical method for what it does. It loops through all the open windows and calls the close() method for each. The one distinction in this example is that, in addition to calling the close() method, closeAll()also removes event listeners for the close event from each window ⓭. This is important because, as you'll see, when we create new windows in this example, we listen for the close event. If we didn't remove the listener before closing the window, we'd create an infinite loop.

The selectHandler() method is the event handler method we're using for the menu's options. We first determine what option the user selected. If he selected the close option ⓮, we call the closeAll() method. Otherwise, if the user selected the new window option ⓯, we run the code to open a new window. To create a new window, we first create a unique title for the window ⓰ by utilizing the count of existing windows, making names such as Window 1, Window 2, and so on. Then we create a new utility window that is 200-by-200 pixels ⑰. We need to take action when the user closes or activates the window, and therefore we register listeners for the corresponding events ⑱. Each window should have a menu item in the windows menu. We add the menu item ⑲ using the window title as the item name, and we store a reference to the window in the menu item's `data` property. The reference is important because it allows the application to activate the window when the user selects it from the menu. Then we simply add the new item to the windows menu ⑳.

There are three events that we still need to handle: selecting a menu item corresponding to a window, activating a window, and closing a window. Selecting a window's menu item results in activating the window via the menu item's `data` property ㉑. Activating a window ㉒ results in looping through the windows menu items and updating the checked state of each, such that only the activated window's menu item is checked. Closing a window ㉓ requires looping through all the menu items to remove the menu item that corresponds to the window.

When you test this application, you have the option to add new windows by selecting the new window item from the windows menu. When you add new windows, you'll see new items added to the windows menu. Selecting windows changes the selected window item in the menu. Closing windows removes the menu items to which they correspond.

USING ICON MENUS

Icon menus are the menus that you can access from the system tray icon (Windows) or dock application icon (OS X) for the application. You can configure and control the icon menu using the `icon.menu` property of the `NativeApplication` object.

```
NativeApplication.nativeApplication.icon.menu = customMenu;
```

This is all that's necessary to customize the icon menu.

With window, application, and icon menus, we've seen how to use menus that can appear external to your application's content. Next we'll look at ways to use menus that appear within your application's content.

USING CONTEXT MENUS

You can display context menus for any display object in a Flash- or Flex-based AIR application. The mechanism for adding context menus to display objects in AIR applications is exactly the same as for web applications. You need to assign the menu to the `contextMenu` property of the display object. This is a standard Flash or Flex skill, even for web-based application development. However, when building AIR applications, there are two important differences:

- Context menus for AIR applications are instances of `NativeMenu`, whereas context menus for web applications are instances of `ContextMenu`.
- Context menus for AIR applications are system-level, meaning they can appear in front of and outside the boundaries of the application window.

Listing 2.28 illustrates a simple context menu.

Listing 2.28   Adding a context menu

```
package {

    import flash.display.MovieClip;
    import flash.display.NativeMenu;
    import flash.display.NativeMenuItem;
    import flash.display.Sprite;

    public class Example extends MovieClip {

        public function Example() {

            var rectangle:Sprite = new Sprite();
            rectangle.graphics.lineStyle(0, 0, 1);
            rectangle.graphics.beginFill(0, 1);
            rectangle.graphics.drawRect(0, 0, 100, 100);
            rectangle.graphics.endFill();
            addChild(rectangle);

            var menu:NativeMenu = new NativeMenu();
            var item:NativeMenuItem = new NativeMenuItem("copy");
            menu.addItem(item);

            rectangle.contextMenu = menu;
        }
    }

}
```

Figure 2.9 shows the result of this example.

There's just one more way to use menus with AIR applications. Next we'll look at using menus as pop-up menus.

POP-UP MENUS

You can display pop-up menus at any time programmatically. Often you'll want to open pop-up menus when the user clicks the mouse or presses a key. Whatever you use as the trigger to open the menu, the code you use to actually display the menu is the same. You simply need to call the `display()` method of a `NativeMenu` object. The `display()` method requires that you specify three parameters: the `Stage` object on which to display the menu, and the x and y coordinates at which to display the menu. Listing 2.29 illustrates a simple pop-up menu.

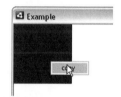

Figure 2.9   AIR context menus can appear outside the boundaries of the application window.

Listing 2.29   Adding a pop-up menu

```
package {

    import flash.display.MovieClip;
    import flash.display.NativeMenu;
    import flash.display.NativeMenuItem;
    import flash.display.Sprite;
    import flash.events.MouseEvent;

    public class Example extends MovieClip {
```

```
private var _menu:NativeMenu;

public function Example() {

    _menu = new NativeMenu();
    var item:NativeMenuItem = new NativeMenuItem("a");
    _menu.addItem(item);
    item = new NativeMenuItem("b");
    _menu.addItem(item);
    item = new NativeMenuItem("c");
    _menu.addItem(item);
    item = new NativeMenuItem("d");
    _menu.addItem(item);

    var rectangle:Sprite = new Sprite();
    rectangle.graphics.lineStyle(0, 0, 1);
    rectangle.graphics.beginFill(0, 1);
    rectangle.graphics.drawRect(0, 0, 100, 100);
    rectangle.graphics.endFill();
    addChild(rectangle);

    rectangle.addEventListener(MouseEvent.MOUSE_DOWN, showMenu);
}
private function showMenu(event:MouseEvent):void {
    _menu.display(stage, mouseX, mouseY);
}

}

}
```

1 Create new menu

2 Create rectangle

Listen for mouseDown event 3

4 Display pop-up menu

In this example, we first create a new menu and add four options to it **1**. Then we create a display object **2** that we'll use to launch the pop-up menu. We'll launch the pop-up menu when the user clicks the rectangle. Therefore we register an event listener for the mouseDown event **3**. When the user clicks the rectangle, we display the pop-up menu at the point where the user is clicking **4**.

You've now seen all the ways you can use menus in AIR applications: window menus, application menus, icon menus, context menus, and pop-up menus. Not only have we wrapped up our discussion of menus, but we've also covered all of the theoretical material in this chapter. Next we'll start applying some of this knowledge in building a sample application.

2.5 *Starting the AirTube application*

Throughout this book, we'll use a variety of smaller example applications. However, we'll also have one central, larger example application that we'll revisit and add to as we cover more and more topics. We're calling the application AirTube because it uses Adobe AIR to provide access to the popular YouTube video service. In this chapter, we'll build the foundation for the rest of the application by creating the windows that the application will use. Furthermore, we'll create some of the other foundational classes and components used by the application.

2.5.1 Overview of AirTube

AirTube uses the public YouTube developer API to create an AIR application that allows users to search the YouTube catalog by keywords, play videos, and store videos for offline playback. AirTube highlights the following features:

- Desktop application with multiple windows
- Search YouTube videos by keyword
- Play back videos
- View YouTube page for videos
- Save videos locally
- Search and play back local videos
- Detect network availability
- Save shortcuts to videos on the desktop

Before we get into the details of how to build the application, we'll first look at two screenshots from the completed application. In figure 2.10, you can see the main screen. The main screen allows users to search for videos using keywords/tags. The results are displayed in a two-column tile list.

Figure 2.10 The main screen of the AirTube application allows for searching and browsing through videos.

Figure 2.11   **The video screen allows you to view a video, go to the YouTube page, or save the video locally.**

Next we look at the video window. Figure 2.11 shows the video window, which not only plays back the selected video, but also allows the user to click through to the YouTube page for the video or to download the video for offline viewing.

In the next sections, we'll walk through the first few steps to begin building the application.

2.5.2   Getting started

Before we can start writing code, there are a few preliminary steps you'll need to take. They are as follows:

- Sign up for a YouTube developer API key
- Download two ActionScript libraries
- Configure a new AIR project

This application relies on the YouTube service. (See www.youtube.com/dev.) This is a free public service that allows developers to build applications that search YouTube's video library and play back the videos. Although the service is free, you do need an account to be able to access it.

1 If you don't have one already, you can sign up for a free YouTube account at www.youtube.com/signup. Simply fill out the form and click Sign Up.

2 Once you've created an account and logged in, you should go to your account page at www.youtube.com/my_account.

3 From your account page, click on the Developer Profile option, or you can go directly to www.youtube.com/my_profile_dev.

4 Request a new developer ID. This is the key that you'll need to access the YouTube service.

Now that you have the necessary YouTube account and key, you'll next need to get set up with the necessary ActionScript libraries. Although you could write your own code in ActionScript to work with the YouTube service directly, it's simpler to leverage existing libraries that are built expressly for that purpose. You'll need to download the as3youtubelib library as well as the as3corelib library. The official sites for these libraries are code.google.com/p/as3youtubelib and code.google.com/p/as3corelib, respectively. But to make sure you're working with the same version of the libraries that we use in this book, you can download those versions from this book's official site at www.manning.com/lott.

The next step is to create a new AIR project for the AirTube application. There's nothing unusual about this project, so you can create a new project in the way you normally would, whether using Flex Builder or configuring the project manually. Once you've created the project, add the as3youtubelib and as3corelib libraries. If you've downloaded the libraries from this book's site, you'll be downloading the source code, and the easiest way to add the code to your project is to unzip the code to the project's source directory.

That's all you need to do to configure your project. Now we can get started building the application.

2.5.3   *Building the data model*

The AirTube application centers around a data model locator that we'll call `ApplicationData`. The `ApplicationData` class uses the Singleton design pattern to ensure there's only one globally accessible instance of the class throughout the application. We use the `ApplicationData` instance to store all the information about the application state: is the application online or offline, are there any video results to a query, is a video currently downloading, and so forth. All that information gets stored in `ApplicationData`.

We're going to build `ApplicationData` (or at least the start of it) in just a minute. But first we have to create another class that we'll use as part of the application's data model. Because AirTube is essentially a video searching and viewing application, the one model class we're going to build is a video model class that we'll call `AirTube-Video`. The `AirTubeVideo` class is a wrapper for the `Video` class from the as3youtube library. The as3youtube `Video` class is how all the data from the API calls gets serialized when it's returned, and contains information such as video title, ID, thumbnail image, and so on. We're creating a wrapper class (`AirTubeVideo`) for modeling video data because, in addition to the information returned by the YouTube API, we're also going to want to store a few extra pieces of data about each video, including the URL for the .flv file and whether we've stored the particular video locally. Follow these steps to create the data model for the AirTube application:

1   Create a new ActionScript class document and save it to com/manning/
    airtube/data/AirTubeVideo.as relative to your project's source directory.

2 Add the code from listing 2.30 to the `AirTubeVideo` class. As you can see, Air-TubeVideo requires a `Video` parameter when constructing a new instance. The class has an accessor (getter) method for the `Video` object as well as two additional pieces of data: the URL for the .flv file and the offline status of the video (whether or not it's been downloaded locally).

Listing 2.30 The `AirTubeVideo` class

```
package com.manning.airtube.data {

    import com.adobe.webapis.youtube.Video;

    import flash.events.Event;
    import flash.events.EventDispatcher;

    public class AirTubeVideo extends EventDispatcher {

        private var _video:Video;
        private var _flvUrl:String;
        private var _offline:Boolean;

        public function get video():Video {
            return _video;
        }

        [Bindable(event="flvUrlChanged")]
        public function get flvUrl():String {
            return _flvUrl;
        }

        public function set flvUrl(value:String):void {
            _flvUrl = value;
            dispatchEvent(new Event("flvUrlChanged"));
        }

        [Bindable(event="offlineChanged")]
        public function set offline(value:Boolean):void {
            _offline = value;
            dispatchEvent(new Event("offlineChanged"));
        }

        public function get offline():Boolean {
            return _offline;
        }

        public function AirTubeVideo(value:Video) {
            _video = value;
        }

    }
}
```

❶ Enable Flex data binding

In the code, you can see that we're using a `[Bindable]` metadata tag ❶ that's used by Flex to enable data binding. We use the same convention throughout the book for the event names and `[Bindable]` metadata tags: the event name is the name of the getter/setter plus `Changed`. For example, in this case, the getter/setter is named `flvUrl` and the event is therefore `flvUrlChanged`.

3 Create a new ActionScript class document and save it to com/manning/air-tube/data/ApplicationData.as relative to your project's source directory.

4 Add the code from listing 2.31 to the ApplicationData class. The ApplicationData class uses the Singleton pattern, which is why it has a static _instance property and an accessor method (getInstance()) to retrieve the one instance of the class. Otherwise, ApplicationData only has two pieces of data at this time: an array of videos and a reference to a currently selected video.

Listing 2.31 The ApplicationData class

```
package com.manning.airtube.data {

    import flash.events.Event;
    import flash.events.EventDispatcher;

    public class ApplicationData extends EventDispatcher {

        static private var _instance:ApplicationData;      ◁┐   Managed
                                                                 instance of
        private var _videos:Array;                           ❶ class
        private var _currentVideo:AirTubeVideo;

        [Bindable(event="videosChanged")]
        public function set videos(value:Array):void {
            _videos = value;
            dispatchEvent(new Event("videosChanged"));
        }

        public function get videos():Array {
            return _videos;
        }

        [Bindable(event="currentVideoChanged")]
        public function set currentVideo(value:AirTubeVideo):void {
            _currentVideo = value;
            dispatchEvent(new Event("currentVideoChanged"));
        }

        public function get currentVideo():AirTubeVideo {
            return _currentVideo;
        }

        public function ApplicationData() {

        }

        static public function getInstance():ApplicationData {   ◁┐
            if (_instance == null) {
                _instance = new ApplicationData();          Accessor to
            }                                          managed instance ❷
            return _instance;
        }
    }
}
```

If you're unfamiliar with the Singleton pattern, there are two key things to look at in this code. First, there's a static property with the same type as the class itself

❶. We use this property to store the one instance of the class. Next, the get-Instance() method **❷** is a public static method that returns a reference to the one instance of the class. You'll see this same pattern used throughout several other classes in the AirTube application.

That's all that's necessary to build the basics of the data model for the AirTube application. Next we'll start building the service that the AirTube uses.

2.5.4 *Building the AirTube service*

The AirTube application is built primarily around the YouTube developer API. We'll write a class called AirTubeService that acts as a proxy to the YouTube API. We'll also add other functionality into the service class over time. The following steps walk you through building the initial stages of the service class:

1 Open a new ActionScript class document and save it to com/manning/airtube/services/AirTubeService.as relative to your AirTube project's source directory.

2 Add the code from listing 2.32 to the AirTubeService class. You'll notice that AirTubeService also uses the Singleton design pattern.

Listing 2.32 The `AirTubeService` class

```
package com.manning.airtube.services {

    import com.adobe.webapis.youtube.YouTubeService;
    import com.adobe.webapis.youtube.events.YouTubeServiceEvent;
    import com.manning.airtube.data.AirTubeVideo;
    import com.manning.airtube.data.ApplicationData;

    import flash.events.Event;

    public class AirTubeService {

        static private var _instance:AirTubeService;

        public function AirTubeService() {
        }

        static public function getInstance():AirTubeService {
            if(_instance == null) {
                _instance = new AirTubeService();
            }
            return _instance;
        }
    }
}
```

3 Add a _proxied property that references an instance of the YouTubeService class from the as3youtube library. This instance allows AirTubeService to make calls to methods of YouTubeService. Listing 2.33 shows AirTubeService with the changes in bold.

Listing 2.33 The `AirTubeService` class with the proxied service requests

```
package com.manning.airtube.services {

    import com.adobe.webapis.youtube.YouTubeService;
    import com.adobe.webapis.youtube.events.YouTubeServiceEvent;
    import com.manning.airtube.data.AirTubeVideo;
    import com.manning.airtube.data.ApplicationData;

    import flash.events.Event;

    public class AirTubeService {

        static private var _instance:AirTubeService;                    ❶ Reference to
                                                                           as3youtube
        private var _proxied:YouTubeService;                               service

        public function set key(value:String):void {     Set
                                                          developer
            _proxied.apiKey = value;                      key
        }


        public function AirTubeService() {         ❷ Create service and
                                                      listen to event
            _proxied = new YouTubeService();
            _proxied.addEventListener(
  YouTubeServiceEvent.VIDEOS_LIST_BY_TAG, getVideosByTagsResultHandler);
        }

    static public function getInstance():AirTubeService {
            if(_instance == null) {
                _instance = new AirTubeService();
            }
            return _instance;
        }

        public function getVideosByTags(tags:String):void {
            if(_proxied.apiKey.length == 0) {
                throw Error("YouTube API key not set");
            }                                                        ❸ Search
            _proxied.videos.listByTag(tags);                           for
                                                                       videos
        }

        private function getVideosByTagsResultHandler(         Video search
  event:YouTubeServiceEvent):void {                            response handler
            var videos:Array = event.data.videoList as Array;
            for(var i:Number = 0; i < videos.length; i++) {   ❹ Loop
                videos[i] = new AirTubeVideo(videos[i]);          through
            }                                                     results
            ApplicationData.getInstance().videos = videos;
        }
                                              Update data model ❺
    }
}
```

The `_proxied` property ❶ is what we'll use to store a reference to an instance of the `YouTubeService` class from the as3youtube library. We'll use the instance to make calls to the YouTube service. You can see that we create an instance of the service in the constructor ❷.

The YouTube service requires a developer key that you created in the getting started section. The YouTubeService class requires that you pass it the developer key via a property called apiKey. We're creating a setter for the AirTubeService that allows you to pass along the developer key to the YouTubeService instance.

The getVideosByTags() method ❸ makes the request to retrieve videos that contain one or more of the tags/keywords specified. This method merely makes a call to the listByTag() method that's available from the YouTube service via the _proxied instance. The only thing we're doing other than relaying the request is ensuring that the developer key is defined. If the key isn't yet defined, the service won't work. Therefore, we throw an error if the key isn't defined.

The getVideosByTagsResultHandler() method is the event handler when a response is returned from the YouTubeService's listByTag() method. This is where we'll take the result set, transform it into usable data, then assign that to the ApplicationData instance. The data is returned as an array of Video objects (from the as3youtube library). The array is stored in a data.videoList property of the event object. We want to loop through all the results and wrap them in AirTubeVideo objects ❹. Once the videos are properly formatted as AirTube-Video objects, we can assign the array to the videos property of the ApplicationData object ❺. That will cause ApplicationData to dispatch an event, notifying listeners that they should update themselves based on the new data.

We've now built the service class for the AirTube application. Next we'll build the windows for the application and wire everything up.

2.5.5 Retrieving .flv URLs

The YouTube API at the time of this writing doesn't return a direct URL to the .flv files for the videos. Instead, when you request videos from YouTube, it returns a URL to the Flash-based video player that in turn accesses the .flv file. In order to retrieve videos that we can download and save locally, the AirTube application needs to get a direct URL to the .flv file for a video. To achieve this feat, we have to resort to a bit of magic. In this section, we'll build a class that retrieves the actual .flv URL for a given video based on its YouTube player URL.

NOTE The mechanism by which we retrieve the URL for an .flv on YouTube is, to put it bluntly, a hack. As a result, we can't guarantee that YouTube will continue to support access to files in this way. Should the system change, please know that we'll make every reasonable effort to find a new working solution and make that available through the book's web site.

At the time of this writing, the URL to retrieve an .flv file from YouTube requires two pieces of information that YouTube calls video_id and t. These two pieces of information can be retrieved by making a request to the player URL as returned by the YouTube service, and then reading the video_id and t values from the URL to which the player URL redirects. An example might help clarify this. The following is an example of a player URL returned from the YouTube service:

```
http://www.youtube.com/v/llRw9UG48Dw
```

If you view that in a web browser, you'll notice that it redirects to the following URL:

```
http://www.youtube.com/swf/l.swf?video_id=llRw9UG48Dw&rel=1&eurl=&i
➥url=http%3A//i.ytimg.com/vi/llRw9UG48Dw/default.jpg&
➥t=OEgsToPDskJtLebBhzjJbUnpN-uo9iSI
```

In the preceding URL, we've shown in bold the video_id and t values to make them easier to see. These are the values we want to retrieve from the URL. With those two values, we can retrieve the .flv file using the following URL, with the video_id and t values we've retrieved being substituted for the italicized text:

```
http://www.youtube.com/get_video.php?video_id=video_id&t=t
```

In order to achieve our goal, we write a helper class called YouTubeFlvUrlRetriever and add a method to the AirTubeService class. Go ahead and complete the following steps:

1   Open a new ActionScript class document and save it as com/manning/airtube/utilities/YouTubeFlvUrlRetriever.as relative to the source directory.
2   Add the code from listing 2.34 to the YouTubeFlvUrlRetriever class.

Listing 2.34   The `YouTubeFlvUrlRetriever` class

```
package com.manning.airtube.utilities {
    import com.manning.airtube.data.AirTubeVideo;
    import flash.display.Loader;
    import flash.events.Event;
    import flash.net.URLRequest;

    import flash.net.URLVariables;


    public class YouTubeFlvUrlRetriever {

        private var _currentVideo:AirTubeVideo;           ❶ Create
        private var _loader:Loader;                          loader

        public function YouTubeFlvUrlRetriever() {
            _loader = new Loader();                        ❷ Store
        }                                                    current
                                                             video
        public function getUrl(video:AirTubeVideo):void {
            _currentVideo = video;                         ❸ Compose
            var request:URLRequest = new                     request to
URLRequest(video.video.playerURL);                           player URL
            _loader.contentLoaderInfo.addEventListener(Event.INIT,
            ➥videoInitializeHandler);
            _loader.load(request);                     ❹ Listen for
        }                                                 init event

        private function videoInitializeHandler(event:Event):void {
            var variables:URLVariables = new URLVariables();
```

```
            variables.decode(                                    5  Decode URL
         ➥_loader.contentLoaderInfo.url.split("?")[1];              variables
            var flvUrl:String = "http://www.youtube.com/get_video.php?" +
                "video_id=" + variables.video_id + "&t=" + variables.t;
            _currentVideo.flvUrl = flvUrl;        ◁        Store         Compose
            _loader.unload();      ◁           Stop      7 URL          URL to .flv  6
        }                                        loading
                                              8 player
    }

}
```

In this code, the first thing we do is construct a new `Loader` object ❶. We use a
`Loader` object to make the HTTP request to the YouTube player URL and
retrieve the `video_id` and `t` variables.

When we're ready to request a URL, the first thing we do is store a reference
to the video ❷ in order to update its `flvUrl` property once we've retrieved the
URL. Next we can create a request that points to the URL of the YouTube player
for the video ❸, and then we load the URL ❹. This will make the request and
receive the redirected URL once it initializes.

When the application receives an init response to the request, the `Loader`
object's `contentLoaderInfo.url` property will be the redirect URL containing
the `video_id` and `t` variables. We're splitting the URL on the question mark to
get just the querystring portion, then running that through `decode()` ❺ in
order to have the `URLVariables` object parse out the variables. That enables us
to construct the URL to the .flv file using the variables we just decoded ❻. Once
we've composed the correct URL, we can update the `flvUrl` property of the current video ❼. And we also need to unload the `Loader` object ❽ to stop downloading the YouTube video player because we only needed to make the request
to retrieve the variables, not the player itself.

3 Open `AirTubeService` and add the method from listing 2.35. This method sets
the `currentVideo` property of `ApplicationData` in order to keep track of the
video that the user has selected, then it tests to see whether the `flvUrl` property
of the video is null. The property will be null if the video hasn't yet been configured by the `YouTubeFlvUrlRetriever`. If the property is null, we run it through
the `YouTubeFlvUrlRetriever`.

> **Listing 2.35 The `configureVideoForPlayback()` method**

```
public function configureVideoForPlayback(video:AirTubeVideo):void {
    ApplicationData.getInstance().currentVideo = video;
    if(video.flvUrl == null) {
        new YouTubeFlvUrlRetriever().getUrl(video);
    }
}
```

We've now successfully written the code to retrieve the .flv URL. Next we'll start building the windows that allow the user to search for videos, see the results, and even play
back video.

2.5.6   *Building the AirTube main window*

The main window for the AirTube application (which you can see in figure 2.10) consists of a search control bar, a list view for video search results, and a button to launch the selected video for playback. In this section, we'll build the main window and wire it up to allow the user to make requests to the YouTube service for video results. Follow these steps:

1 Create a new MXML document and save it as AirTube.mxml to the source directory of the AirTube project.

2 Add the code from listing 2.36 to the document. You'll notice that we've designed AirTube.mxml such that it also uses the Singleton pattern.

> **Listing 2.36   AirTube.mxml**

```
<?xml version="1.0" encoding="utf-8"?>
<mx:WindowedApplication xmlns:mx="http://www.adobe.com/2006/mxml"
 layout="absolute" width="800" height="600"
creationComplete="creationCompleteHandler();">
   <mx:Script>
      <![CDATA[
         import com.manning.airtube.services.AirTubeService;
         import com.manning.airtube.data.ApplicationData;

         static private var _instance:AirTube;

         private var _service:AirTubeService;

         static public function getInstance():AirTube {
            return _instance;       ◁─┐  No lazy                    Run ❷
         }                          ❶  instantiation    initialization
         private function creationCompleteHandler():void {  ◁──────────┘
            _service = AirTubeService.getInstance();    ◁─┐  Get ❸
            _service.key = "YourAPIKey";    ◁─┐  Set        service
            _instance = this;    ◁─┐  Set     developer
         }                          Singleton  key
      ]]>                          instance
   </mx:Script>
   <mx:VBox width="100%">
      <mx:Label text="AirTube: Adobe AIR and YouTube" />
      <mx:HBox>
         <mx:Label text="tags:" />
         <mx:TextInput id="tags" text="Adobe AIR" />
         <mx:Button label="Search For Videos" />
      </mx:HBox>
         <mx:TileList id="videoList"
         dataProvider="{ApplicationData.getInstance().videos}"
         width="100%" height="400"
         columnCount="2" horizontalScrollPolicy="off" />  ◁─┐  Component
      </mx:VBox>                                              to display
</mx:WindowedApplication>                                    results
```

In most cases of the Singleton pattern, the getInstance() method uses lazy instantiation, creating an instance of the class if it hasn't been created already.

In this case, that isn't necessary. We can simply return a reference to _instance
❶ without testing whether _instance is null. Because AirTube.mxml is the
WindowedApplication instance for the AirTube application, we know that it'll
always exist before any other code tries to reference it.

The AirTube.mxml code is wired up to call the creationCompleteHandler()
method ❷ when the creationComplete event occurs. In the creationCom-
pleteHandler() method, we add the code that needs to occur when the application starts. We'll use the AirTubeService instance a lot in this document.
Therefore, we'll just store a reference to it ❸. We then need to set the developer key to use for the YouTube service. You must replace *YourAPIKey* with your
YouTube API key for this to work. And we also need to assign the this instance
to the _instance property. This is part of the Singleton pattern. We know that
there's only one instance of AirTube.mxml ever created, and we know that it's
automatically created when the application starts.

We use a tile list component to display the search results when the user
searches for videos. Note that we're using databinding to wire up the component with the videos property of the ApplicationData instance. Any time the
videos property updates, the tile list will refresh.

3 Add the code that makes the service request for the videos. This requires adding an event handler to the search button. The changes to the code are shown
in bold in listing 2.37.

Listing 2.37 Adding search behavior to AirTube.mxml

```
<?xml version="1.0" encoding="utf-8"?>
<mx:WindowedApplication xmlns:mx="http://www.adobe.com/2006/mxml"
 layout="absolute" width="800" height="600"
 creationComplete="creationCompleteHandler();">
   <mx:Script>
      <![CDATA[
         import com.manning.airtube.services.AirTubeService;
         import com.manning.airtube.data.ApplicationData;

         static private var _instance:AirTube;

         private var _service:AirTubeService;

         static public function getInstance():AirTube {
            return _instance;
         }

         private function creationCompleteHandler():void {
            _service = AirTubeService.getInstance();
            _service.key = "YourAPIKey";
            _instance = this;
         }

         private function getVideosByTags():void {
            _service.getVideosByTags(tags.text);
         }
```

```
        ]]>
    </mx:Script>
    <mx:VBox width="100%">
        <mx:Label text="AirTube: Adobe AIR and YouTube" />
        <mx:HBox>
            <mx:Label text="tags:" />
            <mx:TextInput id="tags" text="Adobe AIR" />
            <mx:Button label="Search For Videos" click=
            ➥"getVideosByTags();" />
        </mx:HBox>
        <mx:TileList id="videoList"
            dataProvider="{ApplicationData.getInstance().videos}"
            width="100%" height="400"
            columnCount="2" horizontalScrollPolicy="off" />
    </mx:VBox>
</mx:WindowedApplication>
```

4 Test your application at this point, and you'll probably see something similar to
   figure 2.12 (assuming you run the search). You'll notice that the search results
   show up simply as text in the list—and not particularly meaningful or useful
   text to most users. We'd like to change that by creating a custom item renderer
   for the tile list. To do that, first open a new MXML document and save it as
   com/manning/airtube/ui/VideoTileRenderer.mxml relative to your project
   source directory.

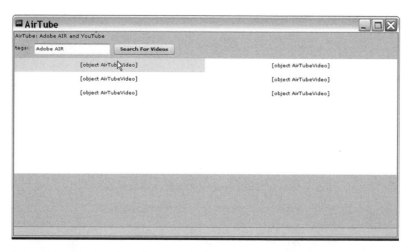

**Figure 2.12   The AirTube main window before customizing the item renderer for the
search results**

5 Add the code from listing 2.38 to the `VideoTileRenderer` component. The
   code is simple. It uses an image and a label to display the thumbnail and the
   title of the video that's passed to the renderer via the `data` property.

Listing 2.38 VideoTileRenderer.mxml

```
<?xml version="1.0" encoding="utf-8"?>
<mx:HBox xmlns:mx="http://www.adobe.com/2006/mxml" width="200"
➥height="100"
 verticalScrollPolicy="off" horizontalScrollPolicy="off">
   <mx:Image source="{data.video.thumbnailUrl}" />
   <mx:Label text="{data.video.title}" />
</mx:HBox>
```

6 Update AirTube.mxml to tell it to use the correct item renderer. All we need to do is update one line of code by adding an `itemRenderer` attribute to the `TileList` tag, as shown in listing 2.39.

Listing 2.39 Using a custom item renderer with the tile list

```
<mx:TileList id="videoList"
        dataProvider="{ApplicationData.getInstance().videos}"
        width="100%" height="400"
        columnCount="2" horizontalScrollPolicy="off"
        itemRenderer="com.manning.airtube.ui.VideoTileRenderer" />
```

Now that we've created the main window, we're going to add two more windows: the video and HTML windows.

2.5.7 *Adding the video and HTML windows*

The AirTube application has two windows in addition to the main window. One allows for the playback of videos and one allows for the viewing of HTML pages. (In this case we're allowing the user to view the YouTube page for a video.) To add these windows to the application, complete the following steps:

1 Create a new MXML document and save it as com/manning/airtube/windows/ VideoWindow.mxml relative to the project's source directory.

2 Add the code from listing 2.40 to the `VideoWindow` component.

Listing 2.40 VideoWindow.mxml

```
<?xml version="1.0" encoding="utf-8"?>                      ⟵ Set width
<mx:Window xmlns:mx="http://www.adobe.com/2006/mxml"           and height
    width="400" height="400"         Set type to utility
    type="utility"            ⟵
    closing="closingHandler(event);"                          ⟵   Handle
    creationComplete="creationCompleteHandler();">  ⟵              closing
                                Handle creationComplete event      event

    <mx:Script>
      <![CDATA[
         import com.manning.airtube.services.AirTubeService;
         import com.manning.airtube.data.ApplicationData;

         [Bindable]
         private var _applicationData:ApplicationData;

         private function creationCompleteHandler():void {
            _applicationData = ApplicationData.getInstance();
```

```
        }
        private function closingHandler(event:Event):void {
            event.preventDefault();                          ┐  Prevent
            visible = false;                                 │  window
        }                                                    │  from
                                                             ① closing
        private function togglePlayback():void {
            if(videoDisplay.playing) {
                videoDisplay.pause();
                playPauseButton.label = "Play";
            }
            else {
                videoDisplay.play();
                playPauseButton.label = "Pause";
            }
        }
    ]]>
</mx:Script>
<mx:VBox>                               Display video title  ②
    <mx:Label text=                                          ┐
    "{_applicationData.currentVideo.video.title}" />         │
    <mx:VideoDisplay id="videoDisplay"
        source="{_applicationData.currentVideo.flvUrl}"   ◁───┐
        width="400" height="300" />
    <mx:HBox>                            Wire up video display ③
        <mx:Button id="playPauseButton" label="Pause"
                click="togglePlayback();" />
    </mx:HBox>
</mx:VBox>
</mx:Window>
```

Notice that when the closing event occurs, we handle it to prevent the default behavior ❶ and instead set the visibility of the window. Also note that the label and video display components use data binding to wire themselves up to properties of the current video ❷ ❸.

3 Create a new MXML document and save it as com/manning/airtube/windows/HTMLWindow.mxml relative to the project's source directory.

4 Add the code from listing 2.41 to HTMLWindow.mxml. This window has no content at this time. We'll add content in chapter 7. You'll notice that this component also handles the closing event in the same way as VideoWindow.

Listing 2.41   HTMLWindow.mxml

```
<?xml version="1.0" encoding="utf-8"?>
<mx:Window xmlns:mx="http://www.adobe.com/2006/mxml" layout="absolute"
    width="800" height="800" closing="closingHandler(event);">
    <mx:Script>
        <![CDATA[

            private function closingHandler(event:Event):void {
                event.preventDefault();
                visible = false;
```

```
        }

      ]]>
    </mx:Script>
</mx:Window>
```

5 Update AirTube.mxml to contain references to instances of the two windows we
   just created, and allow the user to launch the video window and view a selected
   video. Also, add code to close all the windows when the user closes the application. Listing 2.42 shows the changes in bold.

Listing 2.42 Updating AirTube.mxml with the windows

```
<?xml version="1.0" encoding="utf-8"?>
<mx:WindowedApplication xmlns:mx="http://www.adobe.com/2006/mxml"
 layout="absolute" width="800" height="600"
 creationComplete="creationCompleteHandler();"
 closing="closingHandler();">
   <mx:Script>
      <![CDATA[
         import com.manning.airtube.services.AirTubeService;
         import com.manning.airtube.data.ApplicationData;

         static private var _instance:AirTube;

         private var _service:AirTubeService;
         private var _videoWindow:VideoWindow;
         private var _htmlWindow:HTMLWindow;
         static public function getInstance():AirTube {
            return _instance;
         }

         private function creationCompleteHandler():void {
            _service = AirTubeService.getInstance();
            _service.key = "YourAPIKey";
            _instance = this;
            _videoWindow = new VideoWindow();          ➊ Create instance
            _htmlWindow = new HTMLWindow();               of windows
         }

         private function getVideosByTags():void {
            _service.getVideosByTags(tags.text);
         }

         private function playVideo():void {             ➋ Retrieve
            var video:AirTubeVideo =                         selected video
              videoList.selectedItem as AirTubeVideo;
            _service.configureVideoForPlayback(video);
            if(_videoWindow.nativeWindow == null) {      ➌ Get .flv URL
               _videoWindow.open();
            }                              Open video
            else {                         window ➍
               _videoWindow.activate();
            }
         }                                              ➎ Open
                                                           HTML
         public function launchHTMLWindow(url:String):void {   window
```

```
        if(_htmlWindow.nativeWindow == null) {
            _htmlWindow.open();
        }
        else {
            _htmlWindow.activate();
        }
    }
    private function closingHandler():void {
        for(var i:Number = 0; i <
        nativeApplication.openedWindows.length; i++) {
            nativeApplication.openedWindows[i].close();
        }
    }
```

❻ **Close all windows**

```
    ]]>
</mx:Script>
<mx:VBox width="100%">
    <mx:Label text="AirTube: Adobe AIR and YouTube" />
    <mx:HBox>
        <mx:Label text="tags:" />
        <mx:TextInput id="tags" text="Adobe AIR" />
        <mx:Button label="Search For Videos"
        click="getVideosByTags();" />
    </mx:HBox>
    <mx:TileList id="videoList"
        dataProvider="{ApplicationData.getInstance().videos}"
        width="100%" height="400"
        columnCount="2" horizontalScrollPolicy="off" />
    <mx:Button label="Play Selected Video" click="playVideo();"
        enabled="{videoList.selectedItem != null}" />
</mx:VBox>
</mx:WindowedApplication>
```

Button to play video ❼

The application only allows one video window and one HTML window. We reuse these instances for every video and every HTML page the application opens, thus creating instances of each of them ❶. We open them based on user action.

When the user wants to play a video, we need to do several things. First we need to retrieve the video that the user has selected from the list ❷. Then we need to run the video through the configureVideoForPlayback() method to make sure it has the URL to the .flv file ❸. And then we can open the video window instance ❹.

In our code, we've added a method that doesn't get called yet. We're defining the launchHTMLWindow() method ❺ here in order to call it later. This method simply opens the HTML window.

As with most of the applications we build, we want to make sure that, when the user closes the main window, it closes all the windows in the application. We use the closingHandler() method ❻ for this purpose.

We also add a button to play the selected video ❼. When the user clicks on the button, it calls playVideo(). The button is only enabled when a video has been selected from the list.

With that, we've completed the first phase of the AirTube application. Thus far, the user can search for videos and play back a video in the video window. As we continue through subsequent chapters, we'll add more functionality to the application.

2.6 *Summary*

In this chapter, you've learned all the fundamentals of working with applications, windows, and menus. That's a lot of information, and much of it's probably new to you, because the concepts are more relevant to desktop applications than they are to web applications.

Take your time and reread any material from this chapter that you feel you need to review. Here's a summary of some of the key points you'll want to be familiar with:

- Applications and windows are represented programmatically using `Native-Application` and `NativeWindow` objects in pure ActionScript, and `Windowed-Application` and `Window` objects in Flex.
- Creating windows, opening windows, and adding content to windows are independent actions that you need to manage.
- You can create windows that have irregular shapes.
- Applications allow you to do a variety of application-level functions such as detecting user idleness and launching an application in full-screen mode.
- AIR allows you to create native operating system menus and use them in a variety of ways, including window menus, application menus, icon menus, context menus, and pop-up menus.

When you're ready, go ahead to the next chapter, where you'll learn all about working with the file system to do things such as read and write files.

File system integration 3

This chapter is practically brimming over with information, because there's a tremendous amount you can do with the file system capabilities in AIR. In fact, you're limited in large part only by your imagination. We have a lot of ground to cover in this chapter, including the following:

- Referencing files and directories
- Getting directory listings
- Copying and moving files and directories
- Deleting files and directories
- Reading from files
- Writing to files

We're going to tackle all these topics in detail, with lots of examples you can use to follow along. Before long you'll be an old pro at working with the file system.

Before we get to the core file system skills, we're going to talk about the important topic of synchronous and asynchronous programming. This is an important concept for much of AIR programming, and especially important when working with the file system.

3.1 Understanding synchronicity

The concepts of synchronous and asynchronous programming are important when building AIR applications. These concepts aren't unique to working with the file system, but this is the first point in the book when these concepts are going to be important, so we'll cover the topic here.

Synchronous programming is likely familiar to you, because it's the most common and the simplest form of programming. When code executes synchronously, each statement runs in sequence with each statement completing and returning any result before the next statement is executed. Listing 3.1 shows an example of typical synchronous code.

Listing 3.1 Sample synchronous code

```
var devoTracks:Array = new Array("Freedom Of Choice", "Planet Earth",
  "Cold War", "Don't You Know");
devoTracks.push("Mr. B's Ballroom");
var trackCount:int = devoTracks.length;
for(var i:int = 0; i < trackCount; i++) {
  trace(devoTracks[i]);
}
```

In the listing, each statement must complete its execution before the next line of code can execute. For example, the first line of code creates an array with initial values before the next statement can execute, which appends a value to the array. Synchronous programming is so normal and second nature, it's likely that you hardly think of it as anything other than just "programming." While most ActionScript statements are synchronous in nature, there are many statements that are *asynchronous*.

Asynchronous statements don't have to complete execution before the next statement executes. This type of programming may seem chaotic, but it has real value in scenarios where an operation may take a long time to execute, because that could cause an application to halt or freeze up from the user's perspective. Consider the following common scenario: you want to load XML data at runtime from an external XML file in order to use it in an application. Using the `flash.net.URLLoader` class, this task is simple. All you have to do is construct the URLLoader object and call the `load()` method, telling it where to find the XML file. However, depending on the amount of data and the network connection being used, it could take a little or a lot of time to load the data. If the `load()` method of a URLLoader object executed synchronously, everything in the application could freeze up until the XML data had loaded completely. Because of that possibility, the load() method is designed to execute asynchronously. That means that the application doesn't have to wait until the load() method has completely loaded the data before the next statement executes. Listing 3.2 demonstrates this concept.

Listing 3.2   Asynchronous statement execution

```
private var _loader:URLLoader;

private function startXmlRequest():void {
    _loader = new URLLoader();
    _loader.addEventListener(Event.COMPLETE, loaderCompleteHandler);
    _loader.load(new URLRequest("data.xml"));
    trace(_loader.data);
}

private function loaderCompleteHandler(event:Event):void {
    trace(_loader.data);
}
```

In the listing, you can see that there are two trace() statements. The trace() statement that immediately follows the call to the load() method always executes before the trace() statement in the loaderCompleteHandler() method. This is because the load() method of a URLLoader object executes asynchronously. That means that the trace() statement following the call to load() executes before the data completes loading. The implication is that the first trace() statement always outputs null, because the data property of the URLLoader object will be null until the data has completed loading. This is an important implication of asynchronous programming. When a statement executes asynchronously, the results of that operation won't be available immediately after the statement begins execution.

Because the results of asynchronous operations aren't immediately available, asynchronous programming requires a little more careful planning than purely synchronous programming. As an example, you wouldn't want to try to do something with the data from a load() request before it was actually available. Asynchronous programming can prevent your application from appearing to freeze, but it means you need to make sure that code executes in the right sequence. You can ensure the correct sequence of code execution by using events and event listeners. An example of this is shown in listing 3.2. Objects can broadcast events when something of significance occurs. For example, when a URLLoader object completes loading data from a load() request, it broadcasts (or dispatches) an event of type complete. You can register a method with an object such that the method gets called when that object broadcasts a particular event type. The method is then known as an *event listener*. In listing 3.2, the URLLoader object is an event dispatcher that dispatches a complete event, and the loaderCompleteHandler() method is an event listener that gets called when the URLLoader object dispatches the complete event. In that way, you can be sure that the URLLoader object's data will be loaded and available when the loaderCompleteHandler() method is called.

As you can see, while synchronous programming may be the most common sort of programming, even standard ActionScript code has some operations that are inherently asynchronous. Most core ActionScript operations are either synchronous or asynchronous, but not both. But many AIR operations have both synchronous and asynchronous versions. That gives you, the developer, more flexibility in how you code, but it also gives you more responsibility for determining which version to select in a given scenario.

As a general rule, synchronous operations are most appropriate when the operation will execute quickly. Because a synchronous operation that requires a lot of time to execute can cause the application to appear to freeze up, it's usually advisable to use asynchronous versions of operations in such cases.

In this chapter, you'll learn about using the `flash.filesystem.File` class to get a directory listing from the local file system. This is an AIR operation that has both synchronous and asynchronous versions. The synchronous version is the most intuitive to use because it returns an array of the contents of the directory, which you can use immediately. For example, listing 3.3 retrieves the contents of a directory (from a `File` object called `documentsDirectory`), and immediately assigns that result to the `dataProvider` property of a list component.

Listing 3.3 Retrieving a directory listing synchronously

```
directoryContentList.dataProvider =
➥documentsDirectory.getDirectoryListing();
```

If a directory happens to have a large number of files and subdirectories, the operation can take a long time. That will halt all other operations in Flash player. Depending on what's going on in the application at that time, it could potentially mean that the user would be unable to click on buttons, video or animations might halt, audio could be choppy, and the application could generally be unresponsive until the directory listing operation completed. In some cases it isn't problematic if the application appears to freeze during the directory listing operation, but in many cases it isn't ideal. Instead, you can use the asynchronous version of the operation, `getDirectory-ListingAsync()`. The asynchronous version of the operation, as with nearly all ActionScript asynchronous operations, doesn't return a value. Instead, you must register to listen for an event that occurs when the operation has completed. In the case of `getDirectoryListingAsync()`, the `File` object from which you call the method will dispatch a `directoryListing` event when the directory listing operation completes. Because the method doesn't immediately return the directory listing, you must wait until the event occurs before you can read the data or do anything with it. The code snippet in listing 3.4 illustrates how an asynchronous directory listing works.

Listing 3.4 Retrieving a directory listing asynchronously

```
private function getDocumentsDirectoryListing():void {
    var documentsDirectory:File = File.documentsDirectory;
```

```
        documentsDirectory.addEventListener(FileListEvent.DIRECTORY_LISTING,
        ➥directoryListingHandler);
        documentsDirectory.getDirectoryListingAsync();
    }

    private function directoryListingHandler(event:FileListEvent):void {
        directoryListingList.dataProvider = event.files;
    }
```

If you compare listings 3.3 and 3.4, you can see that achieving a result asynchronously requires more code and more complex logic than achieving the same result synchronously. However, asynchronous programming can help you build an application that works without freezing up even when particular operations take a while to execute.

Throughout this chapter and the rest of the book, we'll tell you when there are synchronous and asynchronous versions of an operation, and we'll show you examples of both in many cases. If you need a reminder about the differences between synchronous and asynchronous programming, refer back to this section at any time.

3.1.1 *Canceling asynchronous file operations*

When you make a call to an asynchronous file system operation, you know when it's complete because an event is dispatched. For example, when you make a request for a directory listing asynchronously, the File object from which you've called the method dispatches a directoryListing event when the operation has completed. Even though you know that at some point an operation will likely complete, you don't necessarily have a way of knowing ahead of time how long that operation will take. It's possible that you (as the developer of an AIR application) or a user of your application may decide that an operation is taking too long. For example, retrieving a directory listing, copying, or writing a file may take longer than users are willing to wait. AIR allows you to cancel any asynchronous file system operation by calling the cancel() method on the File object that initiated the request. Keep in mind that, while both File and FileStream objects call asynchronous methods, you call cancel() on the File object to cancel them.

> **NOTE** Not only can synchronous file I/O methods make your application appear to freeze, but normal nonfile I/O code can too. Say your application reads an image file and runs a facial recognition algorithm on the data to isolate the faces for further manipulation. The file may be read asynchronously into memory, but, once loaded, the facial recognition algorithm will be run synchronously. Depending on the design and efficiency of the algorithm, this may make the application appear to freeze. If you have code that's likely to make your application appear frozen, refactor the logic to spread out the processing over multiple frames or intervals of time.

All of the file system operations you'll learn about in this chapter require that you have a reference to an actual directory or file on the user's system. For example, to get a directory listing, you must first have a reference to a directory. In the next section, you'll learn how to get references to files and directories.

3.2   Getting references to files and directories

When you use your computer, there are lots of ways you can get access to a file or directory. You can use the file system explorer to navigate to a file or directory, you can use a shortcut or alias, and you can maybe even access a file or directory from a launch pad or start menu or any number of other options. Just as you have all these options when using your computer, AIR provides lots of ways to access files and directories programmatically. Throughout the following sections we'll look at how to access files and directories in a variety of ways, and we'll explain why you would use each.

3.2.1   Introducing the File class

AIR uses instances of the `flash.filesystem.File` class to represent both files and directories on the user's local file system. In the sections that follow, you'll learn how to get references to files and directories in a variety of ways. Regardless of how you get a reference to a file or directory, you'll be working with a `File` object. Once you have a `File` object, you can call any of the methods available to it in order to do things such as create, read, write, and delete files and directories.

Sometimes you'll have a `File` object but you'll be uncertain as to whether it represents a file or a directory. For example, you might retrieve an array of `File` objects from a directory listing operation, and need to determine which are files and which are directories. You can use a `File` object's `isDirectory` property to determine if it's a directory. If this property is `false`, the object is a file.

Now that you've learned a little about the `File` class, let's look at how you can use the `File` class to retrieve references to common directories on a local file system.

3.2.2   Referencing common directories

Every operating system has several common conceptual directories. For example, both Windows and OS X have a user desktop directory and a documents directory. Because these directories are common, you're likely to want to reference them frequently in your AIR applications. Yet even though they are common, it wouldn't be trivial to determine the correct absolute path to these directories. The good news is that AIR helps us out by providing easy ways to reference these directories via static properties of the `File` class. Not only is it convenient, it's also platform-independent. That means that, even though the actual paths to user desktop directories on your Windows computer and your friend's OS X computer are vastly different, AIR allows you to gain a reference to them in exactly the same way using the `File.desktop-Directory` property. Table 3.1 outlines these directories and the static properties used to access them.

As you might've guessed, all of the static properties listed in table 3.1 are `File` objects themselves. That means you can call any of the methods of the `File` class on

Table 3.1   Platform-independent common directories

Conceptual directory	Description	Property
User's home	Root directory of the user's account	`File.userDirectory`
User's documents	Documents directory typically found in the home directory	`File.documentsDirectory`
Desktop	Directory representing the user's desktop	`File.desktopDirectory`
Application storage	Unique storage directory created for each installed application	`File.applicationStorageDirectory`
Application	Directory where the application is installed	`File.applicationDirectory`

those file objects. For example, if you want to retrieve the directory listing (synchronously) for the user's desktop, all you have to do is run the code as shown in listing 3.5.

Listing 3.5   Reading the directory listing for the user's desktop directory

```
var listing:Array = File.desktopDirectory.getDirectoryListing();
```

There's one other way you can access two of these special directories, application and application storage. When you construct a new `File` object, you can pass the constructor a parameter that specifies the path to the file or directory you'd like to reference using that object. There are two special schemes supported by the `File` class: `app` and `app-storage`.

NOTE   You're probably most familiar with schemes such as `http` or `https` (or perhaps even `file`), as you've seen them used in web browsers. For example, in the address http://www.manning.com, `http` is the scheme. AIR allows you to use `app` and `app-storage` as schemes for `File` objects. When you use them as schemes, you must follow them with a colon and then a forward slash.

The following example creates a reference to the application directory:

```
var applicationDirectory:File = new File("app:/");
```

Note that the preceding code is equivalent to using `File.applicationDirectory`.

Referencing common directories is useful, to be sure. But it's hardly going to meet all the needs of every AIR application by itself. For example, what if you wanted to retrieve a reference to a file in the documents directory rather than the documents directory itself? For this, you'll need to take it a step further by using either relative or absolute referencing. We'll look at relative referencing next.

3.2.3 Relative referencing

One of the great features of AIR is that it enables you to easily create cross-platform applications. Referencing directories can be a challenge when building cross-platform applications. AIR alleviates this challenge to a degree by providing built-in references to common directories, as you've seen in the previous section. Therefore, if you can manage to always reference directories relatively, using the common directories as a starting point, you'll keep the applications you build truly cross-platform.

The alternative to referencing directories relatively is referencing them absolutely. Let's look at an example to contrast the two ways of referencing directories and see where the difficulties arise. For this example, imagine that we're building an application that needs to write a text file to a subdirectory (which we'll name notes) of the user's documents directory. First we consider how to reference that directory in an absolute fashion. To start, we have an obvious problem: the absolute location of a user's documents directory is different on Windows and OS X. On Windows systems, the documents directory for a user is generally located at *DriveLetter:\Documents and Settings\username\My Documents*, where *DriveLetter* is the letter name assigned to the drive (most commonly named C) and *username* is the username of the person currently logged in to the system. On OS X, the user's documents directory is usually at /Users/*username*/Documents, where *username* is the username of the person currently logged in to the system. Even once we've calculated the correct operating system, we're still faced with the dilemma of not knowing the correct username to use. Even assuming we could gather all the necessary information to calculate the correct absolute path to the notes subdirectory of the user's documents directory, it's clearly a lot of work, and surely there must be a better way.

The better way is to reference directories and files relatively instead of absolutely whenever possible. We've already seen how to access a reference to the user's documents directory using `File.documentsDirectory`. All we need now is a way to reference a directory relative to that. The `File` class makes this simple by providing a `resolvePath()` method. The `resolvePath()` method allows you to pass it a string containing a relative path to a directory or file, and it resolves that to a subdirectory or file relative to the File object from which you've called the method. In our example, we can get a reference to the notes subdirectory of the documents directory using the following code:

```
var notesDirectory:File = File.documentsDirectory.resolvePath("notes");
```

You can use the `resolvePath()` method to access a subdirectory or a file within a directory, as in the preceding example. You can also use `resolvePath()` to access a subdirectory or file that's nested further within a directory tree. For example, the following code resolves to a file called reminders.txt within the recent subdirectory of the notes directory located inside the user's documents directory.

```
var reminders:File = File.documentsDirectory.resolvePath(
➥"notes/recent/reminders.txt");
```

You'll notice that the delimiter used between directories and files in a path is the forward slash (/), similar to how a path is represented on a Unix system. You must use a forward slash as the delimiter. The back slash has a special meaning when used within an ActionScript string, and it won't work as a delimiter in a path.

You can also use two dots to indicate one directory up in a path. For example, the following code resolves to the parent directory of the user's documents directory:

```
var parent:File = File.documentsDirectory.resolvePath("..");
```

In addition to using resolvePath() to get relative paths, you can also retrieve a relative path to one file or directory from another using the getRelativePath() method. The method requires that you pass it a reference to a File object to which you'd like the relative path. For example, the following code determines the relative path from the user directory to the documents directory:

```
var relativePath:String = File.userDirectory.getRelativePath(
➥File.documentsDirectory);
```

The documents directory is usually a subdirectory of the user directory. For instance, on a Windows system, the value of relativePath would be My Documents, because the documents directory is a subdirectory of the user directory, and that subdirectory is called My Documents.

If the relative path isn't a subdirectory or a file located within a subdirectory of the File object from which the method was called, then getRelativePath() returns an empty string by default. You can specify an optional second parameter that indicates whether or not to use the dot-dot notation in the path. If you specify a value of true, getRelativePath() returns a value even when the path is outside of the directory from which the method was called.

As we've already stressed, it's better to rely on relative referencing whenever possible. Not only will relative referencing allow you to more reliably build cross-platform and flexible applications, but it's usually a lot easier than the alternative. Relative referencing will work for almost all of your file system needs. But there are cases when you simply need to reference a file or directory absolutely. We'll look at how to do that next.

3.2.4   *Absolute referencing*

When necessary, you can reference directories and files in an absolute manner. The most direct way to do this is to pass the full path to the directory or file to the File constructor, as in the following example:

```
var documentsAndSettings:File = new File("C:/Documents and Settings/");
```

You can see in this example that, even though the path clearly points to a directory on a Windows computer system, the path uses forward slashes. Unlike the resolvePath() method (which requires forward slashes as delimiters), you can use back slashes in the path for the File constructor. Back slashes and forward slashes are interpreted as the same thing in a path passed to the `File` constructor. However, forward slashes are a little easier, because back slashes require that you escape them by using two consecutively, as in the following example:

```
var documentsAndSettings:File = new File("C:\\Documents and Settings\\");
```

When you need to reference files or directories using absolute paths, you need to know the root directories available on the system. For example, in Windows, C:\ is frequently the primary system drive, but you can't rely on that always being true for all systems. You can use the static `File.getRootDirectories()` method to return an array of `File` objects referencing all the root directories.

3.2.5 Accessing a full path

Regardless of whether you're referencing a file or directory absolutely or relatively, you may still want to get the full native path on the system. All `File` objects have a `nativePath` property that tells you this information. Listing 3.6 shows a simple test you can run that outputs the native paths of all the static `File` properties of the `File` class.

Listing 3.6   Native paths of common directories

```
<?xml version="1.0" encoding="utf-8"?>
<mx:WindowedApplication
    xmlns:mx="http://www.adobe.com/2006/mxml"
    layout="absolute"
    creationComplete="creationCompleteHandler();">
  <mx:Script>
    <![CDATA[
        import flash.filesystem.File;                      Output user
                                                           directory path      Output
        private function creationCompleteHandler():void {                     documents
         print(File.userDirectory.nativePath);            ◁──────┘            directory path
         print(File.documentsDirectory.nativePath);                           ◁──────
         print(File.desktopDirectory.nativePath); ◁─┐
                                                     Output desktop path
     print(File.applicationStorageDirectory.nativePath);   ◁────────
         print(File.applicationDirectory.nativePath); ◁─                      Output
        }                             Output application directory path        application
                                                                              storage path
        private function print(string:String):void {
         output.text += ">" + string + "\n";    ◁─
        }                                           Append text
    ]]>                                          ❶ to text area
  </mx:Script>
  <mx:TextArea id="output" width="100%" height="100%" />
</mx:WindowedApplication>
```

The listing uses a `print()` function ❶ to append the `nativePath` values of the common directories to a text area component. The values that this outputs will depend on the following factors: operating system, system user, AIR application name, and AIR application ID. We'll create a fictitious scenario to give you some sample output values. In our scenario, the system user (the user who's logged in to the computer) is

Christina, the Application ID is com.manning.airinaction.ExampleApplication, and the application is named Example Application. In that case, if the application is run on a Windows computer, the output would be as follows:

1   C:\Documents and Settings\Christina
2   C:\Documents and Settings\Christina\My Documents
3   C:\Documents and Settings\Christina\Desktop
4   C:\Documents and Settings\Christina\Application Data\com.manning.airinaction.ExampleApplication. AFA83DFB7118641978BF5E9EE3C49B0A3C82FA13.1\Local Store
5   C:\Program Files\Example Application

With the same set of parameters, the output would be as follows on an OS X computer:

1   /Users/Christina
2   /Users/Christina/Documents
3   /Users/Christina/Desktop
4   /Users/Christina/Library/Preferences/com/manning.airinaction/ExampleAppliction. AFA83DFB7118641978BF5E9EE3C49B0A3C82FA13.1/Local Store
5   /Applications/Example Application.app/Contents/Resources

Although we've only looked at examples that retrieve the native path of the common system directories, you can use the `nativePath` property with any `File` object that references any file or directory on the user's system.

3.2.6   *User referencing*

Thus far we've seen how to create references to files and directories using both relative and absolute techniques. These two techniques work well when the AIR application can determine the file or directory it should reference. For example, if you know that there should be a subdirectory called preloadedAssets in the application directory, then you know that you can reference that directory as follows:

```
var preloadedAssets:File = File.applicationDirectory.resolvePath(
    "preloadedAssets");
```

However, there are plenty of scenarios in which the AIR application simply can't anticipate what file or directory to reference. For example, if the application should show a directory listing of a user-selected directory rather than a predetermined subdirectory in the application directory, you can't use the techniques you've learned thus far. Instead, you need a way to allow the user to specify the reference. AIR allows you to access file and directory references specified by the user using four methods of the `File` class, listed in table 3.2.

Each of these methods opens a dialog box that allows a user to browse her file system and select one (or many, in one case) file or directory. The dialog box opened by each of the methods is similar yet subtly different.

Table 3.2 File class methods that open a dialog box

Method	Description
browseForDirectory()	Lets the user select a directory
browseForOpen()	Lets the user select a file to open
browseForOpenMultiple()	Lets the user select multiple files to open
browseForSave()	Lets the user select a file location to save to

BROWSING FOR A DIRECTORY

The browseForDirectory() method opens a dialog similar to the one you see in figure 3.1. The dialog prompts the user to select a directory. Only directories are available for selection in this dialog. You can also see that below the title bar is a section for text. In the figure, the text says "Select a directory". *This text is configurable using the one parameter of the browseForDirectory() method.*

The starting directory shown in the dialog is determined by which directory the File object that calls the method references. Figure 3.1 shows a dialog that would be opened using the following code:

Figure 3.1
The browseForDirectory()
method opens a dialog such as this.

```
var documents:File = File.documentsDirectory;
documents.browseForDirectory("Select a directory");
```

If you call browseForDirectory() on a File object that points to a file or a directory that doesn't exist, the selected directory in the dialog will be the first directory up the path that does exist. If no part of the path points to a valid existing directory, then the desktop is the default-selected directory.

BROWSING TO SELECT A FILE OR FILES

The browseForOpen() and browseForOpenMultiple() methods both allow you to open a dialog that prompts the user to select files instead of directories. The difference between the two methods is that browseForOpen() allows the user to select only one file, while browseForOpenMultiple() allows the user to select one or more files. Both dialogs look identical. Figure 3.2 shows what they look like.

Both methods require that you specify a string that appears in the title bar of the dialog. In the dialog shown in figure 3.2, the value is "Select a file", though you could specify any value you like. The following code would open the dialog shown in figure 3.2:

```
var desktop:File = File.desktopDirectory;
desktop.browseForOpen("Select a file");
```

Figure 3.2 The browseForOpen() and browseForOpenMultiple () dialogs allow users to select files.

The browseForOpen() and browseForOpenMultiple() methods determine the initial directory for the dialog in the same way browseForDirectory() does. In figure 3.2, you can see that the initial directory is the desktop. That's because the code used to open that dialog called the browseForOpen() method from a File object that references the desktop.

These two methods also allow you to optionally specify filters that determine what types of files to allow the user to select. You can do this by passing the methods a second parameter: an array of flash.net.FileFilter objects. (The FileFilter class is part of the standard ActionScript library, so we're not going to go into detail on its usage in this book.) Each FileFilter element creates a new entry in the Files of type menu within the dialog, allowing the user to filter the view of files by type. The following code demonstrates how you can create an array of filters and use them with the browseForOpen() method:

```
var file:File = File.desktopDirectory;
var filters:Array = new Array();
filters.push(new FileFilter("JPEG Images", "*.jpg"));
filters.push(new FileFilter("GIF Images", "*.gif"));
filters.push(new FileFilter("PNG Images", "*.png"));
filters.push(new FileFilter("All Images", "*.jpg;*.gif;*.png"));
file.browseForOpenMultiple("Select a file", filters);
```

In this example we add four filters: JPEG images, GIF images, PNG images, and all images. Figure 3.3 shows the result in the browse dialog.

There's just one more way in which you can allow users to select a file. We'll look at that next.

BROWSING TO SAVE A FILE

Thus far we've looked at methods for selecting directories and files that are generally intended for reading from the file or directory. There's another scenario in

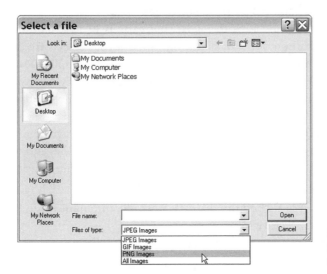

Figure 3.3 Use filters to allow the user to display files of only specific types.

which you'd want to allow the user to browse for files or directories, and that's to allow the user to select where to save a file. The browseForSave() method is intended for this purpose.

Like the other browse methods, the browseForSave() method requires that you pass it a parameter specifying a value to display to the user. Like the browseForOpen() and browseForOpenMultiple() methods, the browseForSave() method displays the parameter value in the title bar of the dialog.

The Save dialog allows the user to browse to and select an existing file or browse to a directory and enter a name for a new file. You can see an example of the Save dialog in Figure 3.4.

The browseForSave() method uses the same rules as the other browse methods to determine the initial directory when the dialog opens.

Figure 3.4 The Save dialog allows users to select a file location to save something from an AIR application.

DETECTING WHEN A USER HAS SELECTED A FILE OR DIRECTORY

Up to this point, you've learned how to invoke the various browse methods. However, we've yet to mention how you can determine what a user selects from the dialog. All of the browse methods happen asynchronously. The application doesn't pause code execution while the browse dialog is open. Instead, it's necessary to listen for specific events that occur when the user either selects a file or directory or cancels the operation.

The `browseForDirectory()`, `browseForOpen()`, and `browseForSave()` methods all dispatch the same type of event when the user selects a directory or file, and they work identically in that regard. When the user selects a directory or file (meaning he's clicked the Open or Save button in the dialog), two things happen:

1 The `File` object that launched the dialog is updated automatically to reference the selected file or directory.

2 The same `File` object dispatches a select event.

Listing 3.7 shows a complete example that allows the user to select a file and then display the information about the selected file in a text area.

Listing 3.7   Listening for select events to determine when a user selects a file

```
<?xml version="1.0" encoding="utf-8"?>
<mx:WindowedApplication xmlns:mx="http://www.adobe.com/2006/mxml"
 creationComplete="creationCompleteHandler();">
    <mx:Script>
    <![CDATA[
        import flash.filesystem.File;

        private function creationCompleteHandler():void {
            var file:File = File.desktopDirectory;
            file.browseForOpen("Select a file");
            file.addEventListener(Event.SELECT, selectEventHandler);
        }

        private function selectEventHandler(event:Event):void {
            var file:File = event.target as File;
            output.text = "File: " + file.name;
            output.text += "\nPath: " + file.nativePath;
        }

    ]]>
    </mx:Script>
    <mx:TextArea id="output" width="100%" height="100%" />
</mx:WindowedApplication>
```

The `browseForOpenMultiple()` method is similar yet slightly different from the other browse methods. When the user selects one or more files in a dialog launched by `browseForOpenMultiple()`, the `File` object dispatches a `selectMultiple` event of type flash.events.FileListEvent. The `FileListEvent` object corresponding to the action has a `files` property that's an array of `File` objects, each referencing one of the files that the user selected. Listing 3.8 shows an example of this.

Listing 3.8   Result of `browseForOpenMultiple()` can be a `selectMultiple` event

```
<?xml version="1.0" encoding="utf-8"?>
<mx:WindowedApplication xmlns:mx="http://www.adobe.com/2006/mxml"
 creationComplete="creationCompleteHandler();">
   <mx:Script>
   <![CDATA[
       import flash.filesystem.File;

       private function creationCompleteHandler():void {
          var file:File = File.desktopDirectory;
          file.browseForOpenMultiple("Select files");
          file.addEventListener(FileListEvent.SELECT_MULTIPLE,
                     selectEventHandler);
       }

       private function selectEventHandler(event:FileListEvent):void {
          var file:File;
          output.text = event.files.length + " files selected";
          for(var i:Number = 0; i < event.files.length; i++) {
             file = event.files[i] as File;
             output.text += "\nFile: " + file.name;
             output.text += "\nPath: " + file.nativePath;
             output.text += "\n\n";
          }
       }

   ]]>
   </mx:Script>
   <mx:TextArea id="output" width="100%" height="100%" />
</mx:WindowedApplication>
```

If the user clicks on the Cancel button from any of the browse dialogs, the result is the same: a cancel event.

3.2.7   *Making paths display nicely*

Under a variety of circumstances, paths to directories and files on a computer might not display in an AIR application exactly as you'd like them to. There are three scenarios:

- The case of the path used by the File object differs from the case of the path on the system (for example, /aPpliCations versus /Applications).
- The path used by the File object is the shortened form (for example, C:/docume~1 versus C:/Documents and Settings).
- The path points to a symbolic link and you'd like to display the path to which the symbolic link points.

In all these cases, there's one solution: the canonicalize() method. The canonicalize() method is a method of the File class that automatically solves each of these problems. All you need to do is call the canonicalize() method on a File object after the path has been set by any of the means we've discussed thus far in the chapter. Listing 3.9 illustrates how this works.

Listing 3.9 Using `canonicalize()` to correct the case of a path

```
<?xml version="1.0" encoding="utf-8"?>
<mx:WindowedApplication xmlns:mx="http://www.adobe.com/2006/mxml"
 creationComplete="creationCompleteHandler();">
   <mx:Script>
   <![CDATA[
      import flash.filesystem.File;

      private var _file:File;

      private function creationCompleteHandler():void {
         _file = new File();
         _file.addEventListener(Event.SELECT, selectHandler);
      }

      private function browse():void {
         _file.browseForOpen("Select a File");
      }

      private function selectHandler(event:Event):void {
         output.text = _file.nativePath;
         _file.canonicalize();
         output.text += "\n" + _file.nativePath;
      }
   ]]>
   </mx:Script>
   <mx:Button label="Browse" click="browse();" />
   <mx:TextArea id="output" width="100%" height="100%" />
</mx:WindowedApplication>
```

1 Browse for file

2 Display path

3 Canonicalize path

4 Display path again

This code allows the user to browse for a file **1**. The key to testing this example properly is to enter the name of a file in the browse dialog rather than select it, and enter the name of the file using a different case than how it appears in the dialog. For example, if you want to select a file called sample.txt, type the value SaMpLe.TxT in the file name input field. Clicking the Open button invokes the `selectHandler()` method, which displays the uncorrected path **2**, canonicalizes the path **3**, then displays the corrected path **4**. The corrected path will show the file name as it appears on the file system (sample.txt instead of SaMpLe.TxT).

The preceding example shows a subtle version of the change that `canonicalize()` can make. Next we'll look at a more drastic example. We'll consider an example in which we set the path to the Flex Builder 3 application folder on Mac OS X (/Applications/Adobe Flex Builder 3). Imagine that you're running this example on a Mac OS X computer and that the path exists on your computer. If you reference this path directly with different capitalization, you'll still get a valid `File` object:

```
var flex:File = new File("/APPlicaTIONs/adoBE flex bUilDER 3");
trace(flex.nativePath);   ⟵  Outputs "/APPlicaTIONs/adoBE flex bUilDER 3"
```

This example outputs /APPlicaTIONs/adoBE flex bUilDER 3 instead of /Applications/Adobe Flex Builder 3. To have the path match the case of the actual files and directories, use the `canonicalize()` method after referencing the path:

```
var flex:File = new File("/APPlicaTIONs/adoBE flex bUilDER 3");
trace(flex.nativePath); ⟵—— Outputs "/APPlicaTIONs/adoBE flex bUilDER 3"
flex.canonicalize();
trace(flex.nativePath); ⟵—— Outputs "/Applications/Adobe Flex Builder 3"
```

After calling canonicalize(), the path case is changed to the case used in the file system. As we'll see later in this chapter, it's possible to create File objects that reference files and directories that don't yet exist (for the purpose of creating them). Therefore, if part of the path the File object points to doesn't exist in the file system, canonicalize()will only adjust the case for the part that does exist. Consider the following example, which references a directory called ADoBe quantum FLEX 8 that doesn't exist on the system. Because the Applications directory does exist, the canonicalize() method will correct the case for the Applications portion of the path, but not for the remainder:

```
var quantumFlex:File = new File("/APPlicaTIONs/ADoBe quantum FLEX 8");
quantumFlex.canonicalize();
trace(quantumFlex.nativePath); ⟵—— Outputs "/Applications/ADoBE quantum FLEX 8"
```

As we've already mentioned, not only does canonicalize() adjust the case, it also converts short names in Windows to their corresponding long names (assuming the path segments exist). For programmatic reasons, Windows requires that all files and directories can be referenced using 8.3 notation, meaning that the names of files and directories must be reducible to 8 characters (plus a three-character file extension for files). The long name is the name you'd usually see within Windows Explorer, and because the long name allows for more characters, it's more user-friendly. Consider the example of the standard path to where Flex Builder is installed on Windows computers, which is C:\Program Files\Adobe\Flex Builder 3. The short name form of that path is C:\Progra~1\Adobe\FlexBu~1. The following code snippet shows how canonicalize() converts from the short form to the long form of the name:

```
var flex:File = new File("C:/Progra~1/Adobe/FlexBu~1");
trace(flex.nativePath); ⟵—— Outputs "C:\Progra~l\Adobe\FlexBu~l"
flex.canonicalize();
trace(flex.nativePath); ⟵—— Outputs "C:\Program Files\Adobe\Flex Builder 3"
```

There's one more use for canonicalize(), which is that it resolves symbolic links (OS X) or junctions (Windows). A symbolic link is almost indistinguishable from the directory to which it points. But, using the isSymbolicLink property of a File object, you can determine whether a File object points to a symbolic link. If it does, you can resolve the path to the directory to which the symbolic link points using the canonicalize() method.

Using canonicalize()is great when your application doesn't know the exact case of file and directory names and you're displaying the paths to the users. Showing accurate cases in the path not only adds a professional touch, it also prevents any confusion for the user.

We've completed our discussion of file and directory listing. Now that you know how to get a reference to a file or directory, you next need to know what more you can do with that reference. That's what we'll discuss throughout the rest of the chapter, starting with retrieving a listing of the contents of a directory, which is covered in the next section.

3.3 *Listing directory contents*

Let's say we're building an application that helps users clean up their cluttered desktops. Clearly the first thing we'd need to do is get a listing of the files and directories on the desktop. Only then can we begin to help the user sort and organize them.

We already know how to retrieve a reference to a user's desktop directory using the `File.desktopDirectory` property. What we need now is a way to get a listing of the contents of that directory. The `File` class provides two convenient ways to accomplish that, one synchronous and one asynchronous. The synchronous method is called `getDirectoryListing()`, and the asynchronous method is called `getDirectoryListingAsync()`. Both methods retrieve an array of `File` objects, each one a reference to a file or directory that's contained within the directory. But the way the array of `File` objects is returned is different depending on which method you use. We'll look at each of these methods, starting with the synchronous version.

3.3.1 *Getting directory listings synchronously*

The `getDirectoryListing()` method runs synchronously and returns an array of `File` objects immediately. This is the simplest way to retrieve a directory listing. The following example illustrates how to retrieve the contents of a user's desktop directory. Because the directory listing is available immediately, the following code loops through all the items and displays them in a text area called `textArea`:

```
var desktopContents:Array = File.desktopDirectory.getDirectoryListing();
for(var i:Number = 0; i < desktopContents.length; i++) {
    textArea.text += dektopContents[i].nativePath + "\n";
}
```

Of course, as we've already discussed, synchronous operations have disadvantages. If the user's desktop had an extraordinarily large number of files, for example, the preceding code would cause the application to freeze up while it executed. For that reason, an asynchronous version of the operation might be better. We'll look at retrieving a directory listing asynchronously next.

3.3.2 *Getting directory listings asynchronously*

You can use the `getDirectoryListingAsync()` method to retrieve a directory listing asynchronously. As with most asynchronous operations, it requires more code and sophistication than the synchronous counterpart. In this case, the directory listing isn't returned immediately. Instead, the `File` object dispatches a `directoryListing` event when the operation executes. The `directoryListing` event is of type `File_ListEvent`, and the event object itself has a `files` property that's an array of the `File` objects for the directory.

Listing 3.10 shows a complete example of an ActionScript class that retrieves a directory listing asynchronously.

Listing 3.10 Asynchronous directory listing example

```
package com.manning.books.airinaction {

    import flash.display.Sprite;
    import flash.events.FileListEvent;
    import flash.filesystem.File;
    import flash.text.TextField;

    public class Example extends Sprite {

        private var _textField:TextField;

        public function Example() {
            _textField = new TextField();
            _textField.width = stage.stageWidth;
            _textField.height = stage.stageHeight;
            addChild(_textField);
            var desktop:File = File.desktopDirectory;
            desktop.addEventListener(FileListEvent.DIRECTORY_LISTING,
                        desktopListingHandler);
            desktop.getDirectoryListingAsync();
        }

        private function desktopListingHandler(event:FileListEvent):void {
            var files:Array = event.files;
            var file:File;
            for (var i:Number = 0; i < files.length; i++) {
                file = files[i] as File;
                _textField.appendText(">" + file.nativePath + "\n");
            }
        }

    }
}
```

① **Create text field**
② **Retrieve desktop reference**
③ **Listen for directoryListing**
Make asynchronous request
④ **Retrieve directory listing**
⑤ **Display path to item**

The preceding example starts by creating a text field ① in order to display the directory listing. We're retrieving the directory listing for the desktop, therefore we next retrieve a reference to the desktop ②. Because the directory listing operation in this case is asynchronous, we need to register an event listener for the directoryListing event ③. Then we can call the getDirectoryListingAsync() method. Once the directoryListing event occurs and the event handler is invoked, we retrieve the array of directory contents from the files property of the event object ④. Then we can loop through all the objects in the array and display the native path of each ⑤.

Everything that we've seen up to this point involves existing file system content. Next we'll look at creating file system content by creating directories.

3.4 Creating directories

Creating directories may seem like a foreign concept from a web developer's standpoint. But when building desktop applications, it's important that your application can create directories. Consider the following scenario: you've just built an application that allows the user to organize all her Word documents on her computer. You want to allow the user to move existing files into new, better-organized directories. To do this, you first need the AIR application to create the necessary directories.

Creating a new directory with AIR is as simple as the following two steps:

1 Create a `File` object that references the new, nonexistent directory.
2 Call the `createDirectory()` method on the `File` object.

The following example illustrates how this works.

Reference ❶
nonexistent
directory

```
var recentDocuments:File = File.documentsDirectory("wordFiles/recent");  ⤶
recentDocuments.createDirectory();  ⟵❷ Create directory
```

In the listing, the first thing we do is create a `File` object that references a subdirectory of the user's documents directory ❶. We're assuming that wordFiles doesn't exist as a subdirectory of the documents directory, and therefore recent doesn't exist as a subdirectory of the wordFiles directory either. This points out two important things:

■ File objects can reference nonexistent directories (and files). Certain operations may not work if a directory or file doesn't exist (for example, you can't move a nonexistent directory), but other operations such as creating a new directory require that you reference a nonexistent directory or file.

■ When you create a new directory using `createDirectory()`, all necessary directories and subdirectories within the path are created. In this example, both the wordFiles directory and its recent subdirectory are created.

In the example, we created a `File` object that references the directory we'd like to create. Once we've done that, all we need to do is call `createDirectory()` ❷ and the system creates the directory on the file system.

If a directory already exists, `createDirectory()` simply won't do anything. That makes `createDirectory()` a relatively safe operation. You needn't be concerned that you might accidentally erase an existing directory by creating a new one with the same name. However, there are cases when you want to determine whether or not a directory already exists. For example, in our previous example, it's possible that the user will already have a directory called wordFiles in her documents directory that she uses for her own purposes independent of the AIR application. Rather than muddying up her wordFiles directory, it would be more polite if the AIR application instead created a new directory with a unique name. To verify whether a directory exists, all you need to do is read the value of the `exists` property of the `File` object that references the directory. The following example illustrates how this might work:

```
var count:int = 0;                                              Create initial reference ❶
var recentDocuments:File = File.documentsDirectory("wordFiles");  ⤶
while(recentDocuments.exists) {  ⟵❷ Test if directory exists
    recentDocuments = File.documentsDirectory("wordFiles" + count);  ⤶
    count++;  ⟵┐      Increment                       Create new
}          ❹ counter                          directory name ❸
```

```
recentDocuments = File.documentsDirectory("wordFiles" + count + "/recent");
recentDocuments.createDirectory();
```
Append recent subdirectory ⑤

In the listing, you can see that we first create a `File` object that references a directory called wordFiles ①. Then we use a `while` statement to test whether the directory already exists ②. As long as the directory exists, we keep updating the directory name ③ with a numeric value that keeps incrementing ④. Once we've determined a unique name for the directory, we just append the recent subdirectory ⑤ and create them both.

Next we'll look at a slightly more comprehensive working example that organizes a user's desktop by placing all the files in subdirectories based on file extension. The code in listing 3.11 can be used as the document class for a Flash-based AIR application.

Listing 3.11 Document class for a Flash-based desktop organizer application

```
package {

    import flash.display.MovieClip;
    import flash.events.MouseEvent;
    import flash.display.Stage;
    import flash.filesystem.File;
    import flash.events.FileListEvent;
    import fl.controls.Button;
    import fl.controls.TextArea;
                                                    Button click  ①
                                                    starts organizing
    public class DesktopOrganizer extends MovieClip {

        public function DesktopOrganizer() {
            _button.addEventListener(MouseEvent.CLICK, startOrganize);
        }
                                          Get reference to target directory  ②
        private function startOrganize(event:MouseEvent):void {
            var organized:File = File.desktopDirectory.resolvePath(
            ➥"Files Organized By Type");    ③  Test if directory exists
            if(!organized.exists) {        ◄─
                organized.createDirectory();         ④  Create
                print("created directory: " + organized.nativePath);    directory
            }                                            ⑤  Get reference
            var desktop:File = File.desktopDirectory  ◄─     to desktop
            desktop.addEventListener(FileListEvent.DIRECTORY_LISTING,
            ➥directoryListingHandler);
            desktop.getDirectoryListingAsync();    ◄─   Retrieve
        }                                      ⑥  directory listing
        private function directoryListingHandler(event:FileListEvent):
        ➥void {
            var files:Array = event.files;
            var file:File;
            var organized:File = File.desktopDirectory.resolvePath(
            ➥"Files Organized By Type");
            var extension:File;
            for(var i:Number = 0; i < files.length; i++) {  ◄─⑦  Loop through files
```

```
            file = files[i] as File;        ❽  Test if file
            if(!file.isDirectory) {     ◁──┘
                extension = organized.resolvePath(file.extension);   ◁──┐
                if(!extension.exists) {      ◁──┐                       Get
                    extension.createDirectory();    Create         reference
                    print("created directory: " +  ❿ directory       to type
                    ➥extension.nativePath);                       directory ❾
                }
            }
        }
    }

    private function print(message:String):void {
        _textArea.text += message + "\n";
    }

}

}
```

This example assumes that there are two UI components placed on the stage of the Flash file: a button named _button and a text area named _textArea. We use the button to allow the user to initiate the organization of the desktop ❶. When the user clicks the button, the first thing we do is get a reference to the directory to which we'll eventually move all the organized files ❷. We're naming that directory Files Organized By Type, and we're placing it on the desktop. If the directory doesn't yet exist ❸, we need to create it ❹. Then we need to get a reference to the user's desktop ❺ and retrieve a listing of all the contents of the desktop ❻. Once the directory listing is returned, we loop through all the contents ❼ and test each to check whether it's a file or a directory ❽. Assuming it's a directory, we next want to determine the path to a subdirectory that has the same name as the file extension ❾. For example, if the file extension is .jpg, we want to eventually move the file to the Files Organized By Type/jpg directory. If that directory doesn't yet exist ❿, we create it ❿. At this point, we haven't learned how to move files. We'll have to wait just a bit, and then we can revisit this example and complete it.

NOTE   In the preceding example, the Files Organized By Type directory would be automatically created when we create subdirectories. Therefore it's not strictly necessary to explicitly create Files Organized By Type in the startOrganize() method. However, we made the decision to create the directory there for the sake of clarity.

There are times when you need to create a directory only temporarily. For example, sometimes you need a directory in which to write files while the application is running, but after the application runs you no longer need the directory. A polite way to do that is to create the directory in the system's temporary directory path. AIR facilitates this with the static File.createTempDirectory() method. The method returns a new File object that references the directory. Every time you run the method, the AIR application will create a new, unique directory in the system's temporary directory path. The following code snippet shows how to use the method:

```
var temporary:File = File.createTempDirectory();          ❶ Output directory path
trace(temporary.nativePath);
```

On a Windows machine, the output of the preceding code ❶ would be something like C:\Documents and Settings*username*\Local Settings\Temp\fla1A.tmp. On a Mac OS X machine, the output ❶ would be something like /private/var/tmp/folders.2119876841/TemporaryItems/FlashTmp0.

You can access to the temporary directory as long as the `File` object exists. Because `createTempDirectory()` always creates a new directory, you won't be able to access the same directory again by calling the method a second time. As long as you need to reference the directory, you'll need a reference to the `File` object the method returns. When you're done with the temporary directory, it's good practice for your application to clean up after itself and delete it. If you don't, it'll be up to the system or the user to remove it. We'll see how to delete directories (and files) in the next section.

3.5 Removing directories and files

There are two ways to remove directories and files. You can permanently delete them or you can move them to the trash. We'll take a look at each of these approaches in this section.

Deleting a directory is as simple as calling the `deleteDirectory()` or `delete-DirectoryAsync()` method. Deleting a file is just as simple, though the methods are different—`deleteFile()` or `deleteFileAsync()`. Of course, these are methods to be used cautiously. You can't undo these actions. It's best to use these methods only under the following circumstances:

- You want to permanently delete a directory or file that the AIR application created and the user doesn't know about or need.
- You've requested the user's permission to permanently delete the directory or file.

The `deleteFile()` and `deleteFileAsync()` methods are identical except that the former is synchronous and the latter is asynchronous. The normal advice applies as far as when to use one over the other: the asynchronous method allows the rest of the code to run without the application freezing even if the file that the system is deleting is large. Neither of these methods requires any parameters.

The `deleteDirectory()` and `deleteDirectoryAsync()` methods are identical except that the first is synchronous and the second is asynchronous. If you know that a directory is large, it's always best to delete the directory asynchronously. By default, both methods only delete empty directories. If the directory has any contents, the methods will throw errors. However, you can optionally pass the methods a Boolean value of `true` to indicate that you'd like to delete the directory as well as all of its contents.

The following example creates a directory and then deletes it:

```
var directory:File = File.createTempDirectory();
directory.deleteDirectory();
```

Moving a directory or file to the trash is a much more polite and appropriate action if you want to remove a directory or file under any circumstances other than those mentioned previously. For example, even if a user decides to delete a directory through the AIR application, it's generally best to merely move it to the trash unless you explicitly ask the user for permission to permanently delete the directory. The methods for moving a file or a directory to the trash are the same. To move a directory or file to the trash, you have two options: moveToTrash() and moveToTrashAsync(). Neither method requires any parameters. They both simply move the directory to the trash, one synchronously and the other asynchronously. If the directory is large, it's generally best to move it to the trash asynchronously.

3.6   *Copying and moving files and directories*

Copying and moving files and directories are common and simple operations. The File class defines methods for each of these operations: copyTo(), copyToAsync(), moveTo(), and moveToAsync(). None of these methods distinguish between directories or files.

Copying and moving are extremely similar. If you think about it, both move a file or directory to a new location in a file structure hierarchy. The difference between them is that the copying operation keeps a copy of the file or directory in the original location as well. Because the two operations are similar, the methods are similar as well. In all cases, the methods require one parameter: a FileReference object pointing to the new location. And all the methods also allow for a second Boolean parameter indicating whether to overwrite any existing content at the new location should it already be there.

> **NOTE**   The File class that we've talked about extensively in this chapter is a subclass of FileReference. That means that you can use a File object any time a FileReference object is required. The copying and moving methods require a FileReference parameter. For all practical purposes, in this chapter you'll always use a File object for this parameter.

As with other synchronous and asynchronous operations, you'll generally find that it's best to have a bias toward the asynchronous copying and moving methods. If you move or copy a large file or directory, the asynchronous methods work better in that they prevent the AIR application from freezing while the file or directory is moved or copied.

In the following example, we're copying a zipFiles directory in the user documents directory to the desktop directory:

Reference source directory ❶

```
var source:File = File.documentsDirectory.resolvePath("zipFiles");
var destination:File = File.desktopDirectory.resolvePath("zipFiles");
source.copyToAsync(destination);
```

Copy directory ❸

Reference destination directory ❷

In this case, we're assuming a directory named zipFiles exists in the documents directory ❶ and that a directory named zipFiles does *not* exist in the desktop directory ❷. This is an important point. As we'll see in a minute, the destination directory must not yet exist for this code to work. Once we've created the references to the source and destination directories, we can copy the source using the `copyToAsync()` method ❸.

If you run this code twice, it will throw an I/O error the second time because the `destination File` object would point to an existing directory. As written, the code assumes that the destination must not yet exist. But if we know that the destination directory could possibly exist, we have a choice: do we want to overwrite the destination with whatever we copy to it? If we do, we need only to pass `true` for the second parameter in the `copyToAsync()` method:

```
source.copyToAsync(destination, true)
```

This optional parameter is `false` by default, but if `true`, `copyToAsync()` will first delete the destination file or folder before copying. Note that this is different from your normal overwrite in that it deletes all files and directories in the destination regardless of whether they're found in the source.

NOTE Everything we've discussed using the specific example of `copyToAsync()` is applicable to the other copy and move methods as well.

All of the copying and moving operations will also throw an I/O error if the source doesn't exist or if the OS is preventing an action due to file locking. The synchronous methods will throw the error directly, and you should wrap them in `try/catch` statements as in the following example:

```
try {
    file.moveTo(destination);
}
catch (error:IOError) {
    trace("an error occurred");
}
```

The asynchronous methods throw errors using error events. You should register listeners for those events if there's a possibility of such an error occurring.

Next we'll revisit the earlier example from listing 3.11. In listing 3.12, you can see how we've now updated the code to actually move the files to the directories based on file extension. The changes are shown in bold.

Listing 3.12 Moving files to new directories based on file extension

```
package {

    import flash.display.MovieClip;
    import flash.events.MouseEvent;
    import flash.display.Stage;
    import flash.filesystem.File;
    import flash.events.FileListEvent;
    import flash.events.Event;
```

```
import fl.controls.Button;
import fl.controls.TextArea;

public class DesktopOrganizer extends MovieClip {

    public function DesktopOrganizer() {
        _button.addEventListener(MouseEvent.CLICK, startOrganize);
    }

    private function startOrganize(event:MouseEvent):void {
        var organized:File = File.desktopDirectory.resolvePath(
        ➥"Files Organized By Type");
        if(!organized.exists) {
            organized.createDirectory();
            print("created directory: " + organized.nativePath);
        }
        var desktop:File = File.desktopDirectory.resolvePath(
        ➥"To Organize");
        desktop.addEventListener(FileListEvent.DIRECTORY_LISTING,
                        directoryListingHandler);
        desktop.getDirectoryListingAsync();
    }

    private function directoryListingHandler(event:FileListEvent):
    ➥void {
        var files:Array = event.files;
        var file:File;
        var organized:File = File.desktopDirectory.resolvePath(
        ➥"Files Organized By Type");
        var extension:File;
        for(var i:Number = 0; i < files.length; i++) {
            file = files[i] as File;
            if(!file.isDirectory) {
                extension = organized.resolvePath(file.extension);
                if(!extension.exists) {
                    extension.createDirectory();
                    print("created directory: " +
                    ➥extension.nativePath);
                }
                file.addEventListener(Event.COMPLETE, completeHandler);   ◁─── Listen for complete event ❶
                file.moveToAsync(extension.resolvePath(file.name));   ◁───
                print("moving file: " + file.name);
            }                                                              Move file ❷
        }
    }

    private function completeHandler(event:Event):void {   ◁───  Notify user when complete ❸
        print("moved file: " + event.target.name);
    }

    private function print(message:String):void {
        _textArea.text += message + "\n";
    }

}
```

You can see that in this example we've opted to move files asynchronously using the moveToAsync() method ❷. To be polite, we're listening for the complete event ❶ and then notifying the user when the file has actually moved ❸.

You've learned how to work with directories extensively, and you've also seen how to copy and move directories and files. Now we're ready to look at some file-specific operations. In the next section, you'll learn how to work with files to do things like read and write and delete files.

3.7   *Reading from and writing to files*

We've seen how to read information about the file system and restructure it by creating new directories as well as moving, copying, and deleting files and directories. But some of the most powerful things you can do with the file system from AIR involve manipulating files and their contents. Using AIR, you can do all sorts of things with files, including reading from a text file, writing a new .png image, downloading a video file from the Web, and much more. All of these tasks involve reading from and/ or writing to files. In the next few sections, we'll look at these topics in more detail.

3.7.1   *Reading from files*

Reading from a file isn't a new concept for most Flash and Flex developers. It is standard or fairly trivial to read from text files or resources using ActionScript or MXML. Furthermore, even for web-based Flash and Flex applications, it's possible to use the ActionScript 3 `flash.net.URLStream` or `flash.net.URLLoader` classes to load files and read and manipulate the binary data. Then what makes AIR any different? The answer is three-part:

- AIR allows an application to access both local and internet files.
- AIR allows an application to read from a `File` object.
- AIR allows the application to write data to a file, completing a cycle that's unavailable normally to Flash and Flex applications on the Web.

As we've mentioned, there are essentially two ways to read from files using AIR:

- Reading from an internet resource
- Reading from a local resource

We'll look at each of these ways of reading from files in the next two sections.

READING FROM INTERNET RESOURCES

Reading from an internet resource is exactly the same from an AIR application as it would be from a web-based application. In the context of our discussions in this chapter, we're only interested in reading the bytes from a file or resource. That means there are two ways to load a resource and read the data: using `URLStream` and using `URLLoader`, two classes that should be familiar to you from your web-based Flash or Flex work. We won't be going into a detailed discussion of how to use these classes, but even if you're not familiar with them, you'll likely be able to pick up the necessary information as you read these sections.

The URLLoader class loads a file or resource in its entirety before making it available for reading. For example, if you use a URLLoader object to download a .jpg file from the internet, the entire file must download to the AIR application before you can read even the first byte from the image. When the resource has been downloaded, the URLLoader object dispatches a complete event, and, as the content is loading, the URL-Loader object dispatches progress events, allowing your AIR application to monitor the download progress.

The URLStream class loads a file or resource and makes the bytes available for reading as the data downloads. For example, if you use a URLStream object to load an .mp3 file from the internet, you can read bytes from the file as soon as they download. URL-Stream objects dispatch progress events as bytes are available.

In certain contexts, the difference between URLLoader and URLStream is similar to the difference between synchronous and asynchronous operations. One such context is when you want to use a URLLoader or URLStream object in the context of reading and manipulating bytes. Because URLLoader doesn't make data available until the entire resource has downloaded, it means you must wait for all the bytes to be available. If you simply want to write those bytes to a local file, it could mean that the application would have to stand by while the entire file downloads and then be presented with a whole bunch of bytes at once, causing the application to momentarily freeze as it tries to write all those bytes to a file. On the other hand, a URLStream object would make the bytes available as the file downloads, meaning the application could write smaller batches of bytes to disk over a period of time, thus minimizing the likelihood of the application freezing.

Listing 3.13 shows a class that downloads an internet resource and outputs the bytes one at a time to an output console using a trace() statement.

Listing 3.13 Downloading a file and reading the bytes

```
package {
    import flash.events.ProgressEvent;
    import flash.net.URLRequest;
    import flash.net.URLStream;

    public class FileDownloader {                        Create      ➊
                                                         URLStream

                                                                    ➋  Listen for
                                                                        progress
        public function FileDownloader(url:String) {
            var stream:URLStream = new URLStream();   ◄──┘
            stream.addEventListener(ProgressEvent.PROGRESS,
              ➥progressHandler);                                    ➌  Make
            stream.load(new URLRequest(url));     ◄───────             request
        }
                                              Handle progress event  ➍

        public function progressHandler(event:ProgressEvent):void {  ◄──
            var stream:URLStream = event.target as URLStream;   ◄──
            while(stream.bytesAvailable) {                                Get stream
                trace(stream.readByte());   ◄──                           reference
            }                              Display bytes  ➏   Loop through
        }                                                    all available
                                                             bytes  ➎
    }
}
```

This example isn't particularly practical as it is, because it merely downloads the file and displays the bytes. But it illustrates the basics of how to request an internet resource and read the bytes as they're available. First you need a URLStream object ❶. Then you need to listen for the progress events ❷ and make the request to load the resource ❸. When the progress events occur ❹, you need to read the available bytes ❺ ❻. There are a variety of ways to read the data from a file. We'll talk about reading binary data in more detail momentarily. First we'll look at how to read from a local resource.

NOTE You can also use a flash.net.Socket object to read binary data from a socket connection. We don't go into detail on using the Socket class in conjunction with files in this book. But you can apply exactly the same principles you learn regarding reading from a URLStream or FileStream object and apply them to working with a Socket object.

READING FROM LOCAL RESOURCES

Reading from a local resource requires using a File object, something you're already familiar with. It also requires using a flash.filesystem.FileStream object, something we haven't yet discussed.

A FileStream object allows you to read (and write) from a file. You must have a File object that points to a file. Then you can use a FileStream object to open that file for reading or writing, using the open() or openAsync() method. Here are the basic preliminary steps for reading from a file:

1 Create a File object that references a file such as the following example:

```
var file:File = File.desktopDirectory.resolvePath("example.jpg");
```

2 Construct a new FileStream object using the constructor as in the following example:

```
var fileStream:FileStream = new FileStream();
```

3 Use the open() or openAsync() method of the FileStream object to open the file for reading. First let's look at how to use the open() method. To do this, you need to pass it two parameters: the reference to the File object you want to open and the value of the flash.filesystem.FileMode.READ constant, as in the following example:

```
fileStream.open(file, FileMode.READ);
```

The open() method makes the file available for reading immediately, because it's a synchronous operation. On the other hand, you can use the openAsync() method to open a file for reading asynchronously. If you open a file for reading asynchronously, you can't read bytes from it until the stream notifies the application that bytes are ready by dispatching a progress event. As bytes are available to be read, the FileStream object will dispatch progress events, just as a URLStream object will dispatch progress events as bytes are available. The following code snippet shows how you can open a file for reading asynchronously and then handle the progress events:

```
private function startReading(fileStream:FileStream, file:File):void {
    fileStream.addEventListener(ProgressEvent.PROGRESS, progressHandler);
    fileStream.openAsync(file, FileMode.READ);
}

private function progressHandler(event:ProgressHandler):void {
    // code for reading bytes
}
```

Once you've opened a file for reading (and bytes are available) by following these steps, you can use all of the `FileStream` object's read methods to read the bytes of the file. For example, the following code reads all the available bytes from a file and writes them to the console or output window using a `trace()` statement:

```
while(fileStream.bytesAvailable) {
    trace(fileStream.readByte());
}
```

Regardless of how you've opened a file or what you read from a file, once you're done reading the data, you should always close the reading access to the file by calling the `close()` method on the same `FileStream` object.

Now that we've seen the general overview for reading both from internet and local resources, we'll next look at how to work with binary data.

UNDERSTANDING BINARY DATA

Humans don't tend to think in terms of binary data. As far as machines do think, they think in terms of binary data. Binary is the format preferred by computers. All files are stored in binary format, and it's only through computer programs that translate that binary data into human-readable form that people can make sense of all that data. In order to work with lower-level file access, humans must pay a price: they must learn to think in binary a little. When we read data from a `URLStream` or `FileStream` object, it's our responsibility to figure out what to do with the binary data that the AIR application can provide.

As we've already stated, all files are binary data. Each file is just a sequence of bits, each having two possible values of either 0 or 1. Bits are further grouped into bytes, which are generally the most atomic data structure we work with in the context of AIR applications and file manipulation. When you string together bytes, you can represent all sorts of data, ranging from plain text to video files. What differentiates these different types of files is not the way in which the data is stored (because they're all just sequences of bytes), but the values of the bytes themselves. Because the type of data is always the same (bytes), an AIR application can read (or write) any file. Theoretically, assuming you know the specification for how to construct a sequence of bytes for a Flash video file, you could build one from scratch using only an AIR application.

Both the `URLStream` and the `FileStream` classes implement an ActionScript interface called `flash.utils.IDataInput`. The `IDataInput` interface requires a set of methods for reading binary data in a variety of ways. These methods are shown in table 3.3.

The `IDataInput` interface also requires a property called `bytesAvailable`. The `bytesAvailable` property returns the number of bytes that are in the object's buffer (see the next section for more information on reading buffers) and allows you to ensure you never try to read more bytes than are currently available.

It would be downright cruel of us to throw all of this information at you without giving a better description of how to work with these methods in a practical way. In the next few sections, we'll see practical examples of how to use these methods in some of the most common ways. We won't go into great detail on the uncommon uses, though you'll likely be able to extrapolate that information.

READING STRINGS

In table 3.3, you can see that there are three methods for reading strings from binary data: `readUTF()`, `readUTFBytes()`, and `readMultiByte()`. For most practical purposes, the `readUTF()` method is not nearly as useful as the other two, so we'll omit that from our discussion and focus on the most useful methods.

Table 3.3   Data formats available for reading from an object that implements `IDataInput`

Format type	Format	Description	Related methods	Related ActionScript object types
Raw bytes	Byte	Single or multiple raw byte	`readByte()` `readBytes()` `readUnsignedBytes()`	int ByteArray
Boolean	Boolean	0 for false, otherwise true	`readBoolean()`	Boolean
Numbers	Short	16-bit integer	`readShort()` `readUnsignedShort()`	int uint
	Integer	32-bit integer	`readInt()` `readUnsignedInt()`	int uint
	Float	Single-precision floating point number	`readFloat()`	Number
	Double	Double-precision floating point number	`readDouble()`	Number
Strings	Multibyte	String using a specified character set	`readMultiByte()`	String
	UTF-8	String using the UTF-8 character encoding	`readUTF()` `readUTFBytes()`	String
Objects	Object	Objects serialized and deserialized using the ActionScript Message Format (AMF)	`readObject()`	Any object that can be serialized with AMF (see "Reading objects" section for more details)

The readUTFBytes() method returns a string containing all the text stored in a sequence of bytes. You must specify one parameter, indicating how many bytes you want. Although not always the case, most frequently you'll want to read the characters for all the available bytes, and therefore you can use the bytesAvailable property to retrieve the value to pass to the readUTFBytes() method.

To illustrate how you might use readUTFBytes(), we'll look at a simple example. This example is a text file reader that reads the data from a file using a FileStream object and the readUTFBytes() method. Listing 3.14 shows the code. This example assumes that the class is being used as the document class for a Flash-based AIR project with a button component called _button and a text area component called _textArea.

Listing 3.14 Using the readUTFBytes() method of a FileStream object

```
package {

    import flash.display.MovieClip;
    import flash.filesystem.File;
    import flash.filesystem.FileStream;
    import flash.filesystem.FileMode;
    import flash.events.Event;
    import flash.events.MouseEvent;
    import flash.events.ProgressEvent;

    public class TextFileReader extends MovieClip {

        public function TextFileReader() {
            _button.addEventListener(MouseEvent.CLICK, browseForFile);
        }

        private function browseForFile(event:MouseEvent):void {
            var desktop:File = File.desktopDirectory;
            desktop.addEventListener(Event.SELECT, selectHandler);
            desktop.browseForOpen("Select a text file");    ◁── Browse for file
        }

        private function selectHandler(event:Event):void {
            var file:File = event.target as File;
            _textArea.text = "";                ◁── Clear text area
            var stream:FileStream = new FileStream();
            stream.addEventListener(ProgressEvent.PROGRESS,        ⎤ Listen for
                        progressHandler);                         ⎟ read events
            stream.addEventListener(Event.COMPLETE, completeHandler); ⎦
            stream.openAsync(file, FileMode.READ);    ◁─┐ Open file for
        }                                              ⎦ reading

        private function progressHandler(event:ProgressEvent):void {
            var stream:FileStream = event.target as FileStream;
            if(stream.bytesAvailable) {               ◁─┐ Verify bytes
                _textArea.text += stream.readUTFBytes( ⎦ available
                ➥stream.bytesAvailable);    ◁─┐ Display bytes
            }                                 ⎦ as string
        }

        private function completeHandler(event:Event):void {
```

```
                event.target.close();   ⟵┐  Close the
            }                            │  file stream
        }
    }
```

You might notice that, using this example, you can read any type of file, not just a text file. But because the code uses `readUTFBytes()` to explicitly interpret the data as a string, the output will only make sense if the file is a text file.

The `readMultiByte()` method is useful for reading text using a specific *code page*. If you're not familiar with code pages, they're the way most systems know which characters correspond to which byte values. Different code pages result in the same data having a different appearance. For example, if you view a text file on a system that uses a Japanese code page, it may not appear the same as it would on a system with a Latin character–based code page. When you use a method such as `readUTFBytes()`, you are using the default system code page. If you want to use a nondefault code page, you need to use `readMultiBytes()`. The `readMultiBytes()` method requires the same parameter as `readUTFBytes()`, but it also requires a second parameter specifying the code page or character set to use. The supported character sets are listed at livedocs.adobe.com/flex/3/langref/charset-codes.html. For example, the following reads from a file stream using the extended Unix Japanese character set:

```
var text:String = stream.readMultiByte(stream.bytesAvailable, "euc-jp");
```

Just because the code says to use a particular character set doesn't mean that the application will necessarily succeed in that effort. For example, if a computer system doesn't have a particular code page, there's no way for the application to interpret the bytes using that code page. In such cases, the AIR application will instead use the default system code page.

READING OBJECTS

Another common way to read data from a file is to read it as objects. This is generally applicable when the file was written from an AIR application to begin with. That's because AIR applications can serialize most objects to a format called *AMF,* write that data to a file, and read the data at a later point and deserialize it back into objects. We'll see several examples of this later in the chapter.

NOTE   AMF is used extensively by Flash Player. `ByteArray`, `LocalConnec-`
`tion`, `NetConnection`, and `URLLoader` are just a few of the classes that
rely on AMF.

Here's how AMF serialization and deserialization work: Flash Player has native support for AMF data. Whenever data might be externalized, it can be serialized to AMF. In most cases, the serialization occurs automatically. For example, if you use a `Net-Connection` object to make a Flash `Remoting` call, the data is automatically serialized and deserialized to and from AMF. Likewise, if you write data to a shared object, it's automatically serialized to AMF. When you read it from the shared object, the data is deserialized back to ActionScript objects.

There are two types of AMF serialization: AMF0 and AMF3. AMF0 is backward-compatible with ActionScript 2, and it isn't generally applicable to AIR applications. AMF3 supports all the core ActionScript 3 data types, and is what you'll usually use for AIR applications. AMF3 is the default AMF encoding. With AMF3 encoding, all the standard, core ActionScript data types are automatically serialized and deserialized. Those data types include `String`, `Boolean`, `Number`, `int`, `uint`, `Date`, `Array`, and `Object`. Initially we'll assume you're only working with these core data types.

When you have a resource that contains AMF data, you can read that data using the `readObject()` method. The `readObject()` method returns one object in the sequence of bytes from the resource. The `readObject()` method's return type is `*`, therefore if you want to assign the value to a variable, you must cast it. Generally speaking, if you're reading an object from a file or other resource, the format of the data and the type of object is already known to you. The following example illustrates reading objects from a file. In this example, we're assuming that the file contains `Array` objects that have been appended one after another in the file:

```
var array:Array;
while(fileStream.bytesAvailable) {
    array = fileStream.readObject() as Array;
    trace(array.length);
}
```

If you could only read standard data types from files, the usefulness would be limited. However, you aren't limited to working with standard data types. In fact, you can read any custom data type you want from a file, as long as the corresponding ActionScript class is known and available to the AIR application. This requires two basic steps:

- Write and compile the ActionScript class for the data type into the application.
- Register the class with an alias.

The first step is one that should be familiar to you. But there are a few things about AMF deserialization that you should know in order to ensure that your class will allow the data to deserialize properly:

- By default, AMF only serializes and deserializes public properties, including getters/setters. That means you must define public properties or getters/setters for every property you want to be able to use with AMF.
- During AMF deserialization, the public properties are set *before* the constructor gets called. That means you should be careful that you don't have an initialization code in your constructor that'll overwrite the values of the properties if they've already been set.

The next step, registering the class with an alias, is one that might be unfamiliar to you. The basic idea is this: when an object is serialized into AMF, it isn't always read by the same program or language that created the data. Therefore, it needs a name that it can use to identify the type. Then any program or language that knows about that name, or alias, will know how to deserialize the data properly. When we talk about writing data, we'll talk more about creating an alias. For the purposes of reading data, all that's necessary is that you know the alias used by the data that's encoded in the file or resource. If you don't know that, you'll need to consult with whoever wrote the data to the resource.

There are two ways you can register a class with an alias. In ActionScript, you can use the `flash.net.registerClassAlias()` method, and for Flex applications you can use the `[RemoteClass]` metadata tag. The two ways accomplish the same thing. If you're using Flex, the `[RemoteClass]` tag is generally the easiest and clearest way to register a class with an alias. To use `[RemoteClass]`, you need only to place the tag just before the class definition and include an `alias` argument that specifies the alias of the data that you want to deserialize. The following example illustrates this:

```
package {
   [RemoteClass(alias="CustomTypeAlias")]
   public class CustomType {
      // Class code goes here
   }
}
```

If you're not using Flex, you'll need to use `registerClassAlias()`. You can call the method from anywhere in the application, but you need to make sure it gets called before you try to read the data from the file. Generally, you'll place `registerClass-Alias()` calls somewhere in the startup sequence for the application. The first parameter is the alias as a string, and the second parameter is a reference to the class. The following example registers the `CustomType` class with the alias `CustomTypeAlias`:

```
registerClassAlias("CustomTypeAlias", CustomType);
```

Once you've registered a class with an alias, you can use `readObject()` to read an object of that type from a resource, and the AIR application will be able to properly deserialize it. If a custom type has properties of another custom type, you'll need to make sure that other custom type is also registered.

We'll see some examples of reading custom types from files a bit later in the chapter when we talk about how to write to files. Before we move on to writing to files, we'll take a bit of time to better understand how reading from files works at a more fundamental level.

UNDERSTANDING THE READ BUFFER

`FileStream` objects use what are known as *read buffers*. You can think of a read buffer as a container with a bunch of slots of bytes. As data is available to be read, it gets placed in the read buffer.

When you use one of the read methods of a `FileStream` object, you're actually reading from the read buffer, which is a copy of bytes from the file, not the file itself.

Generally speaking, there are two broad scenarios for reading from files: reading synchronously and reading asynchronously. You've already seen how to use the `open()` and `openAsync()` methods to start the synchronous and asynchronous versions of the read operation. What we haven't yet discussed is how synchronous and asynchronous reading of files work differently with respect to the read buffer.

When you open a file synchronously for reading, the read buffer is filled entirely. In other words, all the bytes from the file are copied to the read buffer and available for reading. Because all the bytes of a file are available for reading right away in a synchronous operation, the danger of overrunning the buffer is minor, but it's still possible. The `bytesAvailable` property serves as a guide to help make sure you don't request bytes that are outside of the scope of the read buffer. For example, if a file contains 200 bytes (and the read buffer consequently also contains 200 bytes), you wouldn't want to try to read the 202nd byte because it wouldn't exist. That's why you've seen a few examples with the following construct:

```
while(fileStream.bytesAvailable) {
    // Read from the read buffer
}
```

For a synchronous read operation, `bytesAvailable` always tells you the number of bytes from the current read position in the buffer. Reading from a read buffer uses a different technique than reading from an array or other similar operations that you may be more familiar with. Instead of reading from a specific index, the read methods of `FileStream` (and other `IDataInput` types) always reads the next byte or bytes from the current read position. For example, figure 3.5 shows a conceptual diagram of a read buffer. Each of the "slots" for bytes has an index starting with 0. (There are 16 slots in the diagram with indices 0 through 15.) The bytes are placed into those slots, and then they're available for reading. Figure 3.5 shows the read position at the start of the buffer at index 0. At that time, the `bytesAvailable` property returns 16 because there are 16 bytes ahead of the current read position.

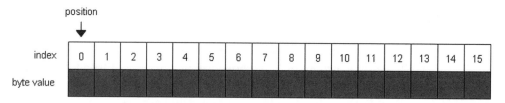

Figure 3.5   A read buffer with the read position at 0

If we were to read four bytes from the read buffer (by calling `readByte()` four times, for example), the read position would be moved to 4, as shown in figure 3.6. The `bytesAvailable` would no longer be 16. Instead, the `bytesAvailable` would be 12, because there would only be 12 bytes ahead of the read position.

When you read a file synchronously, you can move the read position to any available index using the `position` property. For example, if you've already read some or all of the bytes from a `FileStream` object and you want to reread the bytes from the start of the file, you must set the `position` property to 0:

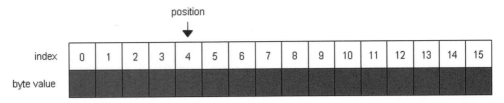

Figure 3.6 **When you read from a FileStream, the position in the read buffer moves.**

```
fileStream.position = 0;
```

Thus far, we've talked only about read buffers for synchronous reading operations. Asynchronous operations interact with read buffers differently. When you open a file to read asynchronously, the read buffer isn't filled right away. Instead, the read buffer gets filled progressively. Each time bytes are added to the buffer, the FileStream dispatches a progress event. Figure 3.7 shows what it might look like when an asynchronous read operation has just started and no bytes have been read into the buffer yet.

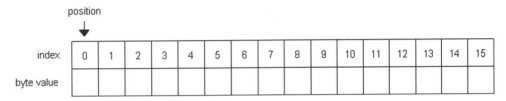

Figure 3.7 **The white squares indicate that no bytes have been read into the buffer yet because the read operation is asynchronous.**

Figure 3.8 shows what the read buffer might look like after the first progress event occurs. In this case, we're assuming that the first progress event occurs after reading just 4 bytes each. This is for the sake of convenience in illustrating the point. In actuality, progress events indicate much larger batches of bytes.

position
↓

index	0	1	2	3	4	5	6	7	8	9	10	11	12	13	14	15
byte value																

Figure 3.8 **The read buffer is partially filled after the first progress event.**

In this example, bytesAvailable will be 4 after the first progress event because there are only four bytes available for reading after the read position. Figure 3.9 shows what the read buffer might look like after the second progress event, assuming another 4 bytes are read in.

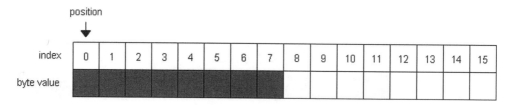

Figure 3.9   The read buffer has yet more bytes available after the second progress event.

In the example, the `bytesAvailable` will be 8 after the second progress event.

You'll notice that, in both figure 3.8 and figure 3.9, the position remains at 0. That's because we're assuming that in each case we're not reading from the buffer yet. But remember that you can read all the available bytes after each progress event. If we did read the bytes from the read buffer after the progress events, the pictures would be different. Figure 3.10 shows what the read buffer would look like after the first progress event if we were to read the available bytes.

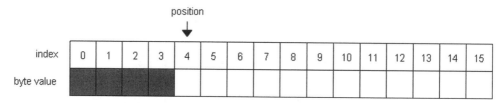

Figure 3.10   Reading the available bytes moves the read position.

If we were to read the bytes as soon as they became available, that would change the value of `bytesAvailable`. Just prior to reading the bytes, `bytesAvailable` would have a value of 4 in the example illustrated by figure 3.10, but, right after reading the bytes, the `bytesAvailable` value would be 0 because there would be no bytes following the read position.

There's another important difference in how the read buffer works when reading from a file synchronously versus asynchronously. As we mentioned earlier, when you read from a file synchronously, you can reread bytes from the read buffer by resetting the `position` property. With an asynchronous read, data is removed from the buffer as it's read and is no longer available unless you save it elsewhere.

That wraps up our discussion of reading from files. Next we'll round out the discussion by talking about how to write to files.

3.7.2   *Writing to files*

In many ways, writing to files is the opposite of reading from files. When you read from files, you're retrieving data from them; when you write to files, you are adding data to them. Because the operations are so similar, you'll see a lot of parity between the reading and writing of files. In the previous section, you learned some of the more challenging concepts involving working with files, including reading binary data. Much of what you learned in that section will be applicable to writing as well, and you'll likely find that, once the reading concepts click for you, the writing concepts will too.

Over the next few sections, we'll talk about all the important concepts you must know to write to files. You'll also see lots of examples that help you to integrate both reading and writing.

SELECTING A WRITING MODE

You'll be glad to know that opening a file for writing is almost exactly the same as opening a file for reading. In both cases, you use a `FileStream` object and call the `open()` or `openAsync()` method. In both cases, you pass the `open()` or `openAsync()` method a reference to the `File` object you want to use. There are three things that differ:

- When you open a file to write, you must specify a file mode parameter of `File-Mode.WRITE`, `FileMode.APPEND`, or `FileMode.UPDATE`.
- When you open a file for writing asynchronously, you must listen for the open event before attempting to write to the file.
- Whereas a file must already exist on the file system before you can read it, that isn't true for writing to a file. If you attempt to open a file that doesn't yet exist on the file system, AIR will create the file and any necessary directories.

The second and third points need little explanation, but we'd be leaving you stranded if we didn't discuss the first point in more detail. When you write to a file, you have three options, as indicated by the three `FileMode` writing constants: `WRITE`, `APPEND`, and `UPDATE`. You need to make sure that you select the correct mode in order to write to the file correctly:

- `WRITE`—Select the `WRITE` mode when you want to create an entirely new file or overwrite an existing file. This mode will truncate an existing file and start writing data from the beginning of the file.
- `APPEND`—Select this mode when you want to append data to the end of an existing file. If the file doesn't already exist, this mode will still create it.
- `UPDATE`—Select this mode if you want to be able to both write to and read from the file at the same time. This mode is similar to the `APPEND` mode in that it doesn't truncate existing content. However, while the `APPEND` mode automatically moves the write position to the end of the file, the `UPDATE` mode keeps the write position at the beginning of the file initially.

The following example opens a file called log.txt in the application storage directory. This code opens the file in `APPEND` mode, meaning any write operations will add to the end of the file:

```
var logFile:File = File.applicationStorageDirectory.resolvePath("log.txt");
var stream:FileStream = new FileStream();
stream.addEventListener(Event.OPEN, openHandler);
stream.openAsync(logFile, FileMode.APPEND);
```

It's important to choose correctly between synchronous and asynchronous operations when opening a file for writing. When reading from a file, the primary determining factor is the size of the file that you intend to read. A large file should generally be opened asynchronously. That same guideline applies to writing as well: if you intend to write a lot of data to a file, you should open it asynchronously.

As with reading from files, once you've written to a file, you should close access to it by using the close() method:

```
fileStream.close();
```

Now that you know how to open a file for writing, we'll look at how to actually write data to it.

WRITING DATA

In table 3.3, you learned all the IDataInput methods for reading from objects such as FileStream objects. You'll be glad to know that the methods for writing maintain parity with the methods for reading. Table 3.4 shows all the methods for writing for a FileStream object.

Table 3.4 IDataOutput methods for writing data

Format type	Format	Description	Related methods	Related ActionScript object types
Raw bytes	Byte	Single or multiple raw byte	writeByte() writeBytes() writeUnsignedBytes()	Int ByteArray
Boolean	Boolean	0 for false, otherwise true	writeBoolean()	Boolean
Numbers	Short	16-bit integer	writeShort() writeUnsignedShort()	Int uint
	Integer	32-bit integer	writeInt() writeUnsignedInt()	int uint
	Float	Single-precision floating point number	writeFloat()	Number
	Double	Double-precision floating point number	writeDouble()	Number
Strings	Multibyte	String using a specified character set	writeMultiByte()	String
	UTF-8	String using the UTF-8 character encoding	writeUTF() writeUTFBytes()	String
Objects	Object	Objects serialized and deserialized using the ActionScript Message Format (AMF)	writeObject()	Any object that can be serialized with AMF

NOTE The methods shown in table 3.4 are required by the IDataOutput interface. FileStream implements the IDataOutput interface, as do many other classes such as ByteArray and Socket.

Most of the write methods work similarly. We're not going to go into detail on each and every method. However, as we did earlier with reading, we'll talk about a couple of the most common ways to write data to a file: text and serialized objects.

Writing text to files mirrors reading text from files: use the writeUTFBytes() and writeMultiByte() methods. The writeUTFBytes() method allows you to specify a string parameter, which it writes to the file. The writeMultiByte() method works similarly except that you must specify a character set to use as well. Listing 3.15 shows an example that writes to a log file using writeUTFBytes(). This example assumes that you're using the class as a document class for a Flash-based AIR project and that there's a button component instance called _button on the stage.

Listing 3.15 Writing to a log file using `writeUTFBytes()`

```
package {

    import flash.display.MovieClip;
    import flash.filesystem.File;
    import flash.filesystem.FileStream;
    import flash.filesystem.FileMode;
    import flash.events.Event;
    import flash.events.MouseEvent;
    import flash.events.ProgressEvent;

    public class LogFileWriter extends MovieClip {

        public function LogFileWriter() {
            _button.addEventListener(MouseEvent.CLICK, addLogEntry);
        }

        private function addLogEntry(event:MouseEvent):void {
            var file:File = File.desktopDirectory.resolvePath("log.txt");
            var stream:FileStream = new FileStream();
            stream.open(file, FileMode.APPEND);
            stream.writeUTFBytes("Log entry " + new Date() + "\n");
            stream.close();
        }

    }

}
```

Writing data as serialized objects shares some similarities with reading serialized objects. Any data that can be serialized using AMF can be written to a file using the writeObject() method. For example, the following writes an array to a file:

```
var array:Array = new Array(1, 2, 3, 4);
fileStream.writeObject(array);
```

In this example, there are no extra steps required to write the array to the file because Array is one of the data types that's inherently supported by AMF serialization. If you want to write a custom data type to a file, you must make sure that you have registered the class with an alias. The process for registering a class with an alias was discussed previously in the section, "Reading objects."

Now that you've learned how to write to files, we'll next look at a more substantial example that uses all this information.

3.8   *Reading and writing music playlists*

In this section, we'll take all the information that we've learned throughout the chapter and create a simple application that allows the user to create playlists of mp3 files on her system. Note that the application doesn't actually play the mp3 files (although that would be possible), but rather we've chosen to keep it focused on the file system operations. You're welcome to add the mp3 playback functionality to the application as a challenge for yourself.

The playlist maker application is fairly rudimentary. It consists of just four classes/ MXML documents:

- PlaylistMaker.mxml
- ApplicationData.as
- Playlist.as
- PlaylistService.as

Over the next few sections, we'll build each of these. The result will look like what you see in figure 3.11.

The PlaylistMaker application has the following features:

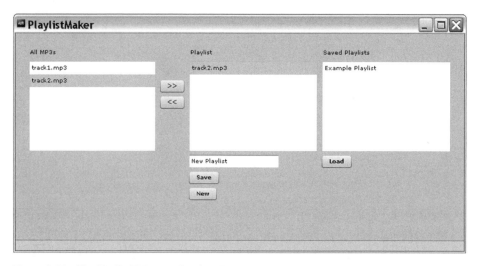

Figure 3.11   The PlaylistMaker application allows users to create playlists from the mp3 files on their computer.

- It searches all the mp3 files on the user's system (given a parent directory) and displays them in a list.
- The user can add and remove tracks to playlists.
- The user can save playlists.
- The user can load saved playlists.

Now that we've had a chance to see how the application is structured, what it looks like, and what it does, we can get to building it.

The first thing we need to do to get started with the PlaylistMaker application is configure the project. If you're using Flex Builder, simply create a new AIR project called PlaylistMaker, and that automatically creates the necessary file system structure as well as the PlaylistMaker.mxml application file. If you're not using Flex Builder, proceed with configuring a project as you normally would, and name the main application file PlaylistMaker.mxml.

Now that you've configured the project, we're ready to create the data model and model locator for the application. We'll do that in the next section.

3.8.1 Building the data model

Our application is quite simple; therefore the data model is simple as well. In fact, we only need one data model class: `Playlist`. `Playlist` objects essentially need only two pieces of information: a name and a collection of the tracks contained within the playlist. The `Playlist` class reflects this simplicity, as you can see in listing 3.16.

In addition to the `Playlist` class, we also need to create something to serve as a model locator, which allows us to store the data for the application in a centralized place. For this purpose, we'll use a class we're calling `ApplicationData`. The `ApplicationData` class contains the data used by the three parts of the application: all the mp3s, the current playlist, and all the saved playlists.

To build the data model and the model locator, complete the following steps:

1 Create a new ActionScript class document and save it as com/manning/playlistmaker/data/Playlist.as relative to the source directory for the project.

2 Add the code from listing 3.16 to the Playlist class.

Listing 3.16 The `Playlist` class

```
package com.manning.playlistmaker.data {
    import flash.events.Event;
    import flash.events.EventDispatcher;                    Make class  ❶
    import flash.filesystem.File;                           serializable

    [RemoteClass(alias="com.manning.playlistmaker.data.Playlist")]
    public class Playlist extends EventDispatcher {
                                  Store playlist tracks
        private var _list:Array;
        private var _name:String;       Name of playlist      ❷ Make properties
                                                                bindable
        [Bindable(event="listChanged")]
        public function get list():Array {
```

```
        return _list;
    }

    public function set list(value:Array):void {
        _list = value;
    }

    [Bindable(event="nameChanged")]
    public function set name(value:String):void {
        _name = value;
    }

    public function get name():String {
        return _name;
    }

    public function Playlist() {          Only create
        if(_list == null) {               array if null
            _list = new Array();
        }
    }

    public function addTrack(value:File):void {      ❸ Add track
        _list.push(value);                              to playlist
        dispatchEvent(new Event("listChanged"));
    }                                                Add only
                                                     name
    public function addTracks(value:Array):void {
        _list = _list.concat(value);                 Notify bound
        dispatchEvent(new Event("listChanged"));    ❹ properties
    }
                                                     Add
    public function removeTrack(value:File):void {   multiple
        for(var i:Number = 0; i < _list.length; i++) { ❺ tracks
            if(_list[i].nativePath == value.nativePath) {
                _list.splice(i, 1);
                break;                                   Remove
            }                                         ❻ a track
        }
        dispatchEvent(new Event("listChanged"));
    }

}
}
```

Although the `Playlist` class is simple, it has some subtleties that require further discussion. First, note that the class starts with a `[RemoteClass]` metadata tag ❶ . This is necessary because later on we're going to write `Playlist` objects to disk, and we need to be able to properly serialize and deserialize the objects. As you'll recall, the `[RemoteClass]` metadata tag tells the application how to map the serialized data back to a class. Note also that both the name and list properties are bindable ❷. That's because we want to wire up UI components later on to display the contents of a playlist. Because we want the list, an array, to be data bindable, we need to provide accessor methods to adding and removing tracks ❸ ❺ ❻. You'll notice that these methods all dispatch `listChanged` events ❹, which triggers data binding changes.

3   Create a new ActionScript class document and save it as com/manning/playlist-
    maker/data/ApplicationData.as relative to the source directory for the project.

4   Add the code from listing 3.17 to the ApplicationData class.

Listing 3.17   The `ApplicationData` class

```
package com.manning.playlistmaker.data {

    import flash.events.Event;
    import flash.events.EventDispatcher;
    import flash.filesystem.File;

    public class ApplicationData extends EventDispatcher {         ❶ Singleton
        static private var _instance:ApplicationData;                instance

        private var _mp3s:Playlist;        ❷ All system mp3s
        private var _playlist:Playlist;                               Current
        private var _savedPlaylists:Array;      Saved           ❸ playlist
                                                ❹ playlists
        [Bindable(event="mp3sChanged")]
        public function get mp3s():Playlist {
            return _mp3s;
        }

        [Bindable(event="playlistChanged")]
        public function set playlist(value:Playlist):void {
            _playlist = value;
            dispatchEvent(new Event("playlistChanged"));
        }

        public function get playlist():Playlist {
            return _playlist;
        }

        [Bindable(event="savedPlaylistsChanged")]
        public function set savedPlaylists(value:Array):void {
            _savedPlaylists = value;
            dispatchEvent(new Event("savedPlaylistsChanged"));
        }

        public function get savedPlaylists():Array {
            return _savedPlaylists;
        }

        public function ApplicationData() {
            _mp3s = new Playlist();
            _playlist = new Playlist();
            _savedPlaylists = new Array();
        }                                          Singleton accessor ❺

        static public function getInstance():ApplicationData {
            if(_instance == null) {
                _instance = new ApplicationData();
            }
            return _instance;
        }                                          Add a playlist to ❻
                                                     saved playlists
        public function addPlaylist(playlist:Playlist):void {
```

```
        if(_savedPlaylists.indexOf(playlist) == -1) {
          _savedPlaylists.push(playlist);
          dispatchEvent(new Event("savedPlaylistsChanged"));
        }
      }
    }
  }
```

The `ApplicationData` class is simple. You can see that it implements the Single-ton design pattern ❶ ❺. The class allows access to three pieces of information: an array of all the system mp3s ❷, the current playlist ❸, and an array of saved playlists ❹. Additionally, the class defines a method for adding a playlist to the saved playlists ❻. This method first verifies that the playlist isn't already in the saved playlists before adding it.

That's all there is to the data model and locator for this application. Next we'll build out the service/controller for the application.

3.8.2   *Building the controller*

The controller for this `PlaylistMaker` application is a class we'll call `PlaylistSer-vice`. This class is responsible for two primary functions: retrieving a list of the mp3s on the system and saving and retrieving playlists to and from disk. To build the con-troller, complete the following steps:

   1 Create a new ActionScript class file and save it as com/manning/playlistmaker/ services/PlaylistService.as relative to the project source directory.

   2 Add the following code to the `PlaylistService` class. This code creates the structure of the class. We'll fill in the methods in subsequent steps:

```
package com.manning.playlistmaker.services {
    import flash.filesystem.File;

    public class PlaylistService {

        public function PlaylistService() {
        }

        public function getMp3s(parentDirectory:File):void {
        }

        private function locateMp3sInDirectory(parentDirectory:File):void {
        }

        private function directoryListingHandler(event:FileListEvent):
        ➥void {
        }

        public function savePlaylists():void {
        }

        public function loadSavedPlaylists():void {
        }

    }
}
```

3 Fill in the getMp3s(), locateMp3sInDirectory(), and directoryListingHand-ler() methods. These methods work together to allow the user to retrieve all the mp3 files within a parent directory.

```
package com.manning.playlistmaker.services {
    import flash.filesystem.File;
    import flash.events.FileListEvent;
    import com.manning.playlistmaker.data.ApplicationData;

    public class PlaylistService {

        public function PlaylistService() {
        }

        public function getMp3s(parentDirectory:File):void {

            locateMp3sInDirectory(parentDirectory);

        }

        private function locateMp3sInDirectory(parentDirectory:File):void {
            parentDirectory.addEventListener(
            FileListEvent.DIRECTORY_LISTING, directoryListingHandler);
            parentDirectory.getDirectoryListingAsync();
        }

        private function directoryListingHandler(event:FileListEvent):
        void {
            var files:Array = event.files;
            var mp3s:Array = new Array();
            var file:File;
            for(var i:Number = 0; i < files.length; i++) {
                file = files[i] as File;
                if(file.isDirectory) {
                    locateMp3sInDirectory(file);
                }
                else if(file.extension == "mp3") {
                    mp3s.push(file);
                }
            }
            if(mp3s.length > 0) {
                ApplicationData.getInstance().mp3s.addTracks(mp3s);
            }
        }
        public function savePlaylists():void {
        }

        public function loadSavedPlaylists():void {
        }

    }
}
```

1 Retrieve .mp3 files

2 Get directory listing

3 Loop through contents

4 Take appropriate action

5 Add to data model

The getMp3s() method merely calls the private method locateMp3s-InDirectory() **1**, which asynchronously retrieves a directory listing **2**. When the directory listing is returned, the handler method loops through the contents **3** and determines the appropriate action for each **4**. If the item is a directory, we call `locateMp3sInDirectory()` recursively. Otherwise, if the file has an extension of .mp3, we add it to an array, which we later add to the data model ❺.

4 Fill in the `savePlaylists()` method as shown in the following code:

```
package com.manning.playlistmaker.services {
    import flash.filesystem.File;
    import flash.events.FileListEvent;
    import com.manning.playlistmaker.data.ApplicationData;
    import flash.filesystem.FileMode;
    import flash.filesystem.FileStream;
    import com.manning.playlistmaker.data.Playlist;

    public class PlaylistService {

        public function PlaylistService() {
        }

        public function getMp3s(parentDirectory:File):void {
            locateMp3sInDirectory(parentDirectory);

        }

        private function locateMp3sInDirectory(parentDirectory:File):void {
            parentDirectory.addEventListener(
            ➥FileListEvent.DIRECTORY_LISTING, directoryListingHandler);
            parentDirectory.getDirectoryListingAsync();
        }

        private function directoryListingHandler(event:FileListEvent):
        ➥void {
            var files:Array = event.files;
            var mp3s:Array = new Array();
            var file:File;
            for(var i:Number = 0; i < files.length; i++) {
                file = files[i] as File;
                if(file.isDirectory) {
                    locateMp3sInDirectory(file);
                }
                else if(file.extension == "mp3") {
                    mp3s.push(file);
                }
            }
            if(mp3s.length > 0) {
                ApplicationData.getInstance().mp3s.addTracks(mp3s);

            }
        }

        public function savePlaylists():void {
            var file:File =
            ➥File.applicationStorageDirectory.resolvePath(
            ➥"savedPlaylists.data");
            var stream:FileStream = new FileStream();
            stream.open(file, FileMode.WRITE);
            var applicationData:ApplicationData =
            ➥ApplicationData.getInstance();
            applicationData.addPlaylist(applicationData.playlist);
```

Create file reference ❶

② Open in write mode

Add current playlist ❸

```
        stream.writeObject(applicationData.savedPlaylists);    ◁───┐
        stream.close();                                            Write all ❹
    }                                                              playlists

    public function loadSavedPlaylists():void {
    }

  }
}
```

When saving the data, we create a reference to the file ❶, open it in write mode ❷, and write the data to the file ❹. In this case, we're writing all the playlists to the file. We also need to make sure the current playlist is added to the saved playlists array in the data model ❸ before writing to disk.

5   Fill in the method that loads the saved playlists. Listing 3.18 shows the completed class with this method filled in.

Listing 3.18   The `PlaylistService` class

```
package com.manning.playlistmaker.services {
    import flash.filesystem.File;
    import flash.events.FileListEvent;
    import com.manning.playlistmaker.data.ApplicationData;
    import flash.filesystem.FileMode;
    import flash.filesystem.FileStream;
    import com.manning.playlistmaker.data.Playlist;

    public class PlaylistService {

        public function PlaylistService() {
        }

        public function getMp3s(parentDirectory:File):void {
            locateMp3sInDirectory(parentDirectory);
        }

        private function locateMp3sInDirectory(parentDirectory:File):void {
            parentDirectory.addEventListener(
            ➥FileListEvent.DIRECTORY_LISTING, directoryListingHandler);
            parentDirectory.getDirectoryListingAsync();
        }

        private function directoryListingHandler(event:FileListEvent):
        ➥void {
            var files:Array = event.files;
            var mp3s:Array = new Array();
            var file:File;
            for(var i:Number = 0; i < files.length; i++) {
                file = files[i] as File;
                if(file.isDirectory) {
                    locateMp3sInDirectory(file);
                }
                else if(file.extension == "mp3") {
                    mp3s.push(file);
                }
```

```
            }
            if(mp3s.length > 0) {
                ApplicationData.getInstance().mp3s.addTracks(mp3s);
            }
        }

        public function savePlaylists():void {
            var file:File =
➡File.applicationStorageDirectory.resolvePath("savedPlaylists.data");
            var stream:FileStream = new FileStream();
            stream.open(file, FileMode.WRITE);
            var applicationData:ApplicationData =
            ➡ApplicationData.getInstance();
            applicationData.addPlaylist(applicationData.playlist);
            stream.writeObject(applicationData.savedPlaylists);
            stream.close();
        }

        public function loadSavedPlaylists():void {
            var file:File =
            ➡File.applicationStorageDirectory.resolvePath(            ❶ Reference
            ➡"savedPlaylists.data");                                     storage file
            if(file.exists) {                                         ❷ If file exists
                var stream:FileStream = new FileStream();
                stream.open(file, FileMode.READ);              ❸ Open for
                var playlists:Array = new Array();                 reading
                while(stream.bytesAvailable) {
                    playlists = stream.readObject() as Array;
                }
                stream.close();                                   ❹ Read data
                                                                     from file
                ApplicationData.getInstance().savedPlaylists = playlists;
            }
        }                                                          Assign array to
    }                                                              savedPlaylists ❺
}
```

When reading the saved playlists, we read from the same file to which we wrote the data ❶. Before we try to read from the file, we verify that it actually exists ❷ or else we might get an error. Then we open the file in read mode ❸, read the data ❹, and write the data to the data model ❺.

That wraps up the controller. Next we need only to build the user interface to the application.

3.8.3 Building the user interface

The user interface for the PlaylistMaker application is PlaylistMaker.mxml, which you already created when configuring the project. Now we need only to add the necessary code to that document in order to make it look like figure 3.11. To do this, open PlaylistMaker.mxml and add the code in listing 3.19.

Listing 3.19 The PlaylistMaker document

```
<?xml version="1.0" encoding="utf-8"?>
<mx:WindowedApplication xmlns:mx="http://www.adobe.com/2006/mxml"
   creationComplete="creationCompleteHandler();" width="800">        ◁─  Register
   <mx:Script>                                                            creationComplete
   <![CDATA[                                                              Handler
      import com.manning.playlistmaker.data.Playlist;
      import com.manning.playlistmaker.services.PlaylistService;
      import com.manning.playlistmaker.data.ApplicationData;
      import flash.filesystem.File;                     Get reference to
                                                        ApplicationData
      [Bindable]
      private var _applicationData:ApplicationData;
      private var _service:PlaylistService;
                                                                   Create
      private function creationCompleteHandler():void {             service
         _applicationData = ApplicationData.getInstance();  ◁─      instance
         _service = new PlaylistService();                    ◁─
         _service.getMp3s(File.documentsDirectory);       ◁─   Request
         _service.loadSavedPlaylists();   ◁┐     Load the    ❶ system mp3s
      }                                    ❷  saved playlists

      private function addToPlaylist():void {
         _applicationData.playlist.addTrack(
         ➥mp3list.selectedItem as File);
      }

      private function removeFromPlaylist():void {
         _applicationData.playlist.removeTrack(
         ➥playlist.selectedItem as File);
      }

      private function newPlaylist():void {
         _applicationData.playlist = new Playlist();
      }

      private function loadPlaylist():void {
         _applicationData.playlist =
         ➥savedPlaylists.selectedItem as Playlist;
      }

      private function savePlaylist():void {
         var playlist:Playlist = _applicationData.playlist;
         playlist.name = playlistName.text;   ◁┐  Set playlist
         _service.savePlaylists();   ◁─ Save the   name
      }                                  playlists
   ]]>
   </mx:Script>
   <mx:HBox width="100%">
      <mx:VBox width="33%">
         <mx:Label text="All MP3s" />
         <mx:List id="mp3list"
               dataProvider="{_applicationData.mp3s.list}"
               labelField="name" width="100%" height="100%" />
      </mx:VBox>
      <mx:VBox>
```

```
            <mx:Spacer height="50" />
            <mx:Button label="&gt;&gt;" click="addToPlaylist();"
               enabled="{mp3list.selectedItem != null}" />
            <mx:Button label="&lt;&lt;" click="removeFromPlaylist();"
               enabled="{playlist.selectedItem != null}" />
         </mx:VBox>
         <mx:VBox width="33%">
            <mx:Label text="Playlist" />
            <mx:List id="playlist"
               dataProvider="{_applicationData.playlist.list}"
               labelField="name"
               width="100%" height="100%" />
            <mx:TextInput id="playlistName"
      text="{_applicationData.playlist.name}" />
            <mx:Button label="Save" click="savePlaylist();" />
            <mx:Button label="New" click="newPlaylist();" />
         </mx:VBox>
         <mx:VBox width="33%">
            <mx:Label text="Saved Playlists" />
            <mx:List id="savedPlaylists"
               dataProvider="{_applicationData.savedPlaylists}"
               labelField="name" width="100%" height="100%" />
            <mx:Button label="Load" click="loadPlaylist();" />
         </mx:VBox>

      </mx:HBox>
   </mx:WindowedApplication>
```

The PlaylistMaker.mxml document isn't too fancy. Primarily it consists of a bunch of UI components wired up (via data binding) to properties in ApplicationData. Otherwise it simply makes a few requests to the service on startup ❶ ❷ and responds to user actions by updating values in ApplicationData. Note that, when requesting the system mp3s, we give the service a parent directory of the user's documents directory ❶. That means we'll only be retrieving the mp3 files from the documents directory. If you wanted to retrieve the files from other locations on the computer, you'd simply need to specify a different starting directory.

That's all there is to PlaylistMaker. You can go ahead and run it and see for yourself how it works.

At this point, you probably think there's not much more we could discuss related to files and storing data locally. After all, we've already covered a great deal of information. Don't worry. We don't have much more to talk about on this topic, but we do have one more important subject to cover: storing data securely. Read on to learn how this works.

3.9   *Storing data securely*

We've seen how to read and write data using files. Much of that data isn't only easily accessible, it's also human-readable. For most data, that's not a problem. In the previous section, we wrote playlist data to files, and there's no problem with storing that data in files that are easily accessible, meaning any user can open them and read them. You probably wouldn't care if your sister, your child, or even a stranger read a playlist you made up. But that's not true of all data. Consider the following example: you build an AIR application that allows users to shop several of their favorite online stores all from one application. As a convenience for the user, you want the application to store billing information. That way the user doesn't have to enter that information every time he wants to make a purchase. Storing that data in a file might seem like a good idea initially, but, unlike a playlist of mp3 tracks, a user's billing information is probably something he doesn't want others to see. Storing that sort of data in a standard file is a bad idea. Not only does it make the data available to other users of the computer, but it also makes the information available to other software running on the computer.

Although writing to a regular file isn't a good idea in cases such as the one just mentioned, AIR does have a solution. The `flash.data.EncryptedLocalStore` class provides access to a secure data storage area on the computer. Each system user of each AIR application gets his own secure data storage area. That means that if you use your shopping application you'll have your own secure data storage area, but if your sister uses the application on the same computer she'll also have her own unique secure data storage area. The `EncryptedLocalStore` class takes care of all the logic behind the scenes, determining which storage area to use. All you have to do is write the code that adds data to the data store, reads from the data store, or removes data from the data store.

All data written to a secure data storage area using `EncryptedLocalStore` is encrypted using AES-CBC 128-bit encryption. Again, `EncryptedLocalStore` takes care of the encryption and decryption. All you need to do is call the correct methods and pass them the correct parameters. We'll look at these methods in a moment. First we need to look at how the data is stored.

Each piece of data in the encrypted data storage area is identified by a unique key. The key is a string that we can use to retrieve the data. For example, if you want to store an email server password, it might make sense to use a key such as `emailServer-Password`. The keys you use are arbitrary, but it's usually a good idea to use names that clearly indicate what the value is. Each key points to a piece of data that you store using `EncryptedLocalStore`, and that piece of data is stored as a `flash.utils.Byte-Array` object. If you're not familiar with the `ByteArray` class, there's no reason to panic. It implements the `IDataInput` and `IDataOutput` interfaces—the same interfaces implemented by `FileStream`. That means you can write and read data to and from a `ByteArray` object just as you would a `FileStream` object. For example, the following code constructs a `ByteArray` object and then writes an array of strings to it using the `writeObject()` method:

```
var array:Array = new Array("a", "b", "c", "d");
var byteArray:ByteArray = new ByteArray();
byteArray.writeObject(array);
```

When you want to write data to the data store, all you need to do is call the static EncryptedLocalStore.setItem() method. The staticItem() method requires that you give it two pieces of information: the key and the data (in the form of a ByteArray object). The following example writes a password value using setItem():

```
var byteArray:ByteArray = new ByteArray();
byteArray.writeUTFBytes("j8ml08*1");
EncryptedLocalStore.setItem("emailServerPassword", byteArray);
```

Once you've written data to the data store, it's likely that at another time you'll want to retrieve that data. You can do that using the getItem() method. The getItem() method requires that you tell it the key of the data you want to retrieve. It then returns a ByteArray object with the data. The following example retrieves the email server password:

```
var byteArray:ByteArray =
➥EncryptedLocalStore.getItem("emailServerPassword");
var password:String= byteArray.readUTFBytes(byteArray.length);
```

What if you want to remove data from the data store? Not a problem. Encrypted-LocalStore provides two static methods for accomplishing that: removeItem() and reset(). The removeItem() method removes an item given the key. For example, the following will remove the email server password from the data store:

```
EncryptedLocalStore.removeItem("emailServerPassword");
```

The reset() method removes all data from the data store:

```
EncryptedLocalStore.reset();
```

We've wrapped up all the core theoretical information, so we have just one more thing to do in this chapter, which is to add to our AirTube application by integrating some of the file system knowledge we just learned.

3.10   *Writing to files with AirTube*

As you probably recall, in chapter 2 we started building the AirTube application, which allows users to search YouTube and play back videos. We made tremendous progress with the application in that chapter. But we've yet to implement one of the key features of the application: allowing the user to download videos for offline play-back. We didn't build that functionality in chapter 2 for good reason: we didn't yet know how to do it. But with the knowledge we've gained in this chapter, we're ready to tackle the job.

Although we've seen the theory behind what we're about to do, we haven't yet seen a practical example of it. Thus far in the chapter, we've seen practical examples of how to read from and write to local files, but not how to read from an internet resource and write that to a local file. That's what we're going to do here. We need to download an .flv file from the internet and save it to a file locally on the user's computer. We'll also use the same process to download the thumbnail image for the video.

To implement this new feature in the AirTube application, complete the following steps:

1 Open the `ApplicationData` class for the AirTube project and update the code to add a `downloadProgress` property as shown in listing 3.20. (Changes are shown in bold.) We'll use this property to monitor download progress for the video. On its own it doesn't do much. But we'll update the value from the service class, as you'll see in just a minute.

Listing 3.20 Adding the `downloadProgress` to the `ApplicationData` class

```
package com.manning.airtube.data {

    import flash.events.Event;
    import flash.events.EventDispatcher;

    public class ApplicationData extends EventDispatcher {

        static private var _instance:ApplicationData;

        private var _videos:Array;
        private var _currentVideo:AirTubeVideo;
        private var _downloadProgress:Number;

        [Bindable(event="videosChanged")]
        public function set videos(value:Array):void {
            _videos = value;
            dispatchEvent(new Event("videosChanged"));
        }

        public function get videos():Array {
            return _videos;
        }

        [Bindable(event="currentVideoChanged")]
        public function set currentVideo(value:AirTubeVideo):void {
            _currentVideo = value;
            dispatchEvent(new Event("currentVideoChanged"));
        }

        public function get currentVideo():AirTubeVideo {
            return _currentVideo;
        }

        [Bindable(event="downloadProgressChanged")]
        public function set downloadProgress(value:Number):void {
            _downloadProgress = value;
            dispatchEvent(new Event("downloadProgressChanged"));
        }

        public function get downloadProgress():Number {
            return _downloadProgress;
        }

        public function ApplicationData() {

        }

        static public function getInstance():ApplicationData {
```

```
        if(_instance == null) {
            _instance = new ApplicationData();
        }
        return _instance;
    }

  }
}
```

2   Open the `AirTubeService` class, and add the code shown in listing 3.21. The
    changes are shown in bold. We're adding one public method called `saveToOff-`
    `line()`, which initiates the download of the thumbnail and video files, and then
    we're adding the necessary handler methods.

```
package com.manning.airtube.services {

  import com.adobe.webapis.youtube.YouTubeService;
  import com.adobe.webapis.youtube.events.YouTubeServiceEvent;
  import com.manning.airtube.data.AirTubeVideo;
  import com.manning.airtube.data.ApplicationData;
  import com.manning.airtube.utilities.YouTubeFlvUrlRetriever;

  import flash.events.Event;
  import flash.events.ProgressEvent;
  import flash.filesystem.File;
  import flash.filesystem.FileMode;
  import flash.filesystem.FileStream;
  import flash.net.URLRequest;
  import flash.net.URLStream;
  import flash.utils.ByteArray;

  public class AirTubeService {

    static private var _instance:AirTubeService;

    private var _proxied:YouTubeService;
    private var _flvFile:File;
    private var _imageFile:File;
    private var _downloadingVideo:AirTubeVideo;

    public function set key(value:String):void {
      _proxied.apiKey = value;
    }

    public function AirTubeService() {
      _proxied = new YouTubeService();
      _proxied.addEventListener(
      ➥YouTubeServiceEvent.VIDEOS_LIST_BY_TAG,
      ➥getVideosByTagsResultHandler);
    }

    static public function getInstance():AirTubeService {
      if(_instance == null) {
        _instance = new AirTubeService();
      }
      return _instance;
```

```
}
public function getVideosByTags(tags:String):void {
   if(_proxied.apiKey.length == 0) {
      throw Error("YouTube API key not set");
   }
   _proxied.videos.listByTag(tags);
}

private function getVideosByTagsResultHandler(
➥event:YouTubeServiceEvent):void {
   var videos:Array = event.data.videoList as Array;
   for(var i:Number = 0; i < videos.length; i++) {
      videos[i] = new AirTubeVideo(videos[i]);
   }
   ApplicationData.getInstance().videos = videos;

}
public function configureVideoForPlayback(video:AirTubeVideo):
➥void {
   ApplicationData.getInstance().currentVideo = video;
   if(video.flvUrl == null) {
      new YouTubeFlvUrlRetriever().getUrl(video);
   }
}
```

Pass in video to save ❶

```
public function saveToOffline(video:AirTubeVideo):void {
   _downloadingVideo = video;

   _flvFile = File.applicationStorageDirectory.resolvePath(
   ➥"videos/" + video.video.id + ".flv");
   var videoLoader:URLStream = new URLStream();
   videoLoader.load(new URLRequest(video.flvUrl));
   videoLoader.addEventListener(Event.COMPLETE,
                     videoDownloadCompleteHandler);
   videoLoader.addEventListener(ProgressEvent.PROGRESS,
   ➥videoDownloadProgressHandler);

   _imageFile = File.applicationStorageDirectory.resolvePath(
   ➥"thumbnails/" + video.video.id + ".jpg");
   var imageLoader:URLStream = new URLStream();
   imageLoader.load(new URLRequest(video.video.thumbnailUrl));
   imageLoader.addEventListener(ProgressEvent.PROGRESS,
   ➥imageDownloadProgressHandler);
}
```

Create destination video path ❷

Create destination image path ❸

```
private function videoDownloadProgressHandler(event:
➥ProgressEvent):void {
   var loader:URLStream = event.target as URLStream;
   var bytes:ByteArray = new ByteArray();
   loader.readBytes(bytes);
   var writer:FileStream = new FileStream();
   writer.open(_flvFile, FileMode.APPEND);
   writer.writeBytes(bytes);
   writer.close();
   var ratio:Number = event.bytesLoaded / event.bytesTotal;
   ApplicationData.getInstance().downloadProgress = ratio;
```

Read available bytes ❹

Write to video file ❺

```
    }

    private function videoDownloadCompleteHandler(event:Event):void {
        _downloadingVideo.offline = true;
        ApplicationData.getInstance().downloadProgress = 0;
    }

    private function imageDownloadProgressHandler(event:
ProgressEvent):void {
        var loader:URLStream = event.target as URLStream;
        var bytes:ByteArray = new ByteArray();
        loader.readBytes(bytes);                        ◁─────┐  Read the
        var writer:FileStream = new FileStream();            ⑥  available
        writer.open(_imageFile, FileMode.APPEND);
        writer.writeBytes(bytes);      ◁───┐  Write to
        writer.close();                    ⑦  image file
    }
  }
}
```

The saveToOffline() method ① uses URLStream objects to start downloading
the video file and the thumbnail, and creates the paths to the destination files
② ③ using the video's ID to create unique file names. As the video and thumbnail download, the progress events get handled by the videoDownloadPro-
gressHandler() and imageDownloadProgressHandler() methods, respectively.
Each of these methods does the same basic thing: uses the readBytes() method
of the URLStream object to read all the available bytes ④ ⑥ and then writes
those bytes to the end of the destination file ⑤ ⑦.

3 Update the video window with a few minor changes. You can do this by opening
   VideoWindow.mxml and adding the code shown in bold from listing 3.22.

Listing 3.22   Updating VideoWindow.mxml to support downloading videos

```xml
<?xml version="1.0" encoding="utf-8"?>
<mx:Window xmlns:mx="http://www.adobe.com/2006/mxml" width="400"
 height="400" type="utility" closing="closingHandler(event);"
 creationComplete="creationCompleteHandler();">
   <mx:Script>
     <![CDATA[
         import com.manning.airtube.services.AirTubeService;
         import com.manning.airtube.data.ApplicationData;

         [Bindable]
         private var _applicationData:ApplicationData;

         private function creationCompleteHandler():void {
            _applicationData = ApplicationData.getInstance();
         }

         private function closingHandler(event:Event):void {
            event.preventDefault();
            visible = false;
         }

         private function saveOffline():void {
```

```
                    AirTubeService.getInstance().saveToOffline(
               ➥_applicationData.currentVideo);
          }

     ]]>
  </mx:Script>
  <mx:VBox>
     <mx:Label text="{_applicationData.currentVideo.video.title}" />
     <mx:VideoDisplay id="videoDisplay"
        source="{_applicationData.currentVideo.flvUrl}"
        width="400" height="300" />
     <mx:HBox id="progressContainer" width="100%"
        visible="{_applicationData.downloadProgress > 0}"
        includeInLayout="{progressContainer.visible}">#1
        <mx:Label text="download progress" />
        <mx:HSlider id="progressIndicator" enabled="false" width="100%"
           minimum="0" maximum="1"
           value="{_applicationData.downloadProgress}" />
     </mx:HBox>
     <mx:HBox>
        <mx:Button id="playPauseButton" label="Pause"
           click="togglePlayback();" />
        <mx:Button id="saveOfflineButton" label="Save Offline"
              visible="{!_applicationData.currentVideo.offline}"
              enabled="{!(_applicationData.downloadProgress > 0)}"
              click="saveOffline();" />
     </mx:HBox>
  </mx:VBox>
</mx:Window>
```

Hide unless downloading ◁

Show download progress ❶

Hide if video already offline ◁

Disable while downloading

❷ **Click to save**

The changes to the code in VideoWindow.mxml are fairly modest. All we've done is add a slider to show download progress ❶ and a button to save the video ❷. The components are data bound to properties in ApplicationData, and when the user clicks to save the video, we just call the service method to save the video.

And that wraps up this stage of the AirTube application. Of course, we haven't yet created a way to view videos the user has saved offline. For that, we'll be using a local database, which is covered in chapter 5. If you run the AirTube application now, you can see the button to save a video for offline playback; if you click it, you'll see the download progress indicator update in the window. Also, if you look in the application storage directory for the AirTube application, you'll see the saved .flv and .jpg files.

3.11 Summary

In this chapter you've acquired a great deal of information related to working with the file system via AIR applications. One of the most fundamental skills when working with the file system is being able to reference files and directories, and that was our starting point in this chapter. From that point, we looked at basic directory skills, such as reading a directory listing and creating new directories. Next we looked at copying, moving, and deleting both directories and files. Then we moved into the most complex topic of the chapter: reading from and writing to files. This topic took us into what might have been new territories when we explored the interfaces for reading and writing binary data.

We've covered a lot of ground in this chapter, and now it's time to move on to the next. In chapter 4, you'll learn all about drag-and-drop operations as well as copy and-paste operations.

Copy-and-paste and drag-and-drop

This chapter covers

- Copying data from AIR applications
- Pasting data into AIR applications
- Dragging data from AIR applications
- Dropping data on AIR applications

Copy-and-paste and drag-and-drop operations are a standardized way for users to interact with an application, so it's a good idea to build these behaviors into AIR applications. For example, if you build an application that displays images from a network source, many users would expect and appreciate the ability to save copies of the images locally by dragging the image from the AIR application to the desktop.

An important thing to understand about drag-and-drop and copy-and-paste in AIR is that they run at the system level. You may be used to enabling these sorts of operations within Flex or Flash applications, but there's a big distinction to be made here. When you build Flex or Flash applications for the Web, all your drag-

and-drop and most of your copy-and-paste operations are limited to the one instance of Flash player. For example, you can't drag an image from a Flash application running in a browser and save it to the desktop. AIR enables these operations to be extended beyond the confines of Flash player. You can allow users to transfer data within, as well as to and from, an AIR application using these operations.

Drag-and-drop and copy-and-paste are simple in many respects. But don't let their simplicity hide their importance. Implementing these simple operations well in AIR applications allows users to interact with them in more intuitive ways, improving their user experience.

Although copy-and-paste and drag-and-drop are different operations, they share a lot of commonality, both in an abstract sense and in practice. That's why we've put these two topics together in this chapter. We'll start by looking at what these operations have in common. Then we'll look at each of the operations in more detail.

4.1   Using a clipboard to transfer data

Drag-and-drop and copy-and-paste are similar in nature. Both operations involve moving or copying data from one location to another. The only thing that differs is how the user interacts with the data in order to move or copy it.

In the case of drag-and-drop, the user clicks on a UI element (an image or text file, for example), drags it to a new location, and then releases the mouse button to complete the transaction, thereby moving or copying the data (the image or text file).

Copy-and-paste requires that the user select a UI element by way of a menu option, keyboard shortcut, or button, and then the user can move or copy to a new location using a menu option, keyboard shortcut, or button in the new location. In both operations, there must be a transfer medium—a place where the data is placed temporarily while it's being moved or copied. In AIR, this transfer medium is called a *clipboard*, and in the next few sections we'll learn more about what a clipboard is and how you can work with it.

4.1.1   What's a clipboard?

The clipboard is the metaphor that computers use for moving or copying data. You're likely already familiar with the system clipboard used by your operating system, which allows you to copy-and-paste. For example, if you want to copy text from your email program and paste it into a Word document, you're using the system clipboard behind the scenes.

In this chapter, we'll be working with two different sorts of clipboards. One type of clipboard is the system clipboard that we just mentioned. You'll see how you can write data to the system clipboard for use in other applications. We'll also work with AIR-specific clipboards. Regardless, AIR treats both of these clipboards in the same way, and you can access them via instances of the `flash.desktop.Clipboard` class.

What can you do with `Clipboard` objects? `Clipboard` objects are relatively simple. You can do just three things with clipboards: add data to them, read data from them, and clear data off of them. Throughout the chapter, we'll elaborate on different ways to accomplish these tasks, but, generally speaking, that's what you can do with Clipboard objects.

If you want to work with a Clipboard object, the first thing you need to do is create a reference to one. We'll be working with both AIR-specific clipboards and the system clipboard. Therefore, you'll need to know how to reference both types. Getting a reference to the system clipboard is as simple as accessing the static Clipboard.generalClipboard property.

```
var systemClipboard:Clipboard = Clipboard.generalClipboard;
```

We'll also use lots of AIR-specific clipboards. In these cases, you'll need to use the Clipboard constructor, which requires no parameters. The following creates a new Clipboard object:

```
var clipboard:Clipboard = new Clipboard();
```

The next step would be to add or retrieve data. However, before we can do that, we need to understand the formats that we can use with a clipboard.

4.1.2   *Understanding data formats*

You may store and retrieve data to and from a clipboard in a variety of formats. You're probably familiar with this concept even if you've never thought about it before. When you use the system clipboard on your computer, you sometimes copy-and-paste text, and you sometimes copy-and-paste files. Text and files are different formats, but you can store both on the system clipboard. When you're working with AIR, the same is true. As a result, you need to be able to specify what format you want to use to store or retrieve data. Many of the Clipboard methods require that you specify a format, including the methods for writing data to and reading data from the clipboard. For example, in the next section we'll look at the setData() method used to write data to the clipboard. This method always requires that you give it a format as well as the data you want to write to the clipboard. For example, the following code writes text to the clipboard, specifying the text format:

```
clipboard.setData(ClipboardFormats.TEXT_FORMAT, "example text");
```

As we just saw in this example, you can use the flash.desktop.ClipboardFormats constants to refer to the most common formats. These constants and their Action-Script equivalents are shown in table 4.1. These are the formats that are most universally understood by other applications. That means that you can add bitmap-formatted or text-formatted data to the clipboard from an AIR application and know it's likely that the user will be able to copy that to another application on her computer (such as Word). The inverse is also true: these are the formats that most applications will write to a clipboard, and therefore they're available for reading into an AIR application.

Constant	ActionScript equivalent
BITMAP_FORMAT	BitmapData
FILE_LIST_FORMAT	Array of File objects
HTML_FORMAT	HTML-formatted String
TEXT_FORMAT	String
URL_FORMAT	String

Table 4.1 `ClipboardFormats` constants and their ActionScript equivalents

In addition to the standard formats listed in table 4.1, you can transfer objects by reference for use in the same application or in a serialized format that might be valid in other applications that know how to interpret the data. For example, suppose you have several pieces of information such as name, street address, city, state/province, and postal code that you want to bundle together into one unit in an instance of a custom Address class. Using the standard formats, it would be possible to write any one of these pieces of data to the clipboard, but not all grouped together. You can use your own custom format name instead. In this example, the format name address might be appropriate. All that's necessary then is that the application that reads from the clipboard knows both the data format name (address) and how to deserialize the data. When we talk about serializing data, that could refer to custom serialization (such as an XML string) or the use of AIR's native support of AMF. (See chapter 3 for more information about AMF.) The following example assumes that userAddress is an Address object (remember that in our scenario Address is a custom class), and it serializes the object automatically using AMF:

```
clipboard.setData("address", userAddress);
```

Now we know what clipboards are and what formats we can store or retrieve from clipboards. The next logical step is to start reading and writing data from and to a clipboard.

4.1.3   Reading and writing data

Clipboards are fairly passive objects. They don't *do* much. Rather, they're storage areas where you can write data and read data. For example, if you want to take a snapshot of an AIR window's contents and make that available to paste into a Word document, you'll want to write that image data to the clipboard. On the flip side, if you've copied a file from your desktop and you want to paste that into an AIR application to add it to a list of files, you'll need to read that file information from the clipboard.

You can write data to a clipboard using the setData() method as we've already seen in the previous section. The setData() method always requires that you specify two parameters: the format and the data to write to the clipboard. The following example writes the current value of a text input control to a clipboard using text format:

```
clipboard.setData(ClipboardFormats.TEXT_FORMAT, textInput.text);
```

You can add more than one format to a clipboard at a time. For example, if a user copies an image from your AIR application, you may want to allow him to paste it into an image-editing program or onto the desktop as an image file. In this case, you'd need to add the data in two formats: BITMAP_FORMAT and FILE_LIST_FORMAT. Each format requires a different type of data for it to make sense to the recipient of the data. The BITMAP_FORMAT data would need to be a BitmapData object, while the FILE_LIST_FORMAT would need to be an array of one or more File objects. We'll see examples illustrating these sorts of scenarios later in the chapter.

You can read data from a clipboard using the getData() method. The getData() method requires just one parameter: the format of the data to retrieve. The following example retrieves the data from a clipboard in text format:

```
var text:String = clipboard.getData(ClipboardFormats.TEXT_FORMAT)
➥as String;
```

You'll notice that, in this example, the return value of getData() is cast as a String. That's because getData() necessarily has a generic return type. If you try to use the value in a way that requires a more specific type (as in assigning the value to a typed variable), you'll need to cast appropriately. Of course, it's up to you to know what the correct type should be for casting. In the case of text format, URL format, and HTML format, you should cast as a String. For bitmap format, you should cast as BitmapData. And for file list format, you should cast as an Array (knowing that each element of the array is a File object). For custom formats, you'll need to know the original format of the data before it was written to the clipboard.

If you're uncertain whether a clipboard has data in a particular format, you can use the hasFormat() method to query for that information. The method requires that you specify a format, and it returns a Boolean value: true if the clipboard has data for that format, and false otherwise.

4.1.4 Removing data from a clipboard

Not only might you want to set and get data on a clipboard, but you might also want to remove data from a clipboard. For example, if you write data to the system clipboard in a particular format, you aren't guaranteed that there aren't already other pieces of data written to that clipboard in other formats. When the user goes to request the data from the clipboard, the results could be unpredictable because different applications might have differing format precedents. For example, Word always pastes text from the clipboard if it's available, ignoring other formats that might be on the clipboard. It's possible that you could write bitmap-formatted data to the system clipboard from an AIR application, and if the user pastes it into a Word document, she might see only other text that she had previously copied from a different program. Therefore, you need methods to remove data from a clipboard.

> **NOTE**   For exactly the reason described in this scenario, you should always clear
> the system clipboard before writing data to it.

The `clearData()` method allows you to clear the data from a clipboard for a particular format. For example, if you want to remove URL format data from a clipboard, you could use the following code:

```
clipboard.clearData(ClipboardFormats.URL_FORMAT);
```

On the other hand, there are times when you simply want to remove all data of all formats from a clipboard. In those cases, you can use the `clear()` method:

```
clipboard.clear();
```

As you can see, the `clear()` method doesn't require any parameters. It just deletes all the data.

You've now seen how to write, read, and delete data. What we haven't yet talked about is how the data gets stored to a clipboard and how that can impact the way in which the data is available, both within an AIR application and outside of AIR. In the following section, we'll talk about how you can use transfer modes to affect the way data is stored.

4.1.5 *Understanding transfer modes*

There are a variety of scenarios in which you might use a clipboard. The basic three are as follows:

- Transferring data within a single AIR application
- Transferring data between AIR applications
- Transferring data between an AIR application and the operating system or another, non-AIR application

The second and third scenarios require that a copy of the data be made. For example, if you want to copy text from an AIR application to a Word document, you must be aware that Word is incapable of reading the text directly from the AIR application. Instead, a copy of the text must be made. This is true between AIR applications as well. If you have a custom `Address` type that's available in two AIR applications and you want to transfer an `Address` object from one AIR application to another, you must make a copy of the `Address` object. The second AIR application can't access the original `Address` object in order to read from it. However, the first scenario is different. When you want to transfer data within a single AIR application, it's possible to access data by reference, not just by value. By default, when you write data to a clipboard, it's always serializable, meaning that both a copy and a reference are written to the clipboard. If you want to explicitly control whether or not the data you write is serializable, you can specify a third Boolean parameter for the `setData()` method. A value of `true` (the default) means a copy and a reference are written, and `false` means that only a reference is written. You only need to use this parameter if you want to make sure that data isn't serialized and copied.

NOTE Even if you set the third parameter of setData() to false, all standard formats are still available to non-AIR applications. Using a value of false only affects data in custom formats for use within AIR applications.

On the flip side, you can also specify how you want to retrieve data when calling get-Data(). You can do this by way of a second, optional parameter that indicates a transfer mode. There are four transfer modes, each with a constant in the flash.desktop.ClipboardTransferMode class. The constants are as follows:

- ORIGINAL_PREFERRED—In this mode, a reference to the original is returned if it's available. If no reference is available, a copy is returned. Remember that references are only available within the same AIR application from which the data originated. If you specify this transfer mode and the data originated from another application, it'll always return the copy of the data. This transfer mode is the default.
- ORIGINAL_ONLY—In this mode, the reference to the original data is returned if it's available. Otherwise, if the original is unavailable, null is returned.
- CLONE_PREFERRED—In this mode, a copy of the data is returned if available. Otherwise, a reference is returned.
- CLONE_ONLY—In this mode, only a copy is returned if available. Otherwise, null is returned.

We have just one more topic to cover before we can jump to actually using clipboards. Next we'll discuss how you can be clever with how and when you write data to a clipboard.

4.1.6 *Deferred rendering*

Generally we write data to a clipboard as soon as the request is made. For example, if a user selects a menu option to copy text from a text area, we probably expect that the application immediately writes the text to the clipboard. However, there are some cases in which it's better to defer the writing of the actual data to the clipboard. Instead, we just want to set a note about where to find the necessary data when the user tries to retrieve it from the clipboard. There are two basic scenarios for this deferral:

- The data is large or it would be computationally intensive to write the data to the clipboard.
- The data might update between the time it's selected and the time it's requested, and you want to always get the most up-to-date data.

Admittedly, both of these are edge cases, but it's good to know that, should you need it, AIR supports deferred rendering. If you want to enable deferred rendering, you shouldn't use setData(). Instead, you should use setDataHandler(). The setDataHandler() method also requires that you specify the format. However, instead of specifying the data, you pass the method a reference to a handler method. When the user requests the data of that format from the clipboard, AIR calls the handler method and uses the value returned by the handler method. That means you must make sure the return value of the handler method is the expected type for the format. Consider the following example:

```
clipboard.setDataHandler(ClipboardFormats.TEXT_FORMAT, getText);
```

In this example, the format is set to text, which means that the handler method (`getText()`) must return a `String` as in the following:

```
private function getText():String {
    return textArea.text;
}
```

If you want to defer rendering by using `setDataHandler()`, you must make sure you haven't set data using `setData()`, because `setData()` will always take precedence over `setDataHandler()`. If you've already written data to a clipboard using `setData()` and you want to use deferred rendering for the same format, just call `clearData()` for that format before calling `setDataFormat()`.

The handler method specified by `setDataHandler()` doesn't get called until the user requests the data (for example, when she pastes into a Word document). But AIR will only call the handler method that once. Subsequent requests for the data will retrieve the same data from the clipboard that was returned when the method was first called.

Now we've covered all the necessary preliminary topics related to clipboards, and we're ready to start writing code that uses clipboards. Next we'll continue with a discussion of copy-and-paste operations, and later we'll cover drag-and-drop operations.

4.2   Copy-and-paste

Copy-and-paste is undoubtedly a familiar concept to you, because it's such an integral part of basic computer usage. For example, when you want to create a copy of a file on your computer, you frequently will select the file, use the system keyboard shortcut or context menu option to copy the file, and then use a keyboard shortcut or context menu option to paste the copy in a new location on the file system. You likewise use a similar procedure to copy-and-paste text from an email program to a text editor or from a web page to an email program. Because copy-and-paste operations are fundamental to computer usage, you'll want to support this sort of behavior in AIR applications that you build. Over the next few sections, we'll take a look at how you can enable copy-and-paste in your AIR applications.

4.2.1   Selecting a clipboard

When you want to enable copy-and-paste, you almost always want to use the system clipboard. Remember that there are two sorts of clipboards you can work with in AIR applications: the system clipboard and AIR-specific clipboards. Although each works the same way, only the system clipboard enables copying and pasting from and to other, non-AIR applications. Generally users expect that if they copy something they'll be able to paste it anywhere on the same system, within the same application or in a different application. For that reason, you'll want to use the system clipboard.

Recall from our earlier discussion that you can retrieve a reference to the system clipboard using the `Clipboard.generalClipboard` property:

```
var clipboard:Clipboard = Clipboard.generalClipboard;
```

Also, when you copy data to the system clipboard, you should clear all the existing data from the clipboard first. As we mentioned in an earlier section, you can use the `clear()` method to delete all the data on a clipboard:

```
clipboard.clear();
```

Once you've done these things, you're ready to copy content to the clipboard.

4.2.2 Copying content

Copying content requires nothing more than writing data to the clipboard using the techniques you've already learned. Let's look at an example. In this example we create two text areas, one with initial text, and allow the user to copy-and-paste selected text between the two using a window or application menu. (See chapter 2 for more information about menus.) Figure 4.1 shows what the completed application looks like.

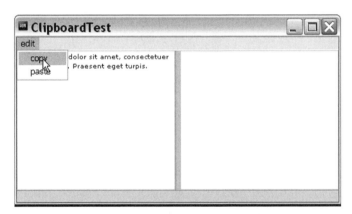

Figure 4.1 In this application, a user can copy-and-paste between two text areas using a menu.

First of all we need to create the basic structure for this application. Listing 4.1 shows this code.

Listing 4.1 Setting up the basic structure for a copy-and-paste application

```
<?xml version="1.0" encoding="utf-8"?>
<mx:WindowedApplication xmlns:mx="http://www.adobe.com/2006/mxml"
    layout="absolute" creationComplete="creationCompleteHandler();">    ⟵
    <mx:Script>                                          Register event
        <![CDATA[                         Selected           listener
                                          text area
            private var _focused:TextArea;  ⟵           Reference to clipboard
            private var _clipboard:Clipboard;   ⟵

            private function creationCompleteHandler():void {
```

```
        _clipboard = Clipboard.generalClipboard;        ◁━━  Assign system
    }                                                         clipboard

    private function copyText(event:Event):void {    ◁━━  Empty method
    }                                                      to handle copy

    private function pasteText(event:Event):void {   ◁━
    }
                                                         Empty method
                                                         to handle paste
    ]]>
</mx:Script>
<mx:HBox width="100%" height="100%">
    <mx:TextArea id="textAreaA" width="50%" height="100%"
        focusIn="_focused = textAreaA;">    ◁━┐
        <mx:text>                               Set focused text area
        Lorem ipsum dolor sit amet, consectetuer adipiscing elit.
        </mx:text>
    </mx:TextArea>
    <mx:TextArea id="textAreaB" width="50%" height="100%"
        focusIn="_focused = textAreaB;" />    ◁━
</mx:HBox>                                        Set focused
</mx:WindowedApplication>                         text area
```

Next, we can add the menu. Listing 4.2 shows the code that adds a window or application menu with one submenu called Edit. The Edit menu has two options: Copy and Paste.

Listing 4.2   Adding a menu to the application

```
<?xml version="1.0" encoding="utf-8"?>
<mx:WindowedApplication xmlns:mx="http://www.adobe.com/2006/mxml"
    layout="absolute" creationComplete="creationCompleteHandler();">
    <mx:Script>
        <![CDATA[

        private var _focused:TextArea;
        private var _clipboard:Clipboard;

        private function creationCompleteHandler():void {
            _clipboard = Clipboard.generalClipboard;              Create
            var menu:NativeMenu = new NativeMenu();               copy
            var editMenu:NativeMenu = new NativeMenu();           item
            var copyItem:NativeMenuItem = new NativeMenuItem("copy");  ◁━
            copyItem.addEventListener(
            ➥Event.SELECT, copyText);          Register copy
            var pasteItem:NativeMenuItem =      event handler
            ➥new NativeMenuItem("paste");       Create paste item
            pasteItem.addEventListener(Event.SELECT, pasteText);  ◁━
            editMenu.addItem(copyItem);                          Register
            editMenu.addItem(pasteItem);        Add the edit     paste
            menu.addSubmenu(editMenu, "edit");  ◁━  submenu      event
            if(NativeApplication.supportsMenu) {                 handler
                nativeApplication.menu = menu;
            }                                    Apply menu to
            else if(NativeWindow.supportsMenu) { window or
                nativeWindow.menu = menu;        application
            }
```

```
        }
        private function copyText(event:Event):void {
        }
        private function pasteText(event:Event):void {
        }
    ]]>
  </mx:Script>
  <mx:HBox width="100%" height="100%">
     <mx:TextArea id="textAreaA" width="50%" height="100%"
        focusIn="_focused = textAreaA;">
        <mx:text>
        Lorem ipsum dolor sit amet, consectetuer adipiscing elit.
        </mx:text>
     </mx:TextArea>
     <mx:TextArea id="textAreaB" width="50%" height="100%"
        focusIn="_focused = textAreaB;" />
  </mx:HBox>
</mx:WindowedApplication>
```

Next we need to add the definition for the copyText() method. This method should determine the selected text from the selected text area, and it should write that text to the clipboard. Listing 4.3 shows this code.

Listing 4.3 Copying the selected text

```
<?xml version="1.0" encoding="utf-8"?>
<mx:WindowedApplication xmlns:mx="http://www.adobe.com/2006/mxml"
   layout="absolute" creationComplete="creationCompleteHandler();">
  <mx:Script>
     <![CDATA[

        private var _focused:TextArea;
        private var _clipboard:Clipboard;

        private function creationCompleteHandler():void {
           _clipboard = Clipboard.generalClipboard;
           var menu:NativeMenu = new NativeMenu();
           var editMenu:NativeMenu = new NativeMenu();
           var copyItem:NativeMenuItem = new NativeMenuItem("copy");
           copyItem.addEventListener(Event.SELECT, copyText);
           var pasteItem:NativeMenuItem = new NativeMenuItem("paste");
           pasteItem.addEventListener(Event.SELECT, pasteText);
           editMenu.addItem(copyItem);
           editMenu.addItem(pasteItem);
           menu.addSubmenu(editMenu, "edit");
           if(NativeApplication.supportsMenu) {
              nativeApplication.menu = menu;
           }
           else if(NativeWindow.supportsMenu) {
              nativeWindow.menu = menu;
           }
        }

        private function copyText(event:Event):void {
```

```
            var text:String = _focused.text.substring(
            ➥_focused.selectionBeginIndex, _focused.selectionEndIndex);
            _clipboard.clear();
            _clipboard.setData(ClipboardFormats.TEXT_FORMAT, text);
        }

        private function pasteText(event:Event):void {
            var text:String =
            _clipboard.getData(ClipboardFormats.TEXT_FORMAT) as String;
            var currentText1:String =
            ➥_focused.text.substr(0, _focused.selectionBeginIndex);
            var currentText2:String =
            ➥_focused.text.substr(_focused.selectionEndIndex);
            _focused.text = currentText1 + text + currentText2;
        }

    ]]>
    </mx:Script>
    <mx:HBox width="100%" height="100%">
        <mx:TextArea id="textAreaA" width="50%" height="100%"
            focusIn="_focused = textAreaA;">
            <mx:text>
            Lorem ipsum dolor sit amet, consectetuer adipiscing elit.
            </mx:text>
        </mx:TextArea>
        <mx:TextArea id="textAreaB" width="50%" height="100%"
            focusIn="_focused = textAreaB;" />
    </mx:HBox>
</mx:WindowedApplication>
```

We'll wrap up this example in the next section, but you can test it as is right now, and you'll see that you can use the Edit > Copy menu item to copy selected text in a text area of the AIR application and paste it into another application such as a text editor. That should prove that you've successfully copied text to the system clipboard.

In the first example, we used a menu to copy text. You aren't limited to using menus to initiate copying and you aren't limited to copying text. Next we'll look at a simple example that allows you to take a snapshot of an AIR application as a bitmap using a button and write that to the system clipboard. In figure 4.2, you can see what the application looks like when it's running.

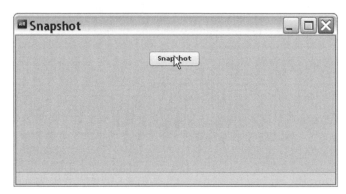

Figure 4.2   Take a snapshot of the application by clicking a button, which allows the user to then paste the snapshot from the clipboard to another application.

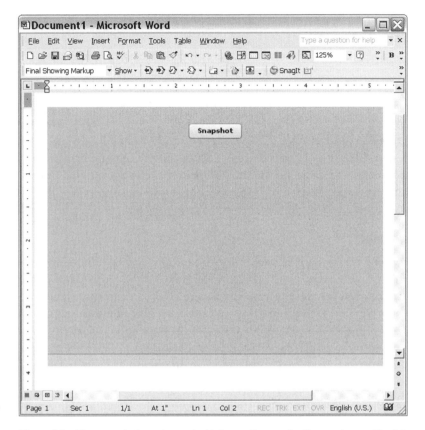

Figure 4.3 The snapshot can be pasted into another application such as a Word document.

Once the user has taken a snapshot by clicking the button, she can paste the bitmap into another application. Figure 4.3 shows an example of how the bitmap can be pasted into a Word document.

Listing 4.4 shows the code for this example, which you'll notice is remarkably simple.

Listing 4.4 Taking a snapshot and writing it to the system clipboard

```
<?xml version="1.0" encoding="utf-8"?>
<mx:WindowedApplication xmlns:mx="http://www.adobe.com/2006/mxml">
   <mx:Script>
      <![CDATA[

         private function takeSnapshot():void {
            var bitmapData:BitmapData = new BitmapData(stage.width,
                                        stage.height);
            bitmapData.draw(stage);
            var clipboard:Clipboard =
               Clipboard.generalClipboard;
```

Create a **1** BitmapData object

2 Take snapshot

Get system clipboard reference

```
                    clipboard.clear();
                    clipboard.setData(ClipboardFormats.BITMAP_FORMAT,
                            bitmapData);
                }
                                                           Write bitmap to   ❸
                                                             clipboard
            ]]>
        </mx:Script>
        <mx:Button label="Snapshot" click="takeSnapshot();" />   ⟵    Use button to
    </mx:WindowedApplication>                                           call method
```

As you can see in this example, all that was required was that we create a `BitmapData` object ❶, copy the stage content to the object ❷, and then write that to the clipboard ❸. You can see that we're using `BITMAP_FORMAT` for the format in this case.

Now that we've thoroughly reviewed copying content, we next need to look at the pasting operation.

4.2.3   *Pasting content*

Pasting content is the reading part of a copy-and-paste operation. Copying writes to the clipboard, but pasting reads from the clipboard. When you paste content in an AIR application, you're reading from the system clipboard, meaning that the content could have originated within the AIR application itself or in another application running on the computer. For example, a user could have copied a file from the system and then might try to paste that into an AIR application.

Pasting content into an AIR application is simply a matter of using the retrieval technique you learned in section 4.1.3. In that section, you learned about the `get-Data()` method. Using the `getData()` method, you can retrieve data from the system clipboard in any format that's currently available. To see an example of this, we continue with the earlier example from listing 4.3. In that example, the user was able to copy text from a text area using the application or window menu. Now we add paste capabilities such that the user can paste content into a text area using the menu as well. Listing 4.5 shows the code that does this.

Listing 4.5   Pasting text into the current text area

```
<?xml version="1.0" encoding="utf-8"?>
<mx:WindowedApplication xmlns:mx="http://www.adobe.com/2006/mxml"
    layout="absolute" creationComplete="creationCompleteHandler();">
    <mx:Script>
        <![CDATA[

            private var _focused:TextArea;
            private var _clipboard:Clipboard;

            private function creationCompleteHandler():void {
                _clipboard = Clipboard.generalClipboard;
                var menu:NativeMenu = new NativeMenu();
                var editMenu:NativeMenu = new NativeMenu();
                var copyItem:NativeMenuItem = new NativeMenuItem("copy");
                copyItem.addEventListener(Event.SELECT, copyText);
                var pasteItem:NativeMenuItem = new NativeMenuItem("paste");
                pasteItem.addEventListener(Event.SELECT, pasteText);
```

```
            editMenu.addItem(copyItem);
            editMenu.addItem(pasteItem);
            menu.addSubmenu(editMenu, "edit");
            if(NativeApplication.supportsMenu) {
                nativeApplication.menu = menu;
            }
            else if(NativeWindow.supportsMenu) {
                nativeWindow.menu = menu;
            }
        }

        private function copyText(event:Event):void {
            var text:String = _focused.text.substring(
            ➥_focused.selectionBeginIndex, _focused.selectionEndIndex);
            _clipboard.clear();
            _clipboard.setData(ClipboardFormats.TEXT_FORMAT, text);
        }

        private function pasteText(event:Event):void {
            if(_focused is TextArea) {                        ◄──   ❶ Is text area
                var text:String = _clipboard.getData(                   selected?
                ➥ClipboardFormats.TEXT_FORMAT) as String;    ❷ Get text
                var currentText1:String = _focused.text.substr(0,   format data
                ➥_focused.selectionBeginIndex);                       Text
                var currentText2:String =                             up to
                ➥_focused.text.substr(           Text after          selection
                ➥_focused.selectionEndIndex);    selection
                _focused.text = currentText1 + text + currentText2;  ◄──
            }                                           Assign new text
        }

    ]]>
    </mx:Script>
    <mx:HBox width="100%" height="100%">
        <mx:TextArea id="textAreaA" width="50%" height="100%"
            focusIn="_focused = textAreaA;">
            <mx:text>
            Lorem ipsum dolor sit amet, consectetuer adipiscing elit.
            </mx:text>
        </mx:TextArea>
        <mx:TextArea id="textAreaB" width="50%" height="100%"
            focusIn="_focused = textAreaB;" />
    </mx:HBox>
</mx:WindowedApplication>
```

In this code, we first verify that the user has selected a text area ❶ to make sure we don't try to access properties of a null reference. Then we retrieve the text format data from the clipboard ❷. The remainder of the new code just inserts the text from the clipboard at the selection.

It's possible that the user might not have any text data copied to the system clipboard. In such a case, the getData() method would return null, and that would be inserted into the text field as the string value null. To correct that, we can add one more test to the code. Listing 4.6 shows what the pasteText() method looks like when we add a call to hasFormat() in the if statement.

Listing 4.6 Testing whether data exists can save on computation

```
private function pasteText(event:Event):void {
    if(_focused is TextArea &&
    ➥_clipboard.hasFormat(ClipboardFormats.TEXT_FORMAT)) {
        var text:String = _clipboard.getData(
        ➥ClipboardFormats.TEXT_FORMAT) as String;
        var currentText1:String = _focused.text.substr(0,
        ➥_focused.selectionBeginIndex);
        var currentText2:String =
        ➥_focused.text.substr(_focused.selectionEndIndex);
        _focused.text = currentText1 + text + currentText2;
    }
}
```

By testing whether the clipboard has data in the specified format, we can avoid needless code execution if there's no data written to the clipboard for the format.

4.2.4 Cutting content

Many applications extend on the copy-and-paste operation by allowing the user to *cut* content. Cutting content is similar to copying it: both copy the content to a clipboard. But cutting content removes the content from the original location as an additional step. You can achieve this same behavior in an AIR application by writing a bit of extra code. In this section, we'll briefly look at how to add the cut feature to the simple application we've worked with in the past two sections.

Listing 4.7 shows what the example looks like when we add the cut feature into the code from listings 4.5 and 4.6.

Listing 4.7 Adding a cut option to the menu

```
<?xml version="1.0" encoding="utf-8"?>
<mx:WindowedApplication xmlns:mx="http://www.adobe.com/2006/mxml"
    layout="absolute" creationComplete="creationCompleteHandler();">
    <mx:Script>
        <![CDATA[

        private var _focused:TextArea;
        private var _clipboard:Clipboard;

        private function creationCompleteHandler():void {
            var menu:NativeMenu = new NativeMenu();
            var editMenu:NativeMenu = new NativeMenu();
            var copyItem:NativeMenuItem = new NativeMenuItem("copy");
            copyItem.addEventListener(Event.SELECT, copyText);
            var cutItem:NativeMenuItem = new NativeMenuItem("cut");      ◁──┐ Create cut
            cutItem.addEventListener(Event.SELECT, cutText);            ◁─┐ │ menu item
            var pasteItem:NativeMenuItem = new NativeMenuItem("paste");   │ │
            pasteItem.addEventListener(Event.SELECT, pasteText);         │ │
            editMenu.addItem(copyItem);                                  │ │ Listen for
            editMenu.addItem(cutItem);        ◁──┐ Add item             │─┘ select event
            editMenu.addItem(pasteItem);         │ to menu
            menu.addSubmenu(editMenu, "edit");
```

```
        if(NativeApplication.supportsMenu) {
            nativeApplication.menu = menu;
        }
        else if(NativeWindow.supportsMenu) {
            nativeWindow.menu = menu;
        }
        _clipboard = Clipboard.generalClipboard;
    }
    private function copyText(event:Event):void {
        var text:String = _focused.text.substring(
        ➥_focused.selectionBeginIndex, _focused.selectionEndIndex);
        _clipboard.setData(ClipboardFormats.TEXT_FORMAT, text);
    }
    private function cutText(event:Event):void {      ⬅──  Handle cut select event ❶
        copyText(event);                              ⬅────── Copy text    ❷ Get text
        var currentText1:String = _focused.text.substr(0,  ⬅──        up to
        ➥_focused.selectionBeginIndex);#6                             selection
        var currentText2:String = _focused.text.substr(   ┃❸ Get text after
        ➥_focused.selectionEndIndex);                     ┃  selection
        _focused.text = currentText1 + currentText2;  ⬅──  ┃ Set
        _focused.setSelection(_focused.selectionBeginIndex, │ selection
        ➥_focused.selectionBeginIndex);
    }                                                 Remove
                                                      selection ❹
    private function pasteText(event:Event):void {
        if(_focused is TextArea) {
            var text:String = _clipboard.getData(
            ➥ClipboardFormats.TEXT_FORMAT) as String;
            var currentText1:String = _focused.text.substr(0,
            ➥_focused.selectionBeginIndex);
            var currentText2:String =
            ➥_focused.text.substr(_focused.selectionEndIndex);
            _focused.text = currentText1 + text + currentText2;
        }
    }
    ]]>
</mx:Script>
<mx:HBox width="100%" height="100%">
    <mx:TextArea id="textAreaA" width="50%" height="100%"
        focusIn="_focused = textAreaA;">
        <mx:text>
        Lorem ipsum dolor sit amet, consectetuer adipiscing elit.
        </mx:text>
    </mx:TextArea>
    <mx:TextArea id="textAreaB" width="50%" height="100%"
        focusIn="_focused = textAreaB;" />
</mx:HBox>
</mx:WindowedApplication>
```

This new code is similar to existing code. You can see that, in the cutText() method
❶, the first thing we do is call the copyText() method to copy the text from the text
area. Then the next few lines of code ❷ ❸ are identical to lines of code from the
pasteText() method. These lines of code retrieve the text in the focused text area up

to and after the selection. Then we update the text in the text area to remove the selected text ❹ and set the selection (the highlighted text) to the index where the previously selected text started.

Whether you're copying or cutting data, one important thing to consider is how the data will be written to the clipboard. Normally custom data types aren't recognized by a clipboard, and the public properties of a custom data type are instead written to a generic object. In the next section, we'll see how you can instruct an application to preserve a custom data type and write and read it using a clipboard.

4.2.5   *Using custom formats*

Earlier in the chapter, we talked about working with custom formats. One of the keys to working with custom formats is making sure that you're serializing data correctly. If you want to copy-and-paste data from one AIR application to another or to another application that understands AMF (see chapter 3 for more information), using AMF serialization is generally the best option, because it's supported natively by AIR and runs nearly automatically. In this section, we'll look at how you can create a custom data format and copy-and-paste between two AIR applications.

In an earlier section, we presented a scenario in which you bundled up a bunch of related variables into an `Address` class. We then talked about the dilemma of making instances of a custom class such as `Address` available to other applications via a clipboard. We'll now build an example that illustrates how to do just that. In this example, we'll create two simple AIR applications, one that allows the user to create a new address and one that views addresses. We'll start by building the address creator. Figure 4.4 shows what it looks like.

The address creator application requires a custom data type that we're calling `Address`. We need to define the custom `Address` class. Listing 4.8 shows what this class looks like. You'll notice that we're using `[RemoteClass]` to tell the application how to map the class to an alias. If you were to build a Flash version of this application, you'd need to instead register the class alias using the `registerClassAlias()` method you learned about in chapter 3.

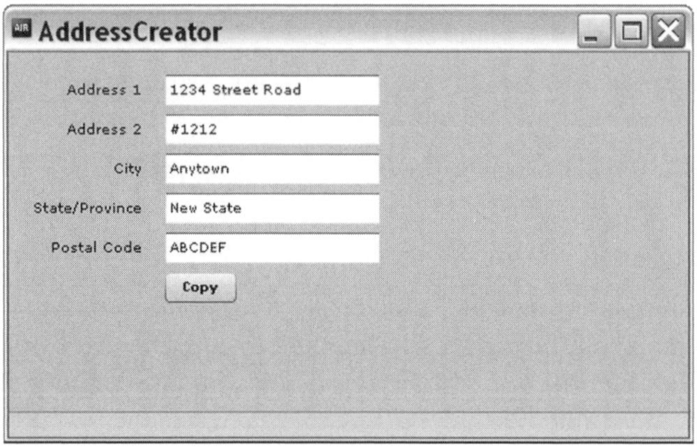

Figure 4.4   The address creator application allows the user to enter a new address and copy it to the system clipboard.

```
package com.manning.airinaction {

   [RemoteClass(alias="com.manning.airinaction.Address")]
   public class Address {

      private var _address1:String;
      private var _address2:String;
      private var _city:String;
      private var _province:String;
      private var _postalCode:String;

      public function set address1(value:String):void {
         _address1 = value;
      }

      public function get address1():String {
         return _address1;
      }

      public function set address2(value:String):void {
         _address2 = value;
      }

      public function get address2():String {
         return _address2;
      }

      public function set city(value:String):void {
         _city = value;
      }

      public function get city():String {
         return _city;
      }

      public function set province(value:String):void {
         _province = value;
      }

      public function get province():String {
         return _province;
      }

      public function set postalCode(value:String):void {
         _postalCode = value;
      }

      public function get postalCode():String {
         return _postalCode;
      }

      public function Address() {
      }

   }
}
```

There's nothing remarkable about the Address class. It's quite straightforward in that it's a simple value object that stores values for address lines 1 and 2, city, province, and postal code.

Next we'll create the address creator application itself. Listing 4.9 shows what this code looks like.

Listing 4.9   The address creator application

```xml
<?xml version="1.0" encoding="utf-8"?>
<mx:WindowedApplication xmlns:mx="http://www.adobe.com/2006/mxml"
    layout="absolute">
    <mx:Script>
        <![CDATA[
            import com.manning.airinaction.Address;         Called when user
                                                            clicks button
            private function copy():void {
                var address:Address = new Address();
                address.address1 = address1.text;
                address.address2 = address2.text;           ❶ Create and
                address.city = city.text;                      populate
                address.province = province.text;              address        Get
                address.postalCode = postalCode.text;                         system
                var clipboard:Clipboard = Clipboard.generalClipboard;         clipboard
                clipboard.clear();                                  Clear
                clipboard.setData("address", address);              clipboard
            }
                                                            Add address
        ]]>                                              ❷ to clipboard
    </mx:Script>
    <mx:Form>
        <mx:FormItem label="Address 1">
            <mx:TextInput id="address1" />
        </mx:FormItem>
        <mx:FormItem label="Address 2">
            <mx:TextInput id="address2" />
        </mx:FormItem>
        <mx:FormItem label="City">
            <mx:TextInput id="city" />
        </mx:FormItem>
        <mx:FormItem label="State/Province">
            <mx:TextInput id="province" />
        </mx:FormItem>
        <mx:FormItem label="Postal Code">
            <mx:TextInput id="postalCode" />
        </mx:FormItem>
        <mx:FormItem>
            <mx:Button label="Copy" click="copy();" />
        </mx:FormItem>
    </mx:Form>
</mx:WindowedApplication>
```

This code uses MXML components to create a simple form that allows the user to fill out the address fields. When the user clicks the button, we construct an Address object and assign the values from the fields to the corresponding properties of that

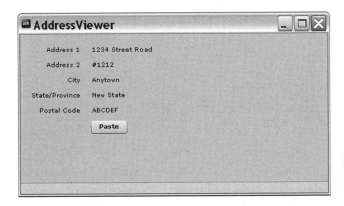

Figure 4.5 The address viewer application allows a user to paste an Address object.

Address object ❶. Then we add the object to the system clipboard using a custom format of address ❷.

At this point, the user has the ability to copy a custom data type, but we next need to create the address viewer application so he can paste the data. Figure 4.5 shows what the address viewer application looks like.

Listing 4.10 shows the code for the address viewer application.

Listing 4.10 The address viewer application

```
<?xml version="1.0" encoding="utf-8"?>
<mx:WindowedApplication xmlns:mx="http://www.adobe.com/2006/mxml"
   layout="absolute">
   <mx:Script>
      <![CDATA[
         import com.manning.airinaction.Address;

         [Bindable]
         private var _address:Address;

         private function paste():void {
            var clipboard:Clipboard = Clipboard.generalClipboard;
            if(clipboard.hasFormat("address")) {
               _address = clipboard.getData("address") as Address;
            }
         }

      ]]>
   </mx:Script>
   <mx:Form>
      <mx:FormItem label="Address 1">
         <mx:Label text="{_address.address1}" />
      </mx:FormItem>
      <mx:FormItem label="Address 2">
         <mx:Label text="{_address.address2}" />
      </mx:FormItem>
      <mx:FormItem label="City">
         <mx:Label text="{_address.city}" />
      </mx:FormItem>
```

❶ **Declare bindable Address property**

Get system clipboard

Get the Address object

Verify address format data ❷

```
        <mx:FormItem label="State/Province">
            <mx:Label text="{_address.province}" />
        </mx:FormItem>
        <mx:FormItem label="Postal Code">
            <mx:Label text="{_address.postalCode}" />
        </mx:FormItem>
        <mx:FormItem>
            <mx:Button label="Paste" click="paste();" />
        </mx:FormItem>
    </mx:Form>
</mx:WindowedApplication>
```

The address viewer application uses a similar MXML form to the one used by the address creator application. The main difference is that, instead of using text input controls, the address viewer uses label controls that are data-bound to properties of an Address object declared as a property of the document ❶. When the user clicks on the Paste button, we verify that the system clipboard has data in the address format ❷. If it does, we simply read that data and assign it to the Address property.

We've just wrapped up our coverage of copy-and-paste functionality in AIR. As you've seen, copy-and-paste is a useful and powerful, though subtle, feature of an application. Next we'll round out our conversation by talking about a related operation: drag-and-drop.

4.3   Drag-and-drop

Up to this point, you've seen the simpler of the two clipboard-related operations: copy-and-paste. The drag-and-drop operation is more complex, and as such we've deferred discussing it until now. But just because it's more complex doesn't mean it's terribly difficult. You'll soon see that drag-and-drop uses much of the same logic as copy-and-paste, albeit in a slightly more sophisticated fashion. Over the next few sections, we'll break it down and look at each step of enabling various types of drag-and-drop operations in AIR applications.

4.3.1   Understanding drag-and-drop

Drag-and-drop operations are fundamentally the same as copy-and-paste in many key ways. Essentially a drag-and-drop operation consists of the following:

- The user initiates the operation via a gesture (such as clicking on an item).
- The transfer data is written to a clipboard.
- The user begins dragging the item.
- The user drops the item, and if the drop occurs over a valid target, the data is retrieved from the clipboard.

As you can see, the underlying operation for drag-and-drop is one of writing to and reading from a clipboard. What differs between copy-and-paste and drag-and-drop operations is primarily the way in which the user interacts with the system.

Drag-and-drop user interaction has the following basic stages:

1 The user clicks on an item, called the *initiator.*
2 The user moves the mouse while holding down the button, thus initiating the dragging of the initiator.
3 The user moves the initiator over another user interface element that's configured to be receptive to dropping behavior. This interface element is called a *drop target.*
4 The system determines whether the drop target can accept an initiator of the type that's moved over it.
5 The user drops the initiator by releasing the mouse button.
6 The system triggers the drop reception code if applicable. Otherwise, if the drop isn't over a suitable drop target, the operation is terminated.

As we'll see in subsequent sections, it's possible that an AIR application can be responsible for the first part of these stages (dragging an item out of an AIR application), the second part of the stages (dragging an item into an AIR application), or all of the stages. Initially, we'll look at the complete set of events that accompany each of the stages.

4.3.2 Drag-and-drop events

Each of the stages of a drag-and-drop operation has an accompanying event. These events, listed in table 4.2, are pivotal for successfully implementing a drag-and-drop operation.

Table 4.2 The drag-and-drop events

Event	`NativeDragEvent` constant	Dispatcher	Dispatch conditions
`nativeDragStart`	`NATIVE_DRAG_START`	Initiator	The user begins the drag.
`nativeDragUpdate`	`NATIVE_DRAG_UPDATE`	Initiator	The drag is in progress.
`nativeDragComplete`	`NATIVE_DRAG_COMPLETE`	Initiator	The user releases the dragged item.
`nativeDragEnter`	`NATIVE_DRAG_ENTER`	Drop target	The drag gesture passes within the target object boundary.
`nativeDragOver`	`NATIVE_DRAG_OVER`	Drop target	The drag gesture remains within the target object boundary.
`nativeDragExit`	`NATIVE_DRAG_EXIT`	Drop target	The drag gesture leaves the target object boundary.
`nativeDragDrop`	`NATIVE_DRAG_DROP`	Drop target	The user releases the dragged item over a drop target that has previously agreed to accept this specific drop.

Of the events in table 4.2, two are most important: `nativeDragEnter` and `native-DragDrop`. The `nativeDragEnter` event is important because it's how you can determine when an initiator has moved over a drop target. This is crucial because by default no interface item is configured to accept a drop. Instead, it must be configured at the time of the `nativeDragEnter` event to accept a drop. (See the next section for more information on how to accomplish this.) The `nativeDragDrop` event is important because it's when the system can run the code to determine what to do in response to the drop. The `nativeDragDrop` event only occurs if the drop target was configured to accept the drop during the most recent `nativeDragEnter` event. We'll see examples of how this all works in the next section.

All the events in table 4.2 are of type `flash.events.NativeDragEvent`. The `NativeDragEvent` class defines static constants for each of the event names that are displayed in table 4.2.

NOTE   All event objects of type `NativeDragEvent` have a `clipboard` property. The `clipboard` property references the `Clipboard` object that contains the data for the drag-and-drop operation. You should always reference a clipboard through the `clipboard` property of the `NativeDragEvent` object when an event occurs. Don't try to reference the `Clipboard` object in another way (except when creating it).

Another event that isn't listed in table 4.2 (because it's not specific to drag-and-drop) is the `mouseDown` event (of type `MouseEvent`). The `mouseDown` event, as you likely know, occurs when the user clicks on an interactive display object. This is one of the more common Flash and Flex events, and it's also utilized during drag-and-drop operations because most often you'll start drag-and-drop operations in response to a `mouseDown` event. In fact, AIR only allows you to call the `doDrag()` method of the `NativeDrag-Manager` (see next section) in response to a `mouseDown` event or a `mouseMove` event (if the mouse button is pressed).

4.3.3   *Using the drag manager*

AIR has a special manager class just for managing native drag-and-drop operations: `flash.desktop.NativeDragManager`. Even if you're using Flex (with its `DragManager` class), the `NativeDragManager` class always supersedes any other drag managers in other libraries, because only `NativeDragManager` allows for system-level drag-and-drop operations.

The `NativeDragManager` class is what you'll use to start drag operations as well as notify the system when to allow a drop on a drop target. These are the two primary functions of the `NativeDragManager` class, and they're available via two static methods: `doDrag()` and `acceptDragDrop()`, which we'll look at in this section.

When a user initiates a drag operation (often via a `mouseDown` event), you need to call the `NativeDragManager.doDrag()` method. The `doDrag()` method requires at least two parameters: a reference to the drag initiator and a `Clipboard` object that contains the transfer data. Listing 4.11 is a simple example that illustrates how to do this.

Listing 4.11 Initiating a native drag operation

```
<?xml version="1.0" encoding="utf-8"?>
<mx:WindowedApplication xmlns:mx="http://www.adobe.com/2006/mxml"
    layout="absolute">
    <mx:Script>
        <![CDATA[                                    Create random value  ❶

            private function startInitiatorDrag():void {      Create
                initiatorLabel.text = String(Math.random());   clipboard
                var clipboard:Clipboard = new Clipboard();
                clipboard.setData(ClipboardFormats.TEXT_FORMAT,  ❷ Write data to
                        initiatorLabel.text);                     clipboard
                NativeDragManager.doDrag(initiatorLabel, clipboard);
            }

        ]]>                                          Start the drag
    </mx:Script>                                      operation  ❸
    <mx:HBox>
        <mx:Canvas width="200" height="50" backgroundColor="#00FF00">
            <mx:Label id="initiatorLabel" width="100%" height="100%"  ❹ Initiator
                mouseDown="startInitiatorDrag();" />
        </mx:Canvas>
        <mx:VBox>
            <mx:Canvas width="200" height="100" backgroundColor="0xFFFF00">
                <mx:Text width="100%" height="100%" />
            </mx:Canvas>                             ❺ Drop target I
            <mx:Canvas width="200" height="100" backgroundColor="0xFFFF00">
                <mx:Text width="100%" height="100%" />
            </mx:Canvas>                             ❻ Drop target 2
        </mx:VBox>
    </mx:HBox>
</mx:WindowedApplication>
```

This example consists of a label ❹ that is the initiator and two text components ❺ ❻ as the drop targets. Thus far we haven't actually wired up the text components as drop targets. We'll do that shortly. All we've done up to this point is wire up the label component to act as the initiator by calling `startInitiatorDrag()` when the user clicks on it. At that point, we assign a random value to the label ❶ to give us a visual indicator that something has changed. We then copy that value to a clipboard ❷. All we need to do after that is call the `doDrag()` method, passing it a reference to the initiator and the clipboard ❸.

NOTE You should never use the system clipboard for drag-and-drop operations. Although you can work with all `Clipboard` objects in the same way once you've obtained a reference, the system clipboard should only be used for copy-and-paste operations. When you want to work with a `Clipboard` object for a drag-and-drop operation, you should always create a new `Clipboard` object using the constructor.

To complete the example from listing 4.11, we need to enable the text components as drop targets. As it is, you can tell that there are no properly configured drop

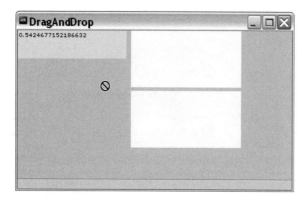

Figure 4.6   When no drop target has been configured to accept a drop, you'll only see the invalid drop target icon (the circle with the slash through it).

targets when you run the example, because, no matter where you drag the mouse, you see only an icon with a circle and a slash through it, as shown in figure 4.6. This icon indicates that the mouse isn't currently over a drop target that accepts the drop from the initiator.

We can configure any interactive object as a drop target by listening for native-DragEnter events on that object. When the nativeDragEnter event occurs, we need to call NativeDragManager.acceptDragDrop(), passing it a reference to the drop target object. This tells the system that it should allow drops from the current initiator on the specified drop target. This also causes a change in the mouse icon, as seen in figure 4.7.

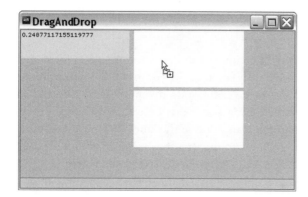

Figure 4.7   When a drop target is configured to accept a drop, the icon changes.

Listing 4.12 shows how we can modify the example to allow for drops on the text components.

Listing 4.12   Allowing drops on targets

```
<?xml version="1.0" encoding="utf-8"?>
<mx:WindowedApplication xmlns:mx="http://www.adobe.com/2006/mxml"
    layout="absolute">
    <mx:Script>
```

```
<![CDATA[

    private function startInitiatorDrag():void {
        initiatorLabel.text = String(Math.random());
        var clipboard:Clipboard = new Clipboard();
        clipboard.setData(ClipboardFormats.TEXT_FORMAT,
                    initiatorLabel.text);
        NativeDragManager.doDrag(initiatorObject, clipboard);
    }

    private function nativeDragEnterHandler(event:NativeDragEvent):
    void {
        NativeDragManager.acceptDragDrop(event.currentTarget
        as Text);                    <─┐  ❶ Make acceptable
    }                                      drop target

]]>
</mx:Script>
<mx:HBox>
    <mx:Canvas id="initiatorObject" width="200" height="50"
        backgroundColor="#00FF00" mouseDown="startInitiatorDrag();">
        <mx:Label id="initiatorLabel" />       ❷ Listen for
    </mx:Canvas>                                   nativeDragEnter
    <mx:VBox>
        <mx:Canvas width="200" height="100" backgroundColor="0xFFFF00">
            <mx:Text width="100%" height="100%"
                nativeDragEnter="nativeDragEnterHandler(event);" />  <─
        </mx:Canvas>
        <mx:Canvas width="200" height="100" backgroundColor="0xFFFF00">
            <mx:Text width="100%" height="100%"
                nativeDragEnter="nativeDragEnterHandler(event);" />  <─┐
        </mx:Canvas>                                    Listen for
    </mx:VBox>                                   nativeDragEnter ❸
</mx:HBox>
</mx:WindowedApplication>
```

The changes we made are minimal, but these few changes allow both of the text components to be valid drop targets for the initiator. All we did was register a listener for the nativeDragEnter event for both the text components ❷ ❸, and then we defined the handler method to call acceptDragDrop() ❶.

There's one more step in order to meaningfully complete the drag-and-drop operation: we need to listen for and handle the nativeDragDrop event for the drop targets. This event occurs when the user drops the initiator on the target. Listing 4.13 shows what this change looks like.

Listing 4.13   Handling the nativeDragDrop event

```
<?xml version="1.0" encoding="utf-8"?>
<mx:WindowedApplication xmlns:mx="http://www.adobe.com/2006/mxml"
    layout="absolute">
    <mx:Script>
        <![CDATA[

            private function startInitiatorDrag():void {
```

```
        initiatorLabel.text = String(Math.random());
        var clipboard:Clipboard = new Clipboard();
        clipboard.setData(ClipboardFormats.TEXT_FORMAT,
                   initiatorLabel.text);
        NativeDragManager.doDrag(initiatorObject, clipboard);
    }

    private function nativeDragEnterHandler(event:NativeDragEvent):
    ➥void {
        NativeDragManager.acceptDragDrop(event.currentTarget
        ➥as Text);
    }

    private function nativeDragDropHandler(event:NativeDragEvent):
    ➥void {
        var text:Text = event.currentTarget as Text;
        var string:String = event.clipboard.getData(          ❶ Retrieve
        ➥ClipboardFormats.TEXT_FORMAT) as String;                clipboard data
        text.text = string;   ◁┐
    }                              ┤   Apply value
                              ❷   to text
    ]]>
</mx:Script>
<mx:HBox>
    <mx:Canvas id="initiatorObject" width="200" height="50"
        backgroundColor="#00FF00" mouseDown="startInitiatorDrag();">
        <mx:Label id="initiatorLabel" />
    </mx:Canvas>
    <mx:VBox>
        <mx:Canvas width="200" height="100" backgroundColor="0xFFFF00">
            <mx:Text width="100%" height="100%"
                nativeDragEnter="nativeDragEnterHandler(event);"
                nativeDragDrop=                      │ Listen for
                ➥"nativeDragDropHandler(event);" />  │ nativeDragDrop
        </mx:Canvas>
        <mx:Canvas width="200" height="100" backgroundColor="0xFFFF00">
            <mx:Text width="100%" height="100%"
                nativeDragEnter="nativeDragEnterHandler(event);"
                nativeDragDrop=                      │ Listen for
                ➥"nativeDragDropHandler(event);" />  │ nativeDragDrop
        </mx:Canvas>
    </mx:VBox>
</mx:HBox>
</mx:WindowedApplication>
```

This example just retrieves the text from the clipboard ❶ and applies it to the text component ❷, signifying that the drop was successful.

You've seen the basics of drag-and-drop operations. But there's still more we can do to liven up and enhance the behavior.

4.3.4   *Adding drag indicators*

As you've likely noticed, the default behavior when dragging an initiator is that a simple icon follows the mouse: a circle with a slash through it when the mouse isn't over an acceptable drop target, and a plus sign when the mouse is over an acceptable drop target. While that default behavior does give some indication as to what's going on, it doesn't give the user the sort of indication she may be used to when dragging an initiator. Most computer users are accustomed to seeing a semitransparent representation of the initiator move along with the mouse as well. AIR allows us to include that sort of behavior without much difficulty.

When you call the doDrag() method, you must always pass it the first two parameters indicating the initiator and the clipboard to use. You can also specify optional parameters, some of which have to do with adding a semitransparent representation of the initiator, or a drag indicator, that follows the mouse. To achieve this effect, you must create a BitmapData object to pass to the doDrag() method as the third parameter. Listing 4.14 shows a continuation of the earlier examples, this time adding a drag indicator. Because the only changes are in the startInitiatorDrag() method, that's all we show in listing 4.14, but you can assume that the rest of the code is identical to the code from listing 4.13.

Listing 4.14 Adding a drag indicator

```
private function startInitiatorDrag():void {
    initiatorLabel.text = String(Math.random());
    var clipboard:Clipboard = new Clipboard();           Create  ❶
    clipboard.setData(ClipboardFormats.TEXT_FORMAT,    BitmapData
            initiatorLabel.text);                          object
    var initiatorImage:BitmapData =
        new BitmapData(initiatorLabel.width, initiatorLabel.height);
    initiatorImage.draw(initiatorLabel.parent);     ◁─┐ Copy
    NativeDragManager.doDrag(initiator, clipboard,        containing
        initiatorImage);   ◁─┐                          ❷ canvas
}                            ❸ Specify drag indicator
```

All we needed to do in this example was create a BitmapData object that had the same dimensions as the drag initiator ❶, draw a copy of the drag initiator (the containing canvas in this case) in the BitmapData object ❷, and then specify that object as the third parameter for the doDrag() method ❸. The BitmapData object is then automatically applied as the drag indicator, and it follows the mouse wherever it goes, even outside the AIR application.

One thing you might notice is that by default the drag indicator always snaps the upper-left corner of the image to the mouse pointer. Often the preferred behavior is that the drag indicator moves relative to the point where the user clicked on the initiator. For example, if the user clicked in the middle of the drag initiator, usually it's preferable that the middle of the drag indicator always appear at the mouse pointer. You can affect the placement of the drag indicator relative to the mouse using yet another parameter with the doDrag() method. A fourth parameter specified as a Point object will tell the system where to place the drag indicator relative to the mouse pointer. Listing 4.15 shows how you can further modify the previous example to align the drag indicator with the mouse according to where the user clicked on the initiator.

Listing 4.15   Aligning the drag indicator to the mouse

```
private function startInitiatorDrag():void {
    initiator.text = String(Math.random());
    var clipboard:Clipboard = new Clipboard();
    clipboard.setData(ClipboardFormats.TEXT_FORMAT,
                initiator.text);
    var initiatorImage:BitmapData =
    ➥new BitmapData(initiator.width, initiator.height);
    initiatorImage.draw(initiator.parent);
    var point:Point = new Point(-initiatorLabel.mouseX,
                        -initiatorLabel.mouseY);
    NativeDragManager.doDrag(initiator, clipboard,
                    initiatorImage, point);
}
```

Now that we've seen the complete picture of drag-and-drop within an AIR application, we can next look at the scenarios that utilize just one part or another of the complete drag-and-drop picture to allow dragging in and out of an AIR application.

4.3.5   *Dragging out of an AIR application*

Sometimes you'll want to enable a user to drag something from an AIR application into another application. For example, you may want to allow a user to drag an image from an AIR application and save it as a file to the desktop, or you may want to allow a user to drag data from a data grid component and drop it into a spreadsheet application. These sorts of behaviors are possible using AIR. In fact, they're possible using just what you've already learned. In this section, we'll look at an example that shows how this works.

When you want to allow a user to drag something from an AIR application to another application, you need only to implement the first part of the complete sequence for a drag-and-drop operation. Basically, you need to listen for a mouse event to trigger the operation, and then write the necessary data to a clipboard and call doDrag(). The drop portion of the operation is handled automatically by the other application, and you don't need to concern yourself with drop targets or anything of the sort. The following example in listing 4.16 allows the user to drag an image from an AIR application into another application (such as a Word document) that accepts bitmap data from a clipboard.

Listing 4.16   Dragging an image out of an AIR application

```
<?xml version="1.0" encoding="utf-8"?>
<mx:WindowedApplication xmlns:mx="http://www.adobe.com/2006/mxml"
    layout="absolute">
    <mx:Script>
        <![CDATA[

        private function startDragImage():void {
            var clipboard:Clipboard = new Clipboard();
            var bitmapData:BitmapData =
```

```
➥(image.content as Bitmap).bitmapData;
    clipboard.setData(ClipboardFormats.BITMAP_FORMAT,
            bitmapData, false);
    var point:Point = new Point(-image.mouseX, -image.mouseY);
    NativeDragManager.doDrag(image, clipboard,
            bitmapData, point);
    }
  ]]>
</mx:Script>
<mx:Image id="image" source="image.jpg"
    mouseDown="startDragImage();" />
</mx:WindowedApplication>
```

1 Get bitmap data

Write data to clipboard

Call doDrag()

2 Display image

In this example, we use an Image component **2** to display an image. (Note that, if you run this yourself, you need to ensure that you have an image called image.jpg in the same directory as the AIR application.) When the user clicks on the image, we retrieve a `BitmapData` object from the component **1**, write that to a clipboard, and call `doDrag()`. This simple code allows the user to drag the image from the AIR application into another application.

4.3.6 *Dragging into an AIR application*

AIR applications not only support dragging content from an AIR application to other applications, but they also allow a user to drag content from another application into an AIR application. As with dragging out of an AIR application, dragging into an AIR application uses knowledge you already have. Dragging into an AIR application is merely part of the drag-and-drop operation. Basically, you need only to configure drop targets and handle the drop event. Listing 4.17 shows an example of dragging into an AIR application. This simple example allows you to create a rudimentary image gallery by dragging images from other applications (such as web browsers) to the AIR application.

Listing 4.17 Creating an image gallery that supports dragging images

```
<?xml version="1.0" encoding="utf-8"?>
<mx:WindowedApplication xmlns:mx="http://www.adobe.com/2006/mxml"
    layout="absolute" creationComplete="creationCompleteHandler();">
    <mx:Script>
        <![CDATA[
            import mx.controls.Image;

            private function creationCompleteHandler():void {
                addEventListener(
                ➥NativeDragEvent.NATIVE_DRAG_ENTER,
                ➥nativeDragEnterHandler);
                addEventListener(
                ➥NativeDragEvent.NATIVE_DRAG_DROP,
                ➥nativeDragDropHandler);
                var directory:File =
                ➥File.applicationStorageDirectory.resolvePath("images");
```

Listen for creationComplete

1 Listen for nativeDragEnter

2 Listen for nativeDragDrop

Get local images directory

```
        if(!directory.exists) {                    Create directory
            directory.createDirectory();           if necessary
        }
        var images:Array = directory.getDirectoryListing();
        for(var i:Number = 0; i < images.length; i++) {   Display all
            displayImage(images[i]);                       images
        }
    }
                                                           Get a
                                                           directory
                                                           listing

    private function displayImage(file:File):void {
        var image:Image = new Image();
        image.source = file.nativePath;
        image.scaleContent = true;
        image.maintainAspectRatio = true;
        image.width = 100;
        tile.addChild(image);
    }

    private function nativeDragEnterHandler(event:NativeDragEvent):
    void {
        if(event.clipboard.hasFormat(
           ClipboardFormats.FILE_LIST_FORMAT)) {      ❸  Accept
            NativeDragManager.acceptDragDrop(this);        drop for files
        }
    }

    private function nativeDragDropHandler(event:NativeDragEvent):
    void {
        var files:Array = event.clipboard.getData(
           ClipboardFormats.FILE_LIST_FORMAT) as Array;   Retrieve
        var file:File;                                     files
        var newLocation:File;
        for(var i:Number = 0; i < files.length; i++) {
            file = files[i] as File;
            newLocation = File.applicationStorageDirectory.   ❹  Save file
               resolvePath("images/image" +                      locally
               (new Date()).getTime() + i + ".jpg");
            file.moveTo(newLocation);
            displayImage(newLocation);
        }                                    ❺  Display the image
    }
    ]]>
</mx:Script>

<mx:Tile id="tile" width="100%" height="100%" />
</mx:WindowedApplication>
```

In this example, the first thing we do is register to listen for the nativeDragEnter and
nativeDragDrop events ❶ ❷ for the entire application. That way the entire application is a drop target. When the user drags something over the application, we only
want to accept the drop if the clipboard contains file-formatted data ❸. Then, when
the user drops the content on the application, we loop through all the files and save
them with unique names ❹ and display them ❺.

We've now seen all sorts of things we can do with drag-and-drop operations, and we've even put them into practice building simple applications such as the image gallery we just built in this section. Next we'll add drag-and-drop behavior into our AirTube application.

4.4 *Adding drag-and-drop to AirTube*

In this section, we'll add a bit of new functionality to the AirTube application, building on what we learned in this chapter. We'll allow the user to write a file to his system by dragging an item from the search results to the file system. We're going to use a custom file extension of .atv (for AirTube video). In later chapters, we'll utilize the file by allowing users to double-click on .atv files to launch the corresponding video in AirTube.

To add the drag-and-drop functionality to AirTube, all you need to do is open the com.manning.airtube.ui.VideoTileRenderer.mxml file and modify the code as shown in listing 4.18.

Listing 4.18 Adding drag-and-drop behavior to AirTube

```
<?xml version="1.0" encoding="utf-8"?>
<mx:HBox xmlns:mx="http://www.adobe.com/2006/mxml" width="200" height="100"
    verticalScrollPolicy="off" horizontalScrollPolicy="off"
    mouseDown="mouseDownHandler();">          ◁─┐ Handle
    <mx:Script>                                    mouseDown
        <![CDATA[
                                                                  Create file ❶
            private function mouseDownHandler():void {
                var file:File = File.applicationStorageDirectory.
                ➥resolvePath("temporary/" + data.video.title + ".atv");
                var writer:FileStream = new FileStream();
                writer.open(file, FileMode.WRITE);         ❷ Write       ❸
                writer.writeUTF(data.video.id);               video ID   Write
                var clipboard:Clipboard = new Clipboard();               file to
                clipboard.setData(ClipboardFormats.FILE_LIST_FORMAT,     clipboard
                ➥[file]);
                var indicator:BitmapData = new BitmapData(width, height);
                indicator.draw(this);
                var point:Point = new Point(-mouseX, -mouseY);
                NativeDragManager.doDrag(this, clipboard, indicator,
                              point);         ◁─┐ Start drag
            }                                    operation
        ]]>
    </mx:Script>
    <mx:Image source="{data.video.thumbnailUrl}" />
    <mx:VBox>
        <mx:Label text="{data.video.title}" />
    </mx:VBox>
</mx:HBox>
```

When the user clicks on the video render item, we first create a new file based on the video title ❶. Then we write the video ID to the file ❷. We need to create this temporary file because this is what we add to the clipboard ❸ using the file list format. Then all we need to do is call doDrag(). The system takes care of the rest. When the user drags an item to the desktop, for example, the system will create a copy of the .atv file on the desktop. Although we're not going to do anything with the .atv files just yet, we will later on.

4.5   *Summary*

In this chapter, you learned about two related operations: copy-and-paste and drag-and-drop. Each of these operations allows users to interact with your AIR applications in intuitive ways. Because these operations are at the system level, you can use them to transfer data to and from AIR applications, interacting with other applications. For instance, you saw an example that allows a user to drag an image from a web page and drop it into an AIR application.

You learned that both copy-and-paste and drag-and-drop use the common transfer medium of a clipboard. Clipboards are represented as Clipboard objects in AIR applications. You can write data to and read data from clipboards in a variety of formats, allowing you to transfer lots of different types of data. Clipboards are at the center of both types of operations, but the actual code necessary for copy-and-paste and drag-and-drop operations is slightly different. As such, we continued on from our conversation about clipboards to a more detailed look at how to transfer data using both of these types of operations.

Now that we've wrapped up our conversation of copy-and-paste and drag-and-drop, we can go ahead to the next chapter. In chapter 5, we'll learn all about working with local databases.

Using local databases

This chapter covers

- Using basic SQL
- Creating databases
- Running SQL statements
- Adding parameters
- Retrieving record sets

In chapter 3, you learned how to work with the file system. Using a file system allows you to store data in a persistent fashion and organize that data in a variety of ways. Writing data to files is a great solution in some cases. For example, files are ideal for writing binary data such as images or videos that your application will need to load at runtime. Files are also great for portability. If you want to output text to a format that a user can easily send to a friend, a file is good for that. But as useful as files may be, they're not a panacea for all things data. In this chapter, we'll look at a more efficient way to work with some types of data: local databases. A database allows you to store data persistently. Most databases also have a language that allows you to store and retrieve data in an efficient way. AIR uses a type of database called *SQLite*, and SQLite databases use a language called *Structured Query Language*, which is usually written as *SQL*.

NOTE   SQL is pronounced differently by different people. Some prefer to spell out the letters, as in *Ess-Cue-El*. Others prefer to pronounce SQL just like the word *sequel*. In this book we've chosen the latter option. That means you'll see us refer to *a* SQL statement instead of *an* SQL statement.

Using SQL, you can work with sets of data in a much more efficient way than if you had to write custom code to parse through it. Throughout this chapter, we'll look at all you need to know to work with local databases from AIR applications. We'll talk about creating new databases, writing data to databases, reading data from databases, updating existing data, and more. We'll also build a few example applications, including updating the AirTube application to support offline mode using a local database.

NOTE   AIR allows you to create nonpersistent databases that are stored in memory while an application is running. These databases are deleted from memory when the application exits. Although these sorts of databases are possible using AIR, our focus in this chapter is strictly on persistent databases that are written to disk. Persistent databases are generally far more useful simply because the data lives for much longer (until it's explicitly deleted).

A basic knowledge of SQL is critical to understanding much of how to work with databases in AIR. We recognize that you might not have much knowledge of SQL. Therefore, where appropriate, we'll give you tips on basic SQL statements for all the behaviors we mention. If you're already a SQL expert, you can feel free to skip over these sections.

NOTE   While we do provide some basic SQL information throughout the chapter, it isn't intended to be a comprehensive SQL tutorial. For that, we recommend you read a book dedicated to the topic. You might also find some tutorials on the Web that are helpful in that regard. One such excellent resource can be found at www.w3schools.com/sql.

Before we start talking about all the implementation details, we first need to talk about what a database is and why you'd want to use one. You'll find all that information in the next section.

5.1   *What is a database?*

As with several sections in this chapter, if you're already a database and SQL expert and you want to get right to the implementation details, you can skip this section entirely. For the rest of us who could use a brief introduction or refresher on some basic database concepts, we'll take just a few minutes to talk about what databases are and what they can do for us.

Simply put, a database is a collection of information organized in some fashion, usually into groups known as *records*. Each record has a uniform set of data. For example, a record in a database that stores addresses might have the following pieces of data: street address 1, street address 2, city, province, postal code, and country. Most often it's convenient to think of these records as rows, much like the rows in a spreadsheet (which is a simple sort of database). Figure 5.1 shows a visual representation of a record for an address.

StreetAddress1	StreetAddress2	City	Province	PostalCode	Country
1212 Road Street	#555	Plainsville	BC	ABCDEF	Canada

Figure 5.1 Databases organize data in records such as the one shown in this image.

There are a variety of ways in which databases can be modeled, including hierarchical, network, and object models. The SQLite engine used by AIR is a relational database engine, meaning that it uses a relational model of *tables*—a popular database model, and one that's easy to grasp conceptually. A table is composed of columns and rows. Columns in a table are sometimes called *attributes*, but more often they're simply called *columns*. For example, the attributes or columns shown in figure 5.1 are StreetAddress1, StreetAddress2, City, Province, PostalCode, and Country. The rows of a table are the *records*, and a record is the smallest unit that can be inserted or deleted from a table. (You can't insert an entry from one column without inserting the entire row.)

NOTE You can learn much more about SQLite by going to the official web site at www.sqlite.org.

Each database can have more than one table as well, and the data in the tables can have relationships, hence the term *relational* database. These relationships are usually based on *keys*. A key allows you to uniquely identify a record. For example, we could add an ID column to the table from figure 5.1. Figure 5.2 shows what this would look like.

ID	StreetAddress1	StreetAddress2	City	Province	PostalCode	Country
0	1212 Road Street	#555	Plainsville	BC	ABCDEF	Canada

Figure 5.2 Use an ID column as a primary key.

A key used as the unique identifier within a row in this way is called a *primary key*. Primary keys allow you to easily establish relationships between data in tables. We can extend our example to illustrate how this might work. Figure 5.3 shows the address table with a second record added to it.

ID	StreetAddress1	StreetAddress2	City	Province	PostalCode	Country
0	1212 Road Street	#555	Plainsville	BC	ABCDEF	Canada
1	4 Route Lane	#8	Lakeview	AK	99999	US

Figure 5.3   We can add more than one record to a table.

We'll next add a new table for employees that contains the employee ID, name, and title. Figure 5.4 shows this table.

ID	Name	Title
0	Sarah	Manager
1	Francois	Auditor
2	Pan	Human Resource Manager
3	Wendy	New Business
4	Sidney	Trainer

Figure 5.4   The employees table shows the employee ID, name, and title.

Next we can establish a relationship between the data in the two tables by adding another table. This new table tells us which employee works at which address. Figure 5.5 shows the table. As you can see, some of the employees work at more than one address. For example, Pan (the employee with ID 2) works at both addresses.

EmployeeID	AddressID
0	0
1	0
1	1
2	0
2	1
3	1
4	0

Figure 5.5   Create relationships between records using the primary keys.

The SQLite database engine used by AIR writes all these tables to a file or files on the system. All of the writing to and reading from files is managed through the use of SQL. That includes creating new tables, deleting existing tables, inserting data, updating data, and deleting data. You can read more about the SQL you'll need for these operations in section 5.2.

Now that you've had a chance to see how databases are structured, you may next be wondering how to determine when to use one. Although there are no fixed rules for making this determination, here are a few guidelines you might find helpful:

- If the AIR application uses data that's relational in nature, it's a good idea to use a database.
- When you want to be able to search data based on various criteria, a database can be a good way to store the data because SQL supports lots of ways to filter, group, and sort data sets.
- A local database is a great way to cache data retrieved from an online source, allowing an AIR application to continue to run from local data even when not online. When the application reconnects to the internet, it can update the local data.

- For an AIR application that connects to internet resources for writing data, a database allows an application to store data that a user inserts or updates even if the application isn't connected to the internet. When the user next connects to the internet, the AIR application can read the data from the local database and write it to the remote resources.

Next we'll take a look at the language you can use to work with AIR databases: SQL.

5.2 *Understanding SQL*

As we mentioned earlier, the topic of SQL is far too broad for us to cover comprehensively in this chapter. But we want to make sure that, even if you're not already familiar with SQL, you'll still be able to get the most out of this chapter. Therefore, in this section you can learn about many of the basic SQL commands you can use. If you're already familiar with these commands, jump ahead to the next section. Or you may still find it useful to quickly read the following information to learn about the SQLite-specific details.

If you're new to SQL or even if you just want to follow along, you may find it helpful to use the SQLTutorial AIR application that you can download from this book's official web site at www.manning.com/lott. The SQLTutorial application looks like figure 5.6.

The SQLTutorial application automatically creates a database to use and allows you to run SQL statements on that database. The upper-left portion of the application displays all the tables available. When you first run the application, there are no tables, just as in figure 5.6. In the following section, you'll add a table to the database. Once you have tables available, you can select one at a time, and the table's contents are shown in a data grid on the right. In the lower portion of the SQLTutorial application window is a text area that allows you to input SQL commands, and you can click the Run button to execute those commands.

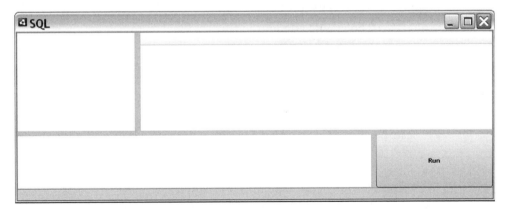

Figure 5.6   The SQLTutorial application allows you to follow along with SQL examples in the following sections.

5.2.1   *Creating and deleting tables*

As we've already mentioned, one of the most basic units of a database is a table. In fact, you can't store data without at least one table. Therefore, creating tables is one of the most primary of SQL commands. You can create a table using the CREATE TABLE command. The command looks like the following:

```
CREATE TABLE tableName (column[, column, ...])
```

The following is a concrete example of a CREATE TABLE statement that creates a new table called musicTracks with the following columns: id, title, artist, album, length, and originalReleaseYear:

```
CREATE TABLE musicTracks (id, title, artist, album, length,
➥originalReleaseYear)
```

SQLite uses a concept of *storage classes*. A storage class allows the database to store data in an efficient way because it only sets aside enough storage space for the type of data it's storing. SQLite supports the following storage classes:

- NULL—Only for null values
- INTEGER—Signed integer values
- REAL—Floating-point numeric values
- TEXT—Text stored in the database encoding such as UTF-8
- BLOB—Data stored literally (that is, you can store binary data)

In order to help the database engine know which storage classes to use for which columns, you can create columns with an *affinity*. Affinity means that the database engine gives preference to a particular data type by trying to coerce data to that type before inserting it. For example, if you specify a column affinity of type INTEGER and you try to insert a string value, the database engine will try to first convert it to an integer. The affinities you can use are as follows:

- TEXT—The engine attempts to convert the data to text before inserting it. That means numeric values are inserted as strings.
- NUMERIC—If possible, the engine converts strings to integers or floating-point numbers and stores them using the appropriate storage class. Null or blob values aren't converted.
- INTEGER—The primary difference between this and NUMERIC is that a string that can be converted to a number with a nonsignificant decimal value (for example, 5.0) will be converted into an integer.
- REAL—All numeric values are converted to floating-point values, even if the value after the decimal point is nonsignificant.
- NONE—No conversion is attempted. This is the default affinity if no other value is specified.

You can declare affinities when creating a table by adding the affinity after the column name. The following example creates the table with id, length, and originalRelease-Year as INTEGER and the rest using TEXT:

```
CREATE TABLE musicTracks (id INTEGER, title TEXT, artist TEXT, album TEXT,
➥length INTEGER, originalReleaseYear INTEGER)
```

Clearly you can only create a table if it doesn't already exist. If you attempt to create a table with the same name as one that already exists, you'll receive an error. However, you can use the IF NOT EXISTS clause in the CREATE TABLE statement to avoid this error. The following creates the musicTracks table only if it doesn't already exist. If it does exist, then nothing happens:

```
CREATE TABLE IF NOT EXISTS musicTracks (id INTEGER, title TEXT,
➥artist TEXT, album TEXT, length INTEGER, originalReleaseYear INTEGER)
```

You can also add column constraints by adding a constraint to each column definition right after the affinity. SQLite supports a variety of constraints, but for the purposes of this book we'll only be interested in the PRIMARY KEY constraint. This constraint requires that the value in the column be unique for each record. (You can only create one primary key column per table.) You can also add the keyword AUTOINCREMENT following the PRIMARY KEY constraint if the affinity is INTEGER. When AUTOINCREMENT is enabled, the value of the column is automatically inserted when adding a row, and it's 1 greater than the previously inserted value. The following creates the table with id as an autoincrementing primary key:

```
CREATE TABLE IF NOT EXISTS musicTracks (id INTEGER PRIMARY KEY
➥AUTOINCREMENT, title TEXT, artist TEXT, album TEXT,
➥length INTEGER, originalReleaseYear INTEGER)
```

If you'd like to test this out for yourself, enter the preceding command in the SQL-Tutorial application text area and click the Run button. You should see the music-Tracks table show up in the tables list. If you select the table from the list, you'll see the columns displayed in the data grid as shown in figure 5.7.

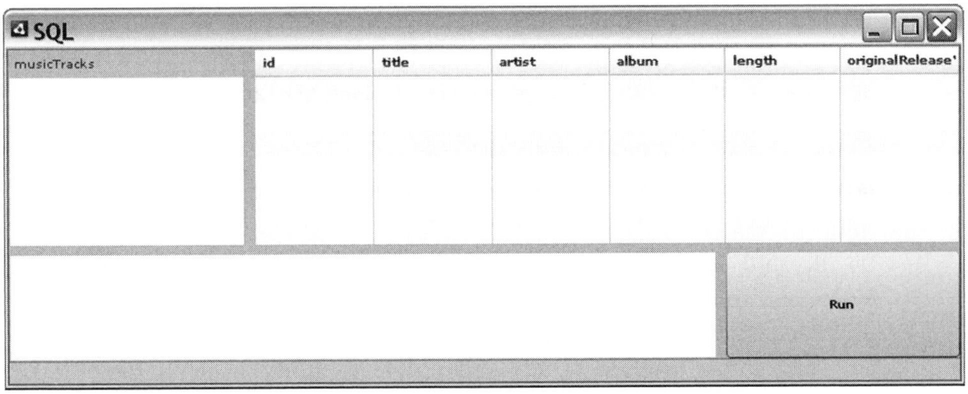

Figure 5.7   After creating a table and selecting it, you can see the columns in the data grid.

Creating tables is half the story as far as tables are concerned. The other half of the story is deleting them. Deleting is considerably simpler than creating. To delete a table, you use the DROP TABLE statement, specifying the table you want to delete. For example, the following deletes the musicTracks table:

```
DROP TABLE musicTracks
```

You can also add an IF EXISTS clause (the analog to the IF NOT EXISTS clause for CREATE TABLE) in order to avoid an error if the table doesn't exist:

```
DROP TABLE IF EXISTS musicTracks
```

NOTE   If you're testing the DROP TABLE code in SQLTutorial, you should make sure to re-create the table before moving on to the next section.

That covers the basics of creating and deleting tables. Next we'll look at how to work with tables by adding data to them.

5.2.2   Adding data to tables

Tables are merely containers for data. Once you have tables created, the next step is to add data to them. In SQL, adding data is called *inserting*, and you insert data using the INSERT command.

The INSERT command looks like the following:

```
INSERT INTO tableName (column[, column, …]) VALUES (value[, value, …])
```

The number and order of columns and values must match. For example, the following statement inserts a new record into the musicTracks table. Note that the column list and the values list both have five items and the order of the items is the same:

```
INSERT INTO musicTracks(title, artist, album, length, originalReleaseYear)
➥VALUES("Just Another Day", "Oingo Boingo", "Dead Man's Party", 243, 1985)
```

One thing you might notice from this example is that we've omitted the id column in the INSERT statement. That's because we placed a PRIMARY KEY AUTOINCREMENT constraint on the id column. Therefore the database engine automatically assigns a value to the id column when inserting a new record.

Another thing you'll notice from this example is that we've placed quotation marks around the text values. If you don't place quotation marks around text values, the database engine tries to interpret the values as column names rather than as literal values. Therefore you must enclose text values in quotation marks. (Either single or double quotation marks work.) You shouldn't place quotation marks around numeric values.

If you'd like to test the code for yourself, go ahead and run the preceding SQL command using SQLTutorial. If you run the code, you'll see the new record show up in the data grid as depicted in figure 5.8.

Once you've inserted data, you can't *re*insert it to make changes to it. Instead you need to update the data using the command discussed in the following section.

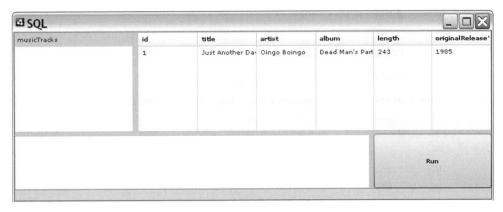

Figure 5.8   Insert a record into a table and it shows up in the data grid.

5.2.3   *Editing data in tables*

Editing existing records in SQL is known as updating, and you use the UPDATE command. The UPDATE command syntax is as follows:

```
UPDATE tableName SET column = value[, column = value, …] WHERE expression
```

The SET clause consists of a list of columns and new value assignments. Typically you follow that with a WHERE clause that indicates which rows to update. If you omit the WHERE clause, all rows are updated, which isn't typically the intended result. The following example updates the musicTracks table by setting the length column to 242 for the record with an id value of 1 (because id is a primary key, this will only update one record):

```
UPDATE musicTracks SET length = 242 WHERE id = 1
```

If you want to create compound WHERE clause expressions, you can use the operators AND and OR. For example, if we wanted to update the artist name for all tracks on the Oingo Boingo album *Dead Man's Party*, we can use the following command:

```
UPDATE musicTracks SET artist = "OINGO BOINGO"
➥WHERE artist = "Oingo Boingo" AND album = "Dead Man's Party"
```

You may have noticed that, in these examples, we surround text values with quotation marks just as we did with text values in INSERT statements.

Again, if you're following along using SQLTutorial, run the preceding SQL statement. When you do, you'll see that the artist name updates from Oingo Boingo to OINGO BOINGO. If you'd inserted other records with the artist name Oingo Boingo but different album names, those records would remain unaffected.

Now that you've seen how to insert and update data, the next step is deleting data, which we'll discuss in the next section.

5.2.4   *Deleting data from tables*

You can delete data from tables using the DELETE command. The syntax for the DELETE command is as follows:

```
DELETE FROM tableName WHERE expression
```

Although the WHERE clause isn't strictly required in the DELETE statement (just like it's not required for an UPDATE statement), it's almost always used. If you omit the WHERE clause, the DELETE statement will delete all the records from the specified table. Generally, you only want to delete one or a few records. The WHERE clause allows you to limit the deletion to only those records that meet the criteria in the expression. For example, the following deletes only the record with the id of 1:

```
DELETE FROM musicTracks WHERE id = 1
```

You can also use compound expressions just as you would with an UPDATE statement. For example, the following deletes all records where the artist is either Devo or Oingo Boingo:

```
DELETE FROM musicTracks WHERE artist = "Devo" OR artist = "Oingo Boingo"
```

We've now covered all the basics of inserting, updating, and deleting data, but we haven't yet shown you how to retrieve data from the database. We'll talk about that in the next section.

5.2.5   *Retrieving data from tables*

Retrieving data from a database can be simple or complex depending on the requirements. For example, retrieving all the records from a table is simple, but retrieving the sum of the values from one column for a particular group of records is more complex. We'll look at how to retrieve data, starting with the simplest examples and moving to more complex examples. If you want to follow along with the examples in this section, you can by using the SQLTutorial application. If you'd like to get exactly the same results as we show in this section, you can run a special command in SQLTutorial that will initialize the musicTracks table with the same values as our sample data set. All you need to do is run the command INITIALIZE musicTracks in SQLTutorial, and you'll see that it creates (if necessary) the musicTracks table and adds data to it. Even if you've already created musicTracks, you can start over by first running the DROP musicTracks command before running INITIALIZE musicTracks.

NOTE   INITIALIZE musicTracks is a special command just for SQLTutorial and isn't a part of standard SQL.

The data set that we'll be working from for the examples in this section is shown in table 5.1.

We'll use this data set for all the examples that follow in this section. Now we're ready to learn about all the basics for retrieving data.

Table 5.1   The data set for all the examples in this section

id	title	artist	album	length	originalReleaseYear
1	Just Another Day	Oingo Boingo	Dead Man's Party	243	1985
2	I Scare Myself	Thomas Dolby	The Flat Earth	299	1984
3	Senses Working Overtime	XTC	English Settlement	270	1984
4	She Blinded Me With Science	Thomas Dolby	The Golden Age of Wireless	325	1982
5	Heaven	The Psychedelic Furs	Mirror Moves	250	1984
6	Dance Hall Days	Wang Chung	Points on the Curve	258	1984
7	Love My Way	The Psychedelic Furs	Forever Now	208	1982
8	Everybody Have Fun Tonight	Wang Chung	Mosaic	287	1986

USING A SELECT STATEMENT

Regardless of how simple or complex the requirements are for how you want to retrieve data, all data retrieval occurs by way of a SELECT command. In its simplest form, the SELECT command syntax is as follows:

```
SELECT column[, column, …] FROM tableName
```

You can simplify things even further by using the * wildcard in place of the column names. The * wildcard allows you to select all the columns from the specified table. For example, the following command retrieves all the columns from all the records from the musicTracks table:

```
SELECT * FROM musicTracks
```

It's always more efficient from the database engine perspective if you list all the columns rather than using the wildcard. Also, listing the columns allows you to control which columns are returned as well as the order in which they're returned. For example, if you wanted to retrieve just the title and artist columns for all the records in the musicTracks table, you could use the following command:

```
SELECT title, artist FROM musicTracks
```

The result would be what is shown in table 5.2.

You can also add a WHERE clause to a SELECT statement. Adding a WHERE clause allows you to filter the results based on an expression. For example, if we want to retrieve all the track titles where the artist is Thomas Dolby, we can use the following command:

```
SELECT title FROM musicTracks WHERE artist = "Thomas Dolby"
```

title	artist
Just Another Day	Oingo Boingo
I Scare Myself	Thomas Dolby
Senses Working Overtime	XTC
She Blinded Me With Science	Thomas Dolby
Heaven	The Psychedelic Furs
Dance Hall Days	Wang Chung
Love My Way	The Psychedelic Furs
Everybody Have Fun Tonight	Wang Chung

Table 5.2   The title and artist columns returned for all the records

The result of this command is shown in table 5.3.

You can use compound expressions as well. For example, the following command retrieves all the tracks that were released in 1984 where the length is greater than 260:

```
SELECT title FROM musicTracks
➥WHERE originalReleaseYear = 1984 AND length > 260
```

The results of this command are shown in table 5.4.

Table 5.3   The titles from musicTracks where the artist is Thomas Dolby

title
I Scare Myself
She Blinded Me With Science

Table 5.4   You can select data based on compound expressions

title
I Scare Myself
Senses Working Overtime

That sums up the basics of working with SELECT statements. In the sections that follow, we'll look at other ways you can further modify a SELECT statement to create more complex queries.

ELIMINATING DUPLICATES

As you've seen, by default all the results meeting the criteria are returned. But sometimes you want to exclude duplicate values. For example, if you were to request all the artists from the musicTracks table using the following command, you'd get duplicate values:

```
SELECT artist FROM musicTracks
```

Table 5.5 shows the results of this command.

If you'd like to exclude duplicate values, you can use the DISTINCT keyword with the SELECT statement as in the following command:

```
SELECT DISTINCT artist FROM musicTracks
```

The results of this command don't contain any duplicate values, as you can see in table 5.6.

Table 5.5 Sometimes result sets can include duplicate values
artist
Oingo Boingo
Thomas Dolby
XTC
Thomas Dolby
The Psychedelic Furs
Wang Chung
The Psychedelic Furs
Wang Chung

Table 5.6 Using the DISTINCT keyword eliminates duplicate values
artist
Oingo Boingo
Thomas Dolby
XTC
The Psychedelic Furs
Wang Chung

Now that you know how to eliminate duplicate values, you're probably wondering how you can sort all the results. Good thing that's what we're going to talk about next.

ORDERING RESULTS

When you retrieve a data set from a database frequently, you may want to order that data in a particular way. For example, when retrieving records from the musicTracks table, you may want to order the results alphabetically by artist name or chronologically by release year. Whatever the case, you can achieve these sorts of results by using an ORDER BY clause with a SELECT statement.

The ORDER BY clause allows you to specify one or more columns by which to sort the data, and you can specify the order: either ascending (default) or descending. Here's an example of a basic ORDER BY clause:

```
SELECT album, originalReleaseYear FROM musicTracks
➥ORDER BY originalReleaseYear
```

This statement orders the results in ascending order based on the release year. The results are shown in table 5.7.

You can explicitly instruct the database engine to sort the data in ascending order using the ASC keyword, or you can specify DESC to indicate that the data should be sorted in descending order. The following statement would sort the results starting with the most recent year:

```
SELECT album, originalReleaseYear FROM musicTracks
➥ORDER BY originalReleaseYear DESC
```

You can add additional columns to the sort expression by using a comma-delimited list. The first column in the list exerts the largest effect because it determines how

album	originalReleaseYear
Forever Now	1982
The Golden Age of Wireless	1982
Points on the Curve	1984
Mirror Moves	1984
English Settlement	1984
The Flat Earth	1984
Dead Man's Party	1985
Mosaic	1986

Table 5.7 Use the ORDER BY clause to sort the data

everything is first sorted. After the data is sorted by the first column, the next column is used to determine how to sort the data more granularly. For example, you may notice that in table 5.7 the data is sorted by release year, but there doesn't seem to be an obvious pattern to how the data is sorted within each release year. The result set has four records with release years of 1984, but the records aren't sorted in any obvious order at that level. We can tell the database engine to sort first by release year and then by album name using the following command:

```
SELECT album, originalReleaseYear FROM musicTracks
➥ORDER BY originalReleaseYear, album
```

The results are shown in table 5.8.

Not only can you order data, but you can also run functions to retrieve specific values from a database, as we'll see in the next section.

album	originalReleaseYear
Forever Now	1982
The Golden Age of Wireless	1982
English Settlement	1984
Mirror Moves	1984
Points on the Curve	1984
The Flat Earth	1984
Dead Man's Party	1985
Mosaic	1986

Table 5.8 Results are now sorted by release year

RUNNING FUNCTIONS

SQL allows you to run functions in queries. The full list of functions allowed by SQLite is documented at www.sqlite.org/lang_expr.html. We'll just show a few examples in this section.

Suppose you want to find out the average length of a song from the musicTracks table. You could retrieve all the records and use ActionScript to calculate the average. But using the SQL avg() function is a lot simpler. All you need to do is use the function in a SELECT statement as follows:

```
SELECT avg(length) FROM musicTracks
```

This statement will return a result set with one column called avg(length) that has a value of 267.5. The column name avg(length) in the result set isn't very friendly. If we want the query to return a result set with a nicer column name, we can specify an *alias* using the AS keyword. An alias allows us to refer to any element in the columns list (whether a function or not) using the alias we specify. For example, we can use an alias of averageLength as follows:

```
SELECT avg(length) AS averageLength FROM musicTracks
```

What if, instead of getting the average length of all the songs in the table, you wanted to get the average length of a song by each artist? That sort of behavior is possible using the GROUP BY clause. The GROUP BY clause allows you to specify a column to use to filter how the aggregate function (such as avg()) is run:

```
SELECT artist, avg(length) as averageLength
➥FROM musicTracks GROUP BY artist
```

The results of this statement are shown in table 5.9.

Artist	averageLength
Oingo Boingo	243
The Psychedelic Furs	229
Thomas Dolby	312
Wang Chung	272.5
XTC	270

Table 5.9 Using a GROUP BY clause we can affect how the aggregate function is applied

If you'd like to further filter which results are returned, you can add a HAVING clause as well. The HAVING clause allows you to specify an expression that determines which results to return. For example, the following specifies that the command should only return results where the average length is greater than 250:

```
SELECT artist, avg(length) as averageLength FROM musicTracks
➥GROUP BY artist HAVING averageLength > 250
```

The results are shown in table 5.10.

artist	averageLength
Thomas Dolby	312
Wang Chung	272.5
XTC	270

Table 5.10 Results with average length greater than 250

That wraps up working with functions in your SQL statements.

NOTE Thus far we've only seen how to work with data in one table. Working with data in more than one table is important for many applications of moderate or greater complexity. While this information is beyond the scope of this book, you can find many good resources on the subject, including the free online resource we mentioned earlier, www.w3schools.org/sql.

Now that we've covered all the basics of working with SQL, we can next look at the specific implementation details for working with SQL from your AIR applications.

5.3   *Creating and opening databases*

Consider for a moment that you want to rent a movie from a local video store. You know that you'd like to rent a movie starring your favorite actor, Humphrey Bogart. You want to know which movies the video store has in stock. What do you do? You might pick up the phone and call the video store. Once the clerk answers, you can ask if they have any movies starring Humphrey Bogart in stock. Upon getting your answer, you can thank the clerk and hang up the phone. Believe it or not, this is analogous to working with a database. When you work with a database, the first thing you must do is make a connection. Once you've established a connection, you can execute statements (such as making queries), and when you're done, you can disconnect from the database. In this section, we're going to look at the first and last steps: opening and closing connections to databases.

SQLite databases are written to files. In chapter 3, you learned how to work with files, and when you work with databases, you'll be leveraging some of those skills. The first thing you need to do when you work with a database is create a `File` object referencing the database file to use. As we'll see in a minute, we can ask AIR to automatically create the file when trying to open the database connection. Therefore the `File` object doesn't need to reference a file that already exists. All you need to do is create a `File` object that points to the file where data is stored or where you want to store data. The following example creates a `File` object that points to a file named example.db in the application storage directory:

```
var databaseFile:File = File.applicationStorageDirectory.resolvePath(
➥ "example.db");
```

Once you've created a `File` object that points to the file in which to store the data, you next must create a `flash.data.SQLConnection` object. You'll use the SQL-Connection object to create the connection to the database file, and all SQL statements must have a `SQLConnection` reference in order to run. The `SQLConnection` constructor doesn't require any parameters. The following shows how to construct a new `SQLConnection` object:

```
var connection:SQLConnection = new SQLConnection();
```

The next step is to connect the object to the database file. You can open a `SQLConnection` object's connection to the database file synchronously or asynchronously. You can open a connection synchronously using the `open()` method. If you open a connection synchronously, all SQL statements will execute on that connection in a synchronous fashion. Generally this isn't advisable for the same reasons that most synchronous operations aren't advisable if they could potentially take a long time to run. (See the discussion in chapter 3 for more detail.) A far better alternative is to open a connection asynchronously using the `openAsync()` method. Both methods require the same parameter: a reference to the `File` object that points to the database file. For example, the following code will open a connection to the database file that we created earlier in this section:

```
connection.openAsync(databaseFile);
```

When you open a connection, you have the option to specify what mode the connection should use. There are three modes: read, update, and create. The read mode specifies that the connection can only be used to read existing data from the database. The update and create modes both allow for both reading and writing of data, but the create mode will create the database file if it doesn't already exist, while the update mode will fail. The default mode is create. If you want to explicitly set the mode, you can pass a second parameter to the `open()` or `openAsync()` method using one of the three `flash.data.SQLMode` constants of `READ`, `UPDATE`, or `CREATE`. For example, the following opens a connection in read mode:

```
connection.openAsync(databaseFile, SQLMode.READ);
```

When you open a connection asynchronously, you must listen for an `open` event before executing any SQL commands. The `open` event is of type `flash.events.SQLEvent`.

Once you're done with a database connection, you should close it. Closing a connection is as simple as calling the `close()` method.

5.4   Running SQL commands

In the previous section, we talked about the three basic steps in working with a database: opening a connection, running commands, and closing the connection. We used an analogy in which you wanted to find out which movies your local video store has in stock. In that analogy, the step in which you ask the clerk which movies are in stock is analogous to running SQL commands on a database. That is what we're going to look at next: how to run SQL commands once you've established a connection to a database.

All SQL statements (`CREATE TABLE`, `INSERT`, `DELETE`, `SELECT`, and so on) should be run using an instance of the `flash.data.SQLStatement` class. In the next few sections, we'll look at working with `SQLStatement` objects.

5.4.1 Creating SQL statements

When you want to run a SQL statement, the first thing you should do is create a new SQLStatement object using the constructor. The constructor requires no parameters. Therefore, the following shows how to construct a new SQLStatement object:

```
var statement:SQLStatement = new SQLStatement();
```

When you want to run a statement, you must tell the SQLStatement object what SQL-Connection object to use. You do that by setting the sqlConnection property as in the following code snippet:

```
statement.sqlConnection = connection;
```

Next you need to specify the SQL statement that you want to run. You can do that by assigning the string value to the text property of the SQLStatement object. For example, the following assigns a SELECT statement to the text property of a SQL-Statement object:

```
statement.text = "SELECT DISTINCT album FROM musicTracks";
```

That's all there is to setting up a basic SQL statement to run. Next we'll look at how to actually run it.

5.4.2 Running SQL statements

Running a SQL statement is as simple as calling the execute() method. When you call the execute() method synchronously, either it runs successfully (and any results are available immediately following) or it throws an error. If you run execute() when using an asynchronous connection, the effect isn't immediate. Instead it results in one of two events: a result event or an error event. When you call the execute() method with no parameters, you must register listeners for these events directly with the SQL-Statement object. For example, the following registers a listener for a result event:

```
statement.addEventListener(SQLEvent.RESULT, statementResultHandler);
```

It's also possible to use a flash.net.Responder object to handle the effect of running a SQL statement. When you use a Responder object, you don't listen for result or error events on the SQLStatement object. Instead, you pass the Responder object to the execute() method as a parameter. The execute() method allows for two parameters. The first is a paging parameter that we'll look at in section 5.4.5. For now, we'll just use the default value of -1 to always return all the results. The second parameter is the Responder object. The following shows how to call the execute() method using a Responder object:

```
statement.execute(-1, new Responder(statementResultHandler,
➥statementErrorHandler));
```

That is all there is to running a SQL statement. Next we'll look at how to retrieve the results of a SELECT statement.

5.4.3 Handling SELECT results

You should listen for error and result events for most if not all statements. It's generally important that an application be capable of knowing when a statement executes successfully or throws an error. That way, the application can respond appropriately. For example, if an error occurs, the application may need to alert the user or retry the statement. However, SELECT statements are the type of SQL statements that always require that you handle the result. After all, if you don't handle the result of a SELECT statement, how will you know when the data you just requested is available?

When you handle the result of a SELECT statement, you'll want to retrieve the resultant data set, which you can do by calling the getResult() method of the SQLStatement that just executed. The getResult() method returns a flash.data.SQLResult object, which contains a data property that's an array of the data returned. By default, the elements of the array are of type Object, and each element has properties with the names of the columns returned in the data set. For example, the following code shows a method that handles a result event and uses a trace() statement to write the album names to the console or output window. You can assume this method handles the result of the SQL statement SELECT DISTINCT album FROM musicTracks:

```
private function statementResultHandler(event:SQLEvent):void {
    var statement:SQLStatement = event.target as SQLStatement;
    var result:SQLResult statement.getResult();
    if(result != null && result.data != null) {
        var dataset:Array = result.data;
        for(var i:Number = 0; i < dataset.length; i++) {
            trace(dataset[i].album);
        }
    }
}
```

As we just said, by default all results are generic Object instances. However, in the next section, we'll see what other options might exist.

5.4.4 Typing results

Sometimes when you write data to a database, you are serializing custom ActionScript types. For example, if you were writing data to a musicTracks database table, you might be writing instances of a custom ActionScript class called MusicTrack that you've written for your application. The MusicTrack class might have the following properties: id, title, artist, album, length, and originalReleaseYear. You then write the objects to the database by writing the properties to the columns with the same names. This is a typical workflow. Therefore, when you retrieve the data by executing a SELECT statement, it would be convenient if you could get AIR to automatically convert the results to objects of type MusicTrack. And AIR allows you to do just that.

In order to get AIR to automatically convert results to typed objects, all you need to do is set the itemClass property of the SQLStatement object prior to calling the execute() method. You should assign the itemClass property a reference to the class of objects that you want AIR to use to automatically type all the results. For example, the following tells AIR to type the results for the `SQLStatement` object to `MusicTrack`:

```
statement.itemClass = MusicTrack;
```

In order for this to work, the names of the columns in the result set and the names of the properties of the class must be the same. That doesn't mean the names of the columns in the database table must be the same as the names of the properties of the class, because you can use column aliases to map table column names to different names in the result set.

5.4.5   *Paging results*

Thus far, we've seen how to retrieve all the results of a `SELECT` statement at once. However, for really large data sets, it may be more practical to retrieve only the records needed at any point in time. For example, if a query could potentially return hundreds of thousands of records but your application only uses 100 at a time (perhaps displaying them to the user), there's no sense in retrieving all the records until and unless the user explicitly requests them. You can tell AIR to retrieve a maximum number of records when you call the `execute()` method by passing that number as the first parameter. The default value of `-1` tells AIR to retrieve all the records, but a positive number tells AIR to retrieve only up to that many records. For example, the following tells AIR to retrieve only up to 20 records:

```
statement.execute(20);
```

When you limit the number of possible results in this way, you need a way to page through the rest of the results. You shouldn't call `execute()` again in order to do that. Instead, you should call the `next()` method for the same `SQLStatement` object. The `next()` method accepts the same parameters as `execute()` and causes the same events. The difference is that `execute()` always retrieves just the first set of records, whereas `next()` retrieves the next set from that which was most recently retrieved. For example, if you call `execute()` with a value of 20, then when you call `next()` with a value of 20, AIR will retrieve records 21–40 (if there are that many). You retrieve the result of a `next()` method call just as you would the result of an `execute()` method call: once the result event occurs, you call `getResult()` on the `SQLStatement` object. Each call to `next()` adds another `SQLResult` object to the queue, and `getResult()` always returns the first `SQLResult` on the queue until there are no more in the queue, at which point `getResult()` returns null.

5.4.6   *Parameterizing SQL statements*

When running SQL statements, frequently you'll draw on variable values. For example, you may want to insert a new music track into a table based on user input. As a Flash or Flex developer, this probably seems like a remedial task to you: clearly all you need to do is take the variables and put them together in a string, as in the following example.

```
statement.text = "INSERT INTO musicTracks(album, artist) VALUES('" +
➥albumInput.text + "', '" + artistInput.text + "')";
```

However, this approach potentially opens up your application to malicious or accidental negative effects, because it allows the user to indirectly inject code into a SQL statement. A better approach is to parameterize SQL statements using the built-in AIR SQL statement parameterization technique.

To parameterize a SQL statement, use @ or : as the initial character to denote a parameter in a SQL statement that you want to assign to the text property of the SQL-Statement object. For example, we can rewrite the preceding statement as follows:

```
statement.text = "INSERT INTO musicTracks(album, artist) VALUES(@album,
➥@artist)";
```

Then you can use the parameters property of the SQLStatement object to define the parameter values. The parameters property is an associative array to which you can add properties and values. The properties should be the names of the parameters used in the SQL statement, and the values should be the values to use in place of the parameters:

```
statement.parameters["@album"] = albumInput.text;
statement.parameters["@artist"] = artistInput.text;
```

AIR automatically makes sure that none of the values assigned to the parameters property are going to cause unintended problems.

What we've just looked at is how to use named parameters. If you prefer, you can also use ordered parameters instead of named parameters. Ordered parameters are denoted by the ? character in the SQL statement. For example:

```
statement.text = "INSERT INTO musicTracks(album, artist) VALUES(?, ?)";
```

Then you can specify an ordered array of values for the parameters property:

```
statement.parameters[0] = albumInput.text;
statement.parameters[1] = artistInput.text;
```

In addition to removing malicious characters and SQL code, this type of statement parameterization (both named and ordered) helps to improve application performance in some cases. The first time that a SQL statement is run, it must be compiled by the AIR application, which takes a small amount of time. Subsequent calls to the statement run faster. However, if you change the text property value, the statement must be recompiled. If you parameterize a statement, you can change the values of the parameters without causing AIR to recompile the statement.

5.4.7 *Using transactions*

Normally when you run a statement, it runs autonomously, and for many scenarios that's appropriate. But there are also cases when it's advantageous to group statements together to run as a batch. A common example is when you want to insert a record into a table, retrieve the new record's ID, and then use that ID to insert a record into another table. Although this requires at least two SQL statements, it's one logical group of statements, and it makes sense to run it all together if possible. That way, if any error occurs at any point, it would be possible to undo any changes. Consider what would happen if you ran all the statements as normal:

- The first statement runs successfully, inserting a record.
- The second statement fails.

In this scenario, the record for the first statement is still in the database even though logically it shouldn't be, because the entire batch of statements didn't complete successfully. You could write your own code to handle such exceptions by removing the first record if the second statement fails. However, a much simpler and more efficient way to deal with this sort of scenario is to use a feature built in to AIR: SQL statement transactions.

A transaction allows you to group together statements that run using the same SQLConnection object. The way that you can create a transaction is as follows:

1 Call the begin() method of the SQLConnection object.
2 Handle the begin() method of the SQLConnection object, and execute SQL statements using the SQLConnection. Execute these methods normally.
3 If an error occurs at any point, call the rollback() method of the SQLConnection object.
4 If all the statements execute successfully, call the commit() method of the SQLConnection object to write the results to disk.

As you can see in these steps, all SQLStatement objects that run using a particular SQLConnection object get grouped together from the point that begin() is called. All those SQLStatement objects run in memory only. The transaction continues until one of two things happens: either the rollback() method gets called or the commit() method gets called. Either method stops the transaction. The rollback() method cancels all the statements that had already run in the transaction, never writing the results to disk. For example, if the first four statements in a transaction all are INSERT statements, then none of those records will actually get written to the database file if a rollback() method gets called. The commit() method, on the other hand, stops the transaction and writes the results to disk.

Another advantage to using transactions is that you can lock the database you want to use over the course of the transaction. This ensures that no other process can modify the database and potentially affect the results of your operation. One example of the usefulness of this would be a case where two pieces of code need to read and modify the same record in a table. If both processes read and then write to the record at the same time, the edits of one process might be lost.

You can lock the database by passing an optional parameter to the begin() method. You have the option of making the database read-only for other connections or making the database completely inaccessible for other connections. You can also

Table 5.11   Transaction lock types

Constant	Description
SQLTransactionLockType.DEFERRED	Lock the database on the first read or write operation.
SQLTransactionLockType.EXCLUSIVE	Lock the database as soon as possible. No other connection can read or write to the database.
SQLTransactionLockType.IMMEDIATE	Lock the database as soon as possible. No other connection can write to the database, but reading is still possible.

defer locking the database until your transaction needs to read or write from the database. You can use constants of the `flash.data.SQLTransactionLockType` class for these values: `DEFERRED`, `EXCLUSIVE`, and `IMMEDIATE`. Table 5.11 describes these values. You would lock the database in a `begin()` method call as follows:

```
connection.begin(SQLTransactionLockType.IMMEDIATE);
```

Now that we've covered all the basics of running SQL statements, we'll next put this all to use by building a sample application.

5.5   *Building a ToDo application*

In this section, we're going to build an application that puts all of the database knowledge we just learned to use. The ToDo application allows users to add and edit to-do items to a database, or delete those items if they want. The application also displays all the current items. Figure 5.9 shows what the application looks like.

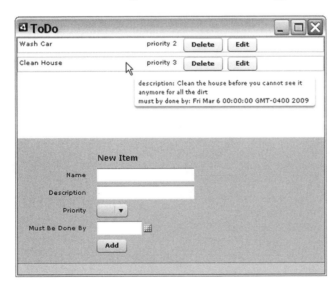

Figure 5.9   The ToDo application lists to-do items, and allows the user to add new items and edit or delete existing items.

To build this application, we'll take the following steps:

1 Build a data model class for a to-do item.
2 Create a component to display each to-do item.
3 Create the database.
4 Create an input form.
5 Add the SQL statements.

In the next section, we'll tackle the first step.

5.5.1   *Building the to-do item data model class*

We'll create a simple ActionScript class to model each to-do item. For our application, each to-do item has the following properties: an ID, name, description, priority, and a date by which it must be complete. Listing 5.1 shows the ToDoItem class.

Listing 5.1   The ToDoItem class is the data model class for to-do items

```
package com.manning.todolist.data {
    import flash.events.Event;
    import flash.events.EventDispatcher;

    public class ToDoItem extends EventDispatcher {

        private var _id:int;
        private var _name:String;
        private var _description:String;
        private var _priority:int;
        private var _mustBeDoneBy:Date;

        [Bindable(event="idChanged")]
        public function set id(value:int):void {
            _id = value;
            dispatchEvent(new Event("idChanged"));
        }

        public function get id():int {
            return _id;
        }

        [Bindable(event="nameChanged")]
        public function set name(value:String):void {
            _name = value;
            dispatchEvent(new Event("nameChanged"));
        }

        public function get name():String {
            return _name;
        }


        [Bindable(event="descriptionChanged")]
        public function set description(value:String):void {
            _description = value;
            dispatchEvent(new Event("descriptionChanged"));
        }
```

```
        public function get description():String {
           return _description;
        }

        [Bindable(event="priorityChanged")]
        public function set priority(value:int):void {
           _priority = value;
           dispatchEvent(new Event("priorityChanged"));
        }

        public function get priority():int {
           return _priority;
        }

        [Bindable(event="mustBeDoneByChanged")]
        public function set mustBeDoneBy(value:Date):void {
           _mustBeDoneBy = value;
           dispatchEvent(new Event("mustBeDoneByChanged"));
        }

        public function get mustBeDoneBy():Date {
           return _mustBeDoneBy;
        }

        public function ToDoItem() {
        }

    }
}
```

The ToDoItem class doesn't do anything unusual. It merely creates private properties as well as accessors and mutators for each of the properties. We also add [Bindable] metadata tags to enable data binding in Flex.

5.5.2   *Creating a to-do item component*

As you can see in figure 5.9, we display each to-do item in a list in the upper portion of the application. We'll next create the MXML component for that purpose. The ToDo-ListRenderer component is this component, and we'll save it in a directory called com/manning/todolist/ui/ToDoListRenderer.mxml. The code is as follows in listing 5.2.

Listing 5.2   The ToDoListRenderer component displays a to-do item

```
<?xml version="1.0" encoding="utf-8"?>
<mx:VBox xmlns:mx="http://www.adobe.com/2006/mxml"
   borderStyle="solid" width="100%"
   toolTip="{'description: ' + data.description
        + '\nmust by done by: ' + data.mustBeDoneBy}">          Add a tool tip
   <mx:HBox>
      <mx:Label text="{data.name}" width="200" />
      <mx:Label text="priority {data.priority}" />
      <mx:Button label="Delete"
      ➥click="dispatchEvent(new Event('delete'));" />
      <mx:Button label="Edit"
      ➥click="dispatchEvent(new Event('edit'));" />
```

```
    </mx:HBox>
  </mx:VBox>
```

As you can see, all this code does is display the values from the data property. In this case, we're assuming that the data property is always going to be assigned a ToDoItem object.

5.5.3   *Creating the database*

Now we need to create the database. The database in this case is simple. It has just one table with the following columns: id, priority, name, description, and mustBeDoneBy. Notice that the columns of the table are identical to the properties of the ToDoItem class. This allows us to easily retrieve data from the table as typed objects later on.

For this application, we simplify everything by placing all the SQL code in the application MXML file. Therefore, we place the database creation code in the application MXML file, which we'll call ToDo.mxml. We start by adding the code shown in listing 5.3 to ToDo.mxml.

Listing 5.3   The ToDo.mxml file creates the database and its table

```
<?xml version="1.0" encoding="utf-8"?>
<mx:WindowedApplication xmlns:mx="http://www.adobe.com/2006/mxml"
  layout="absolute" creationComplete="creationCompleteHandler();">
  <mx:Script>
    <![CDATA[                                          The
                                                       connection
      private var _connection:SQLConnection;   ←──┘   object

      private function creationCompleteHandler():void {
        var file:File =
File.applicationStorageDirectory.resolvePath("database.db");   Listen for
        _connection = new SQLConnection();                      open event
        _connection.addEventListener(SQLEvent.OPEN, openHandler);   ←──┘
        _connection.openAsync(file, SQLMode.CREATE);   ←──┐
      }                                                   Open connection
                                                          asynchronously
      private function openHandler(event:SQLEvent):void {
        var sql:SQLStatement = new SQLStatement();
        sql.sqlConnection = _connection;
        sql.text = "CREATE TABLE IF NOT EXISTS todo(" +
              "id INTEGER PRIMARY KEY AUTOINCREMENT, " +
              "priority INTEGER, " +                          Create
              "name TEXT, " +                                 the table
              "description TEXT, " +
              "mustBeDoneBy DATE)";
        sql.execute();
      }

    ]]>
  </mx:Script>
</mx:WindowedApplication>
```

Note that in this code we use the CREATE TABLE IF NOT EXISTS statement to only create the table if it doesn't already exist. Now that we've created the table (if it doesn't yet exist), we can next add the code for inserting, updating, retrieving, and deleting items.

5.5.4 Creating an input form

We'll next create an input form, allowing the user to enter values for the to-do item. Then we'll add a view state that allows the user to use the same form to edit data. In the edit state, the labels on the form change and the button calls a different method. Listing 5.4 shows the updated code.

Listing 5.4 Adding an input form to the application

```
<?xml version="1.0" encoding="utf-8"?>
<mx:WindowedApplication xmlns:mx="http://www.adobe.com/2006/mxml"
   layout="absolute" creationComplete="creationCompleteHandler();">
  <mx:Script>
    <![CDATA[

        private var _connection:SQLConnection;

        private function creationCompleteHandler():void {
           var file:File =
           ➥File.applicationStorageDirectory.resolvePath("database.db");
           _connection = new SQLConnection();
           _connection.addEventListener(SQLEvent.OPEN, openHandler);
           _connection.openAsync(file, SQLMode.CREATE);
        }

        private function openHandler(event:SQLEvent):void {
           var sql:SQLStatement = new SQLStatement();
           sql.sqlConnection = _connection;
           sql.text = "CREATE TABLE IF NOT EXISTS todo(" +
                   "id INTEGER PRIMARY KEY AUTOINCREMENT, " +
                   "priority INTEGER, " +
                   "name TEXT, " +
                   "description TEXT, " +
                   "mustBeDoneBy DATE)";
           sql.addEventListener(SQLEvent.RESULT, selectToDoItems);
           sql.execute();
        }
        private function addItem(event:MouseEvent):void {        ◁┐ ❶ Handle
        }                                                           adding
                                                                    item
        private function updateItem(event:MouseEvent):void {     ◁┐ Handle
        }                                                           editing
                                                                 ❷ item
    ]]>
  </mx:Script>                                    ❸ Create form
<mx:VBox width="100%" height="100%">
   <mx:Form>                                    ◁┘
       <mx:FormHeading id="formHeading" label="New Item" />
       <mx:FormItem label="Name">
          <mx:TextInput id="itemName" text="{_selectedItem.name}" />
       </mx:FormItem>
       <mx:FormItem label="Description">
          <mx:TextInput id="itemDescription"
             text="{_selectedItem.description}" />
       </mx:FormItem>
       <mx:FormItem label="Priority">
```

```
                    <mx:ComboBox id="itemPriority"
                        selectedItem="{_selectedItem.priority}">
                        <mx:dataProvider>
                            <mx:ArrayCollection>
                                <mx:Number>1</mx:Number>
                                <mx:Number>2</mx:Number>
                                <mx:Number>3</mx:Number>
                                <mx:Number>4</mx:Number>
                            </mx:ArrayCollection>
                        </mx:dataProvider>
                    </mx:ComboBox>
                </mx:FormItem>
                <mx:FormItem label="Must Be Done By">
                    <mx:DateField id="itemMustBeDoneBy"
                    ➥selectedDate="{_selectedItem.mustBeDoneBy}" />
                </mx:FormItem>
                <mx:FormItem>
                    <mx:Button id="formButton" label="Add"
                        click="addItem(event);" />
                </mx:FormItem>
            </mx:Form>
        </mx:VBox>
        <mx:states>                            ❹ Define edit
            <mx:State name="Edit">   ◁───────── state         ❺ Change form
                <mx:SetProperty target="{formHeading}"            heading
                    name="label" value="Edit Item" />
                <mx:SetProperty target="{formButton}"
                    name="label" value="Update" />    ❻ Change
                <mx:SetEventHandler target="{formButton}"  button label
                    name="click" handlerFunction="updateItem" />   ❼ Change
            </mx:State>                                              button click
        </mx:states>                                                 handler
    </mx:WindowedApplication>
```

In the code, we defined a form ❸ that contains input elements for all the values of a to-do item. The default state of the form is for a new to-do item. We also defined a state for editing ❹ an item. In this state, we need to change the form heading ❺ and button label ❻ to reflect that the action is different. Then we set the button's click handler ❼ to call a different method. In the code at this point, we've defined methods to handle when the user clicks the button to add an item ❶ or edit the item ❷, but we haven't actually written the code that runs the necessary SQL statements yet. We'll do that next.

5.5.5 Adding SQL statements

Next we'll write the code that adds new items to the database, as well as the code that edits and retrieves existing data. Listing 5.5 shows the code that we're adding to ToDo.mxml.

Listing 5.5　Code to add, edit, retrieve, and delete records

```
<mx:Script>
  <![CDATA[
    import com.manning.todolist.data.ToDoItem;
    import com.manning.todolist.ui.ToDoListRenderer;

    private var _connection:SQLConnection;

    [Bindable]
    private var _selectedItem:ToDoItem;        ◁── Reference
                                                   selected item
    private function creationCompleteHandler():void {
      var file:File =
      ➥File.applicationStorageDirectory.resolvePath("database.db");
      _connection = new SQLConnection();
      _connection.addEventListener(SQLEvent.OPEN, openHandler);
      _connection.openAsync(file, SQLMode.CREATE);
    }

    private function openHandler(event:SQLEvent):void {
      var sql:SQLStatement = new SQLStatement();
      sql.sqlConnection = _connection;
      sql.text = "CREATE TABLE IF NOT EXISTS todo(" +
              "id INTEGER PRIMARY KEY AUTOINCREMENT, " +
              "priority INTEGER, " +
              "name TEXT, " +
              "description TEXT, " +
              "mustBeDoneBy DATE)";
      sql.addEventListener(SQLEvent.RESULT, selectToDoItems);   ◁─┐
      sql.execute();                                              │
    }                                          Retrieve items     │
                                               after execution ❶──┘
    private function addItem(event:MouseEvent):void {
      var sql:SQLStatement = new SQLStatement();
      sql.sqlConnection = _connection;
      sql.text = "INSERT INTO todo(priority, name, " +         Create
              "description, mustBeDoneBy)" +              ❷ parameterized
              "VALUES(@priority, @name, " +                  SQL statement
              "@description, @mustBeDoneBy)";
      sql.parameters["@priority"] = itemPriority.value;
      sql.parameters["@name"] = itemName.text;
      sql.parameters["@description"] = itemDescription.text;
      sql.parameters["@mustBeDoneBy"] =
      ➥itemMustBeDoneBy.selectedDate;
      sql.addEventListener(SQLEvent.RESULT, selectToDoItems);
      sql.execute();
    }

    private function updateItem(event:MouseEvent):void {
      var sql:SQLStatement = new SQLStatement();
      sql.sqlConnection = _connection;
      sql.text = "UPDATE todo SET priority = @priority, " +
              "name = @name, description = @description, " +     ❷
              "mustBeDoneBy = @mustBeDoneBy WHERE id = @id";
      sql.parameters["@priority"] = itemPriority.value;
      sql.parameters["@name"] = itemName.text;
```

```
            sql.parameters["@description"] = itemDescription.text;
            sql.parameters["@mustBeDoneBy"] =
        ⇒ itemMustBeDoneBy.selectedDate;
            sql.parameters["@id"] = _selectedItem.id;
            sql.addEventListener(SQLEvent.RESULT, selectToDoItems);
            sql.execute();                               Create
            currentState = "";                           parameterized
            _selectedItem = null;                        SQL statement  ❷
        }

        private function selectToDoItems(event:SQLEvent = null):void {
            var sql:SQLStatement = new SQLStatement();
            sql.sqlConnection = _connection;
            sql.text = "SELECT id, priority, name, " +
                    "description, mustBeDoneBy " +            ❸  Set the
                    "FROM todo ORDER BY mustBeDoneBy, priority";     type for
            sql.itemClass = ToDoItem;                              results
            sql.addEventListener(SQLEvent.RESULT, selectHandler);
            sql.execute();
        }

        private function selectHandler(event:SQLEvent):void {      Handle
        }                                                          SELECT
                                                              ❹   results
    ]]>
</mx:Script>
```

In this code, we fill in the addItem() and updateItem() methods with parameterized SQL statements ❷ that draw on the data from the input form. We also add a method that contains a SQL statement that retrieves all the items from the database. We added an event listener on startup ❶ that calls the selectoToDoItems() method once AIR either creates the database table or verifies that it already exists. And we told AIR to use ToDoItem as the type for all items returned by the SELECT statement ❸. At this point, the selectHandler() method ❹ is empty. When we retrieve the data, we want to display it using the MXML component we created previously. Therefore, we'll need to add a container to the layout code, to which we can add the items. Listing 5.6 shows what ToDo.mxml looks like with the addition of the container and the update to selectHandler().

Listing 5.6 Adding a display container and handling SELECT results

```
<?xml version="1.0" encoding="utf-8"?>
<mx:WindowedApplication xmlns:mx="http://www.adobe.com/2006/mxml"
    layout="absolute" creationComplete="creationCompleteHandler();">
    <mx:Script>
        <![CDATA[
            import com.manning.todolist.data.ToDoItem;
            import com.manning.todolist.ui.ToDoListRenderer;

            private var _connection:SQLConnection;

            [Bindable]
            private var _selectedItem:ToDoItem;
```

```
private function creationCompleteHandler():void {
   var file:File =
   ➥File.applicationStorageDirectory.resolvePath("database.db");
   _connection = new SQLConnection();
   _connection.addEventListener(SQLEvent.OPEN, openHandler);
   _connection.openAsync(file, SQLMode.CREATE);
}

private function openHandler(event:SQLEvent):void {
   var sql:SQLStatement = new SQLStatement();
   sql.sqlConnection = _connection;
   sql.text = "CREATE TABLE IF NOT EXISTS todo(" +
           "id INTEGER PRIMARY KEY AUTOINCREMENT, " +
           "priority INTEGER, " +
           "name TEXT, " +
           "description TEXT, " +
           "mustBeDoneBy DATE)";
   sql.addEventListener(SQLEvent.RESULT, selectToDoItems);
   sql.execute();
}

private function addItem(event:MouseEvent):void {
   var sql:SQLStatement = new SQLStatement();
   sql.sqlConnection = _connection;
   sql.text = "INSERT INTO todo(priority, name, ";
           "description, mustBeDoneBy)" +
           "VALUES(@priority, @name, " +
           "@description, @mustBeDoneBy)";
   sql.parameters["@priority"] = itemPriority.value;
   sql.parameters["@name"] = itemName.text;
   sql.parameters["@description"] = itemDescription.text;
   sql.parameters["@mustBeDoneBy"] =
   ➥itemMustBeDoneBy.selectedDate;
   sql.addEventListener(SQLEvent.RESULT, selectToDoItems);
   sql.execute();
}

private function updateItem(event:MouseEvent):void {
   var sql:SQLStatement = new SQLStatement();
   sql.sqlConnection = _connection;
   sql.text = "UPDATE todo SET priority = @priority, " +
           "name = @name, " +
           "description = @description, " +
           "mustBeDoneBy = @mustBeDoneBy " +
           "WHERE id = @id";
   sql.parameters["@priority"] = itemPriority.value;
   sql.parameters["@name"] = itemName.text;
   sql.parameters["@description"] = itemDescription.text;
   sql.parameters["@mustBeDoneBy"] =
   ➥itemMustBeDoneBy.selectedDate;
   sql.parameters["@id"] = _selectedItem.id;
   sql.addEventListener(SQLEvent.RESULT, selectToDoItems);
   sql.execute();
   currentState = "";
   _selectedItem = null;
}
```

```
private function selectToDoItems(event:SQLEvent = null):void {
    var sql:SQLStatement = new SQLStatement();
    sql.sqlConnection = _connection;
    sql.text = "SELECT id, priority, name, description, " +
            "mustBeDoneBy FROM todo " +
            "ORDER BY mustBeDoneBy, priority";
    sql.itemClass = ToDoItem;
    sql.addEventListener(SQLEvent.RESULT, selectHandler);
    sql.execute();
}

private function selectHandler(event:SQLEvent):void {
    var result:SQLResult = event.target.getResult();
    items.removeAllChildren();
    var item:ToDoListRenderer;
    if(result != null && result.data != null) {
        for(var i:Number = 0; i < result.data.length; i++) {
            item = new ToDoListRenderer();
            item.data = result.data[i];
            item.addEventListener("delete",
                deleteItem, false, 0, true);
            item.addEventListener("edit",
                editItem, false, 0, true);
            items.addChild(item);
        }
    }
}

private function deleteItem(event:Event):void {
}

private function editItem(event:Event):void {
}
```

- **1** Get result
- Remove existing items
- **2** Loop through new items
- Listen for delete event
- Listen for edit event
- Assign item to data property

```
]]>
</mx:Script>
<mx:VBox width="100%" height="100%">
    <mx:VBox id="items" width="100%" height="50%"
        backgroundColor="#FFFFFF" />
    <mx:Form>
        <mx:FormHeading id="formHeading" label="New Item" />
        <mx:FormItem label="Name">
            <mx:TextInput id="itemName" text="{_selectedItem.name}" />
        </mx:FormItem>
        <mx:FormItem label="Description">
            <mx:TextInput id="itemDescription"
                text="{_selectedItem.description}" />
        </mx:FormItem>
        <mx:FormItem label="Priority">
            <mx:ComboBox id="itemPriority"
                selectedItem="{_selectedItem.priority}">
                <mx:dataProvider>
                    <mx:ArrayCollection>
                        <mx:Number>1</mx:Number>
                        <mx:Number>2</mx:Number>
                        <mx:Number>3</mx:Number>
                        <mx:Number>4</mx:Number>
```

```
                    </mx:ArrayCollection>
                  </mx:dataProvider>
                </mx:ComboBox>
              </mx:FormItem>
              <mx:FormItem label="Must Be Done By">
                <mx:DateField id="itemMustBeDoneBy"
                ➡selectedDate="{_selectedItem.mustBeDoneBy}" />
              </mx:FormItem>
              <mx:FormItem>
                <mx:Button id="formButton" label="Add"
                  click="addItem(event);" />
              </mx:FormItem>
            </mx:Form>
        </mx:VBox>
        <mx:states>
          <mx:State name="Edit">
            <mx:SetProperty target="{formHeading}" name="label"
              value="Edit Item" />
            <mx:SetProperty target="{formButton}" name="label"
              value="Update" />
            <mx:SetEventHandler target="{formButton}" name="click"
              handlerFunction="updateItem" />
          </mx:State>
        </mx:states>
      </mx:WindowedApplication>
```

This code uses getResult() ❶ to get the data set. It then loops through the records ❷, creates new ToDoListRenderer component instances, and assigns each record to the data property of a component ❸. When the user clicks on the Edit or Delete buttons in the component, we handle those events. Thus far, we haven't specified the code for those methods. Next we'll fill them in. Listing 5.7 shows what these methods look like.

Listing 5.7 Deleting and editing items

```
private function deleteItem(event:Event):void {
    var item:Object = event.currentTarget.data;
    var sql:SQLStatement = new SQLStatement();
    sql.sqlConnection = _connection;
    sql.text = "DELETE FROM todo WHERE id = @id";
    sql.parameters["@id"] = item.id;
    sql.addEventListener(SQLEvent.RESULT, selectToDoItems);
    sql.execute();
}
private function editItem(event:Event):void {
    var item:ToDoItem = event.currentTarget.data;
    _selectedItem = item;
    currentState = "Edit";
}
```

You can see that deleteItem() merely creates a parameterized statement to delete the selected item. The editItem() method simply sets the _selectedItem property and changes the current state.

That wraps up the ToDo application. At this point, you can add new items and view them in the list. You can then edit or delete those items.

5.6   *Working with multiple databases*

These days, most phone companies offer phone plans and options that allow for three-way calling or conference calling, where lots of people can speak together in one phone conversation. This feature isn't appropriate for every phone call. Sometimes you want to have a conversation with just one person. But sometimes it's useful and appropriate to gather many people in one phone conversation. For example, you may be working on a project with several people. While you could talk with each of them individually, it might be more productive if you could all talk together at the same time. Then you can share information and make decisions more quickly. The same is true with databases. In many cases, you only need to connect to one database. But there are other times when your application will need to connect to more than one database. In this section, we'll look at strategies for connecting to more than one database.

Using what you've already learned, you could open a connection to a second database using a second SQLConnection object. However, there are at least two significant drawbacks to that:

- If you use two SQLConnection objects, you can't use both databases in one SQL statement. (For example, you can't select values from across tables in both databases at the same time.)
- SQL connections are expensive from a processing perspective. Therefore, it's generally better to open multiple databases using the same SQLConnection object. You always open the first connection in the way you've already learned: using the open() or openAsync() method. For subsequent connections, you can use the attach() method.

You always need to specify a name for the database when you attach it. The name isn't the name of the database file. Instead, it's the name by which you'll reference the database in SQL statements. Although we haven't mentioned it up to this point, the main database has a name as well: main. You can reference the main database using its name in SQL statements. For example, the following SQL statements are equivalent where musicTracks is a table in the main database:

```
SELECT album FROM main.musicTracks
SELECT album FROM musicTracks
```

NOTE   It's actually more efficient to always reference the database name as well as the table name in SQL statements. If you want your AIR applications to run at top speed, be sure to include the database name, even if it's otherwise assumed.

When you attach a database, you reference its tables using the alias you specify as the first parameter for the attach() method.

Most commonly, when you use the attach() method, you're opening a connection to a different database than the main database and therefore want to specify a second parameter for the attach() method as well: a File object pointing to the database file. You can't specify a mode as you can with open() or openAsync() because any databases attached using attach() automatically use the same mode as the main database. That means that, if you use the create mode for the main database, all attached databases also use the create mode. The following example attaches a database with an alias of userCustomData:

```
connection.attach("userCustomData",
⇒File.applicationStorageDirectory.resolvePath("userdata.db"));
```

Although you may not use the attach feature often, it's useful when you need it.

5.7 *Adding database support to AirTube*

Now that we've learned all the basic skills for working with databases, and we've even put them to work in a ToDo application, we can update our AirTube application with a database-dependent feature. In chapter 3, we allowed the user to download a video file locally. But at that time we didn't know how to work with databases in AIR. Therefore we didn't add the functionality that would allow users to also store the data for the video and search and play back offline videos within the application. That is what we'll do in the following sections. To accomplish this, we'll need to do the following:

- Add online property to ApplicationData.
- Add UI button to toggle online/offline.
- Add service methods to handle offline mode.

We'll start with the first step: updating ApplicationData.

5.7.1 *Updating ApplicationData to support online/offline modes*

Up to now, the AirTube application has only had one mode: online. We'd like to allow the user to select between online or offline mode. In order to support this, we need to add a property to the ApplicationData class. This property, which we'll call online, is a Boolean value indicating whether the application should run in online or offline mode. Listing 5.8 shows what ApplicationData looks like with this added property.

Listing 5.8 Adding an online property to ApplicationData

```
package com.manning.airtube.data {

    import flash.events.Event;
    import flash.events.EventDispatcher;

    public class ApplicationData extends EventDispatcher {

        static private var _instance:ApplicationData;

        private var _videos:Array;
        private var _currentVideo:AirTubeVideo;
        private var _downloadProgress:Number;
```

```
private var _online:Boolean;

[Bindable(event="videosChanged")]
public function set videos(value:Array):void {
   _videos = value;
   dispatchEvent(new Event("videosChanged"));
}

public function get videos():Array {
   return _videos;
}

[Bindable(event="currentVideoChanged")]
public function set currentVideo(value:AirTubeVideo):void {
   _currentVideo = value;
   dispatchEvent(new Event("currentVideoChanged"));
}

public function get currentVideo():AirTubeVideo {
   return _currentVideo;
}

[Bindable(event="downloadProgressChanged")]
public function set downloadProgress(value:Number):void {
   _downloadProgress = value;
   dispatchEvent(new Event("downloadProgressChanged"));
}

public function get downloadProgress():Number {
   return _downloadProgress;
}

[Bindable(event="onlineChanged")]
public function set online(value:Boolean):void {
   _online = value;
   dispatchEvent(new Event("onlineChanged"));
}

public function get online():Boolean {
   return _online;
}

public function ApplicationData() {

}

static public function getInstance():ApplicationData {
   if(_instance == null) {
      _instance = new ApplicationData();
   }
   return _instance;
}

   }
}
```

The online property is straightforward. We merely create a private Boolean property and then create a standard accessor and mutator for it along with typical Flex data-binding metadata. Now that we've added the property, we next need to create a way for the user to toggle between modes, which we'll do in the next section.

5.7.2 Adding a button to toggle online/offline modes

We can now edit AirTube.mxml, adding to it a button that allows the user to toggle the mode between online and offline. Listing 5.9 shows this code.

Listing 5.9 Updating AirTube.mxml with a button to toggle modes

```
<?xml version="1.0" encoding="utf-8"?>
<mx:WindowedApplication xmlns:mx="http://www.adobe.com/2006/mxml"
    layout="absolute" width="800" height="600"
    creationComplete="creationCompleteHandler();"
closing="closingHandler();">
   <mx:Script>
      <![CDATA[
         import com.manning.airtube.data.AirTubeVideo;
         import com.manning.airtube.windows.HTMLWindow;
         import com.manning.airtube.windows.VideoWindow;
         import com.manning.airtube.services.AirTubeService;
         import com.manning.airtube.data.ApplicationData;

         static private var _instance:AirTube;

         private var _service:AirTubeService;
         private var _videoWindow:VideoWindow;
         private var _htmlWindow:HTMLWindow;

         static public function getInstance():AirTube {
            return _instance;
         }

         private function creationCompleteHandler():void {
            _service = AirTubeService.getInstance();
            _service.key = "YourAPIKey";
            _instance = this;
            _videoWindow = new VideoWindow();
               _htmlWindow = new HTMLWindow();
         }

         private function getVideosByTags():void {
            _service.getVideosByTags(tags.text);
         }

         private function playVideo():void {
            var video:AirTubeVideo =
            ➥videoList.selectedItem as AirTubeVideo;
            _service.configureVideoForPlayback(video);
            if(_videoWindow.nativeWindow == null) {
               _videoWindow.open();
            }
            else {
               _videoWindow.activate();
            }
         }

         public function launchHTMLWindow(url:String):void {
            if(_htmlWindow.nativeWindow == null) {
               _htmlWindow.open();
            }
```

```
        else {
            _htmlWindow.activate();
        }
    }

    private function closingHandler():void {
        for(var i:Number = 0; i <
        ➥nativeApplication.openedWindows.length; i++) {
            nativeApplication.openedWindows[i].close();
        }
    }

    private function changeOnlineStatus():void {
        ApplicationData.getInstance().online =
        ➥!ApplicationData.getInstance().online;
    }

    ]]>
</mx:Script>
<mx:VBox width="100%">
    <mx:Label text="AirTube: Adobe AIR and YouTube" />
    <mx:HBox>
        <mx:Label text="tags:" />
        <mx:TextInput id="tags" text="Adobe AIR" />
        <mx:Button label="Search For Videos"
            click="getVideosByTags();" />
        <mx:Button label="Online" toggle="true"
            selected="{ApplicationData.getInstance().online}"
            click="changeOnlineStatus();" />
    </mx:HBox>
    <mx:TileList id="videoList"
        dataProvider="{ApplicationData.getInstance().videos}"
        width="100%" height="400"
        columnCount="2" horizontalScrollPolicy="off" />
    <mx:Button label="Play Selected Video" click="playVideo();"
        enabled="{videoList.selectedItem != null}" />
</mx:VBox>
</mx:WindowedApplication>
```

The preceding code adds just one button component and one method. The button is a toggle button in which the selected state is bound to the online property of ApplicationData. When the user clicks the button, the event handler method merely toggles the value of the ApplicationData instance's online property.

That's all that we need to do as far as the user interface is concerned. Next we'll update the service code to support both online and offline modes.

5.7.3 *Supporting offline saving and searching*

The majority of the new code we need to write to support online and offline modes is in the AirTubeService class. Listing 5.10 shows the code. Although there's a fair amount of new code, don't be concerned. We'll explain it all in just a minute. All we're adding is basic database code for creating a connection, creating a table, and adding and retrieving data.

Listing 5.10 Updating AirTubeService to include offline support

```
package com.manning.airtube.services {

    import com.adobe.webapis.youtube.YouTubeService;
    import com.adobe.webapis.youtube.events.YouTubeServiceEvent;
    import com.manning.airtube.data.AirTubeVideo;
    import com.manning.airtube.data.ApplicationData;
    import com.manning.airtube.utilities.YouTubeFlvUrlRetriever;
    import com.adobe.webapis.youtube.Video;

    import flash.events.Event;
    import flash.events.ProgressEvent;
    import flash.filesystem.File;
    import flash.filesystem.FileMode;
    import flash.filesystem.FileStream;
    import flash.net.URLRequest;
    import flash.net.URLStream;
    import flash.utils.ByteArray;
    import flash.events.SQLEvent;
    import flash.data.SQLConnection;
    import flash.data.SQLMode;
    import flash.data.SQLResult;
    import flash.data.SQLStatement;

    public class AirTubeService {

        static private var _instance:AirTubeService;

        private var _proxied:YouTubeService;
        private var _flvFile:File;
        private var _imageFile:File;
        private var _downloadingVideo:AirTubeVideo;
        private var _connection:SQLConnection;

        public function set key(value:String):void {
            _proxied.apiKey = value;
        }

        public function AirTubeService() {
            _proxied = new YouTubeService();
            _proxied.addEventListener(
    ➥YouTubeServiceEvent.VIDEOS_LIST_BY_TAG, getVideosByTagsResultHandler);
            var databaseFile:File =
            ➥File.applicationStorageDirectory.resolvePath("AirTube.db");
            _connection = new SQLConnection();
            _connection.addEventListener(SQLEvent.OPEN,
                            databaseOpenHandler);
            _connection.openAsync(databaseFile, SQLMode.CREATE);
        }

        static public function getInstance():AirTubeService {
            if(_instance == null) {
                _instance = new AirTubeService();
            }
            return _instance;
        }
```

Create database ❶
connection

```
private function databaseOpenHandler(event:Event):void {
   var sql:SQLStatement = new SQLStatement();
   sql.sqlConnection = _connection;
   sql.text = "CREATE TABLE IF NOT EXISTS videos(" +
      "id TEXT PRIMARY KEY, title TEXT, " +
      "url TEXT, tags TEXT)";
   sql.execute();
}
```

② **Create table**

```
public function getVideosByTags(tags:String):void {
   if(_proxied.apiKey.length == 0) {
      throw Error("YouTube API key not set");
   }
   if(ApplicationData.getInstance().online) {
      _proxied.videos.listByTag(tags);
   }
   else {
      var sql:SQLStatement = new SQLStatement();
      sql.addEventListener(SQLEvent.RESULT,
                  getOfflineVideosResultHandler);
      sql.sqlConnection = _connection;
      var text:String = "SELECT * FROM videos WHERE 1 = 0";
      var tagsItems:Array = tags.split(" ");
      for(var i:Number = 0; i < tagsItems.length; i++) {
         text += " OR tags LIKE ?";
         sql.parameters[i] = "%" + tagsItems[i] + "%";
      }
      sql.text = text;
      sql.itemClass = Video;
      sql.execute();
   }
}
```

③ **Test for mode**

④ **Compose offline SELECT**

```
private function getVideosByTagsResultHandler(
➥event:YouTubeServiceEvent):void {
   var videos:Array = event.data.videoList as Array;
   for(var i:Number = 0; i < videos.length; i++) {
      videos[i] = new AirTubeVideo(videos[i]);
   }
   ApplicationData.getInstance().videos = videos;
}
```

```
private function getOfflineVideosResultHandler(event:SQLEvent):
➥void {
   var statement:SQLStatement = event.target as SQLStatement;
   var result:SQLResult = statement.getResult();
   var videos:Array = new Array();
   var video:AirTubeVideo;
   if(result != null && result.data != null) {
      for(var i:Number = 0; i < result.data.length; i++) {
         video = new AirTubeVideo(result.data[i]);
         video.offline = true;
         video.flvUrl =
         ➥File.applicationStorageDirectory.resolvePath("videos/" +
         ➥video.video.id + ".flv").nativePath;
```

⑤ **Wrap result in AirTubeVideo**

Retrieve file references

```
        video.video.thumbnailUrl =
➥File.applicationStorageDirectory.resolvePath("thumbnails/" +
        ➥video.video.id + ".jpg").nativePath;
        videos.push(video);
      }
    }
    ApplicationData.getInstance().videos = videos;
}
public function configureVideoForPlayback(video:AirTubeVideo):
➥void {
    ApplicationData.getInstance().currentVideo = video;
    if(video.flvUrl == null) {
        new YouTubeFlvUrlRetriever().getUrl(video);
    }
}

public function saveToOffline(video:AirTubeVideo):void {
    _downloadingVideo = video;

    _flvFile =
    ➥File.applicationStorageDirectory.resolvePath("videos/" +
    ➥video.video.id + ".flv");
    var videoLoader:URLStream = new URLStream();
    videoLoader.load(new URLRequest(video.flvUrl));
    videoLoader.addEventListener(Event.COMPLETE,
                        videoDownloadCompleteHandler);
    videoLoader.addEventListener(ProgressEvent.PROGRESS,
    ➥videoDownloadProgressHandler);

    _imageFile =
    ➥File.applicationStorageDirectory.resolvePath("thumbnails/" +
    ➥video.video.id + ".jpg");
    var imageLoader:URLStream = new URLStream();
    imageLoader.load(new URLRequest(video.video.thumbnailUrl));
    imageLoader.addEventListener(ProgressEvent.PROGRESS,
imageDownloadProgressHandler);
  }

private function videoDownloadProgressHandler(event:ProgressEvent):
➥void {
    var loader:URLStream = event.target as URLStream;
    var bytes:ByteArray = new ByteArray();
    loader.readBytes(bytes);
    var writer:FileStream = new FileStream();
    writer.open(_flvFile, FileMode.APPEND);
    writer.writeBytes(bytes);
    writer.close();
    var ratio:Number = event.bytesLoaded / event.bytesTotal;
    ApplicationData.getInstance().downloadProgress = ratio;

  }

private function videoDownloadCompleteHandler(event:Event):void {
    _downloadingVideo.offline = true;
    ApplicationData.getInstance().downloadProgress = 0;
    var sql:SQLStatement = new SQLStatement();
    sql.sqlConnection = _connection;
```

Retrieve file
references

```
        sql.text = "INSERT INTO videos(" +              Create parameterized  6
            "title, id, url, tags) VALUES(" +                      statement
            "@title, @id, @url, @tags)";
        sql.parameters["@title"] = _downloadingVideo.video.title;
        sql.parameters["@id"] = _downloadingVideo.video.id;
        sql.parameters["@url"] = _downloadingVideo.video.url;
        sql.parameters["@tags"] = _downloadingVideo.video.tags;
        sql.execute();
    }

    private function imageDownloadProgressHandler(event:ProgressEvent):
    ➡void {
        var loader:URLStream = event.target as URLStream;
        var bytes:ByteArray = new ByteArray();
        loader.readBytes(bytes);
        var writer:FileStream = new FileStream();
        writer.open(_imageFile, FileMode.APPEND);
        writer.writeBytes(bytes);
        writer.close();
    }
    }
}
```

Although we've added a lot of code, it should mostly be clear to you now that you've worked with AIR databases throughout the chapter. Initially we need to create a connection to the database ❶. Once we've connected to the database, we need to create the table for the data if it doesn't already exist ❷. In this case, we're creating just one table with id, title, url, and tags as the columns. Next, in the method that searches videos, we need to test for the current mode ❸. If the mode is online, then we can search online videos as normal. Otherwise, we now want to search all the offline videos. We compose a SELECT statement ❹ based on the keywords that the user has specified. Once the results are returned, we loop through each of the records (which we've typed as com.adobe.webapis.youtube.Video objects) and wrap them in Air-TubeVideo objects ❺. On the flip side, when the user saves a video to offline, we now need to do more than just save the video file. We also need to save the data for the video to the database ❻.

And that's all there is to this stage of the AirTube application. When you test the application now, you should be able to save videos locally, and then toggle to offline mode and search for those videos (and play them back).

5.8   *Summary*

In this chapter, you learned about using the local database feature of AIR. Using local databases, you can store data persistently, and you can read and write it using SQL, a standard language for working with data. You learned that AIR uses a database engine called SQLite, and how to use this database engine to create databases and tables, write data to the database, read the data, update the data, and delete the data. Not only did you learn the theory of working with databases, but you had an opportunity to put it into practice when we built a ToDo application, as well as when we updated the AirTube application to use a feature that uses local databases.

As you read earlier in this chapter, one of the ways in which you can use local data-bases is to store data for sometimes-connected applications so that they can run when offline. You've now learned everything you need to know about local databases to store and retrieve data for that purpose. But you don't yet know how to detect network connectivity. Proceed to chapter 6 to learn about this topic.

Network communication

This chapter covers

- Monitoring HTTP connectivity
- Monitoring socket connectivity

Suppose for a moment that you're building an application that allows users to edit text documents that live on a server connected to the internet. When the user starts the application, it connects to the server and retrieves a list of available documents. She can select a file, and the text is downloaded and made available for editing. When she saves the file, the application sends the new text to the server, where it's saved. That application may work perfectly when the user is connected to the internet. But when the user isn't connected, there's a problem: she has no way to edit or save files, because those behaviors require an internet connection. Using AIR, you can build a better application, one that knows when the user is connected to the internet. By detecting whether the user is connected to the internet or whether a particular internet resource is available, the AIR application can respond appropriately. You can build the application to take different actions depending on network availability. For example, if a user of the text document–editing application starts the application while connected to the internet, she can start to edit a file. But if she has disconnected before trying to save the file (perhaps she has gotten on a plane), then it saves the data to a local database until the network is available again.

In this chapter, you'll have a chance to learn how to use the different AIR-specific networking features. These include monitors to detect network availability.

6.1 *Monitoring network connectivity*

The enhanced version of the application we described in the introduction to this chapter is an example of a *sometimes-connected application*. That means that the application is designed to work both in an online and an offline mode, and generally users don't have to change their workflow significantly between online and offline modes. In fact, in some cases, users can be completely oblivious to whether they're online or offline at any given time because the application works seamlessly by adapting to the current state. Although sometimes-connected applications can vary greatly in terms of complexity, content, and functionality, they all have one thing in common: they must monitor network connectivity. That is the topic that we'll look at in this section.

AIR allows you to build applications that monitor network connectivity through service monitors. There are two types of service monitors available in AIR: `URLMonitor` and `SocketMonitor`. Both of these classes do essentially the same thing, which is watch a network connection to verify that it's available. When the availability status changes for the monitored connection, the monitor object dispatches an event. What differs between `URLMonitor` and `SocketMonitor` is the *type* of connection each can monitor. `URLMonitor` can watch HTTP connections, while `SocketMonitor` can watch lower-level connections.

The `URLMonitor` and `SocketMonitor` classes aren't part of the standard AIR libraries. That means that, if you try to compile an AIR application that uses these classes, you must include the necessary library. These classes are stored in an .swc file called servicemonitor.swc:

- If you're using Flex Builder, you don't need to manually include the library because Flex Builder does it automatically.
- If you're using the Flex SDK, you'll find the .swc file in the frameworks/libs/air directory.
- If you're using Flash CS3, you'll find the .swc file in the AIK/frameworks/libs/ air directory of the Flash CS3 installation directory.

Next we'll look at how to use `URLMonitor`.

6.1.1 *Monitoring HTTP connectivity*

When you want to monitor HTTP connectivity, you can use the `air.net.URLMonitor` class. The first thing you should do is construct an instance of the class. The constructor requires that you pass it a `flash.net.URLRequest` object specifying the HTTP address that the object should monitor. The following creates a `URLMonitor` object to monitor the Manning web site:

```
var monitor:URLMonitor =
➥new URLMonitor(new URLRequest("http://www.manning.com"));
```

As we mentioned earlier, all monitor objects dispatch events when the connectivity status changes. The type of event is a `status` event, and you can use the `Status-Event.STATUS` constant for the name when registering a listener. The following example registers a listener for the `status` event:

```
monitor.addEventListener(StatusEvent.STATUS, statusHandler);
```

Once you've constructed a `URLMonitor` object and registered a listener for the `status` event, you should next start the monitor. If you don't, nothing will happen. You can start the monitor by calling the `start()` method:

```
monitor.start();
```

Once a monitor object is running, you need to be able to query it to determine the current availability of the connection monitored by the object. You can request this information using the `available` property, which returns a Boolean value: `true` if the connection is available and `false` otherwise. You can test for the value of the available property at any time, though it most often makes sense to test the value when a `status` event occurs.

The code in listing 6.1 is a simple network availability tester. It monitors the availability of www.manning.com. If the availability status changes, the user is notified in a text area component.

Listing 6.1   Using a `URLMonitor` object to monitor HTTP resource availability

```
<?xml version="1.0" encoding="utf-8"?>
<mx:WindowedApplication xmlns:mx="http://www.adobe.com/2006/mxml"
    creationComplete="creationCompleteHandler();">
    <mx:Script>
        <![CDATA[
            import air.net.URLMonitor;

            private var _monitor:URLMonitor;

            private function creationCompleteHandler():void {
                _monitor =
                ➥new URLMonitor(new URLRequest("http://www.manning.com"));
                _monitor.addEventListener(StatusEvent.STATUS,
                                statusHandler);
                _monitor.start();
            }

            private function statusHandler(event:StatusEvent):void {
                textArea.text += "www.manning.com available? " +
                ➥_monitor.available + "\n";
            }

        ]]>
```

```
    </mx:Script>
    <mx:TextArea id="textArea" width="100%" height="100%" />
</mx:WindowedApplication>
```

You can test this example for yourself. Run the application, then toggle network availability either by disconnecting and reconnecting a network cable or by disabling and reenabling a network device.

Normally, monitor objects don't actually poll the network resource at an interval. Instead, they only poll the resource once when the monitor starts and then each time network status changes occur. That means that, by default, a monitor object is really testing to see whether a user's computer has network access, more than it's testing whether the network resource is available in general. Consider the application from listing 6.1. When the network status of the user's computer changes, she is notified. But as long as the user is connected to the internet, she wouldn't receive a notification if the server for www.manning.com suddenly became unavailable on the internet. If you want to test for the availability of a specific resource in addition to a user's network status, you need to tell the monitor object to poll more frequently. You can do that by setting the value of the pollInterval property. The default value is 0, which means the object doesn't poll on an interval. Any integer value larger than 0 causes the object to poll that frequently in milliseconds. For example, the following code causes the object to poll the resource every 10 seconds:

```
monitor.pollInterval = 10000;
```

By default, a URLMonitor object will interpret the following status codes as successful responses, meaning the resource is available: 200, 202, 204, 205, and 206. If you want to alter the list of acceptable status codes, you can do that in one of two ways: pass an array of codes as a second parameter to the URLMonitor constructor or assign an array of codes to the acceptableStatusCodes property of the object.

Once you've started a monitor object, its running property will be true. You can stop a monitor object by calling the stop() method.

6.1.2 *Monitoring socket connectivity*

You can use the air.net.SocketMonitor class to monitor connectivity to sockets other than HTTP connections. For example, if your application connects to a server for video streaming, you may want to use a SocketMonitor object to monitor the server's availability.

When you work with a SocketMonitor object, the first thing you need to do is construct it. The SocketMonitor constructor requires two parameters: the name of the server and the port number. The following creates a SocketMonitor object to monitor the availability of an FTP server:

```
var monitor:SocketMonitor = new SocketMonitor("ftp.exampleserver.com", 21);
```

SocketMonitor and URLMonitor both inherit from air.net.ServiceMonitor, and therefore they behave similarly. Once you've constructed a SocketMonitor object, it works almost identically to a URLMonitor object. You can listen for status events, you

can start and stop the monitoring using the start() and stop() methods, you can
test the current status using the available property, and you can set the object to poll
at an interval using the pollInterval property.

Listing 6.2 shows an example that uses a SocketMonitor object to determine what
to display to a user in an application that retrieves the current time from a National
Institutes of Standards and Times (NIST) server on port 13.

Listing 6.2 Getting the time using a Socket object

```
<?xml version="1.0" encoding="utf-8"?>
<mx:WindowedApplication xmlns:mx="http://www.adobe.com/2006/mxml"
    layout="absolute" creationComplete="creationCompleteHandler();">
    <mx:Script>
        <![CDATA[
            import air.net.SocketMonitor;

            private var _monitor:SocketMonitor;
            private var _socket:Socket;
            private var _timer:Timer;

            private const SERVER:String = "time-A.timefreq.bldrdoc.gov";
            private const PORT:int = 13;

            private function creationCompleteHandler():void {          ❶ Create
                _monitor = new SocketMonitor(SERVER, PORT);               monitor
                _monitor.addEventListener(StatusEvent.STATUS,
                            statusHandler);
                _monitor.start();                                     Start
                                                                      monitor
                _socket = new Socket();
                _socket.addEventListener(ProgressEvent.SOCKET_DATA,
                            socketDataHandler);
                                                                      ❷ Create
                _timer = new Timer(10000);                              timer
                _timer.addEventListener(TimerEvent.TIMER, timerHandler);
            }

            private function statusHandler(event:StatusEvent):void {
                if(!_monitor.available) {                             Test network status
                    timeText.text = "Server unavailable.
                    ➥Will reconnect when the server is next available.";
                    _timer.stop();                                    Stop
                }                                                   ❸ timer
                else {
                    timerHandler();
                    _timer.start();                                   Restart
                }                                                   ❹ timer
            }

            private function socketDataHandler(event:ProgressEvent):void {
                var fullTime:String =
                ➥_socket.readUTFBytes(_socket.bytesAvailable);   Read time
                var time:String = fullTime.split(" ")[2];
                timeText.text = "The current time (UTC) is: " + time;
                _socket.close();                                  Close
            }                                                     socket
```

```
        private function timerHandler(event:TimerEvent = null):void {
            if(_monitor.available && !_socket.connected) {        ◄──┐  Test for
                _socket.connect(SERVER, PORT);    ◄── Connect to      │  network
            }                                          socket         │  connection
        }
    ]]>
    </mx:Script>
    <mx:Text id="timeText" width="100%" height="100%" />
</mx:WindowedApplication>
```

In this example, we use a monitor ❶ to watch a connection to a NIST server on port
13. We also use a timer ❷ to make the requests for the current time from the server
every 10 seconds. When the network status changes, we want to take the appropriate
action. If the network connection is unavailable, we display a message to the user and
stop the timer ❸. If the connection has been reestablished, we restart the timer ❹.
When the server responds to requests, the format of the data for this server is something like the following: 54540 08-03-15 18:06:11 50 0 0 348.3 UTC(NIST) *. You can
see that the time of day is the third group of characters delimited by spaces. Therefore, we retrieve the data from the socket using readUTFBytes() and then get just the
third group of characters to display to the user.

6.2 Adding network monitoring to AirTube

In this section, we'll add network monitoring to the AirTube application. Using a URL-
Monitor object, we can monitor whether or not the system is currently connected to
the internet, and we can configure the application to run in online or offline mode
automatically.

We first add a property to the ApplicationData class. The networkAvailable
property is a Boolean property that we can use to determine whether the application
has network availability. Listing 6.3 shows what ApplicationData looks like with this
added property.

> **Listing 6.3 Adding a `networkAvailable` property to the `ApplicationData` class**

```
package com.manning.airtube.data {

    import flash.events.Event;
    import flash.events.EventDispatcher;

    public class ApplicationData extends EventDispatcher {

        static private var _instance:ApplicationData;

        private var _videos:Array;
        private var _currentVideo:AirTubeVideo;
        private var _downloadProgress:Number;
        private var _online:Boolean;
        private var _networkAvailable:Boolean;

        [Bindable(event="videosChanged")]
        public function set videos(value:Array):void {
            _videos = value;
```

```
      dispatchEvent(new Event("videosChanged"));
   }

   public function get videos():Array {
      return _videos;
   }

   [Bindable(event="currentVideoChanged")]
   public function set currentVideo(value:AirTubeVideo):void {
      _currentVideo = value;
      dispatchEvent(new Event("currentVideoChanged"));
   }

   public function get currentVideo():AirTubeVideo {
      return _currentVideo;
   }

   [Bindable(event="downloadProgressChanged")]
   public function set downloadProgress(value:Number):void {
      _downloadProgress = value;
      dispatchEvent(new Event("downloadProgressChanged"));
   }

   public function get downloadProgress():Number {
      return _downloadProgress;
   }

   [Bindable(event="onlineChanged")]
   public function set online(value:Boolean):void {
      _online = value;
      dispatchEvent(new Event("onlineChanged"));
   }

   public function get online():Boolean {
      return _online;
   }

   [Bindable(event="networkAvailableChanged")]
   public function set networkAvailable(value:Boolean):void {
      if(value != _networkAvailable) {
         _networkAvailable = value;
         if(!_networkAvailable) {
            online = false;
            videos = null;
         }
         dispatchEvent(new Event("networkAvailableChanged"));
      }
   }

   public function get networkAvailable():Boolean {
      return _networkAvailable;
   }

   public function ApplicationData() {

   }

   static public function getInstance():ApplicationData {
      if(_instance == null) {
         _instance = new ApplicationData();
```

```
        }
        return _instance;
    }

  }
}
```

You can see that the setter method does little more than simply assign the new value to the `private` property. In this case, we want to set the application mode to offline if the network is unavailable. Also in that event, we set the `videos` array to null to ensure the user can't try to view videos that are only available online if the system doesn't have network availability.

The next step is to add a `URLMonitor` object to the service class. You can edit AirTubeService.as. First add a new private property called `_monitor` as shown in the following line of code:

```
private var _monitor:URLMonitor;
```

Then modify the constructor as follows:

```
public function AirTubeService() {
   _proxied = new YouTubeService();
   _proxied.addEventListener(YouTubeServiceEvent.VIDEOS_LIST_BY_TAG,
                    getVideosByTagsResultHandler);
   var databaseFile:File =
   ➥File.applicationStorageDirectory.resolvePath("AirTube.db");
   _connection = new SQLConnection();
   _connection.addEventListener(SQLEvent.OPEN, databaseOpenHandler);
   _connection.openAsync(databaseFile, SQLMode.CREATE);
   _monitor = new URLMonitor(new URLRequest("http://www.youtube.com"));
   _monitor.addEventListener(StatusEvent.STATUS, networkStatusHandler);
   _monitor.start();
}
```

As you can see, we're using a `URLMonitor` object to monitor connectivity to www.youtube.com. Next add a `networkStatusHandler()` method as follows:

```
private function networkStatusHandler(event:StatusEvent):void {
   ApplicationData.getInstance().networkAvailable = _monitor.available;
}
```

This method merely sets the `networkAvailable` property of `ApplicationData` when network connectivity status changes occur. That triggers the changes to the online and videos values as well, as we saw in listing 6.3.

The only remaining step is to update AirTube.mxml to indicate the current network status to the user. All we need to do is add a `label` component as shown in the following code. The bolded label is the new code. The rest of the code is shown to give you context:

```
<mx:VBox width="100%">
   <mx:Label text="AirTube: Adobe AIR and YouTube" />
   <mx:HBox>
      <mx:Label text="tags:" />
```

```
<mx:TextInput id="tags" text="Adobe AIR" />
<mx:Button label="Search For Videos" click="getVideosByTags();" />
<mx:Button label="Online" toggle="true"
    selected="{ApplicationData.getInstance().online}"
    click="changeOnlineStatus();" />
<mx:Label text="{ApplicationData.getInstance().networkAvailable ?
    'Network Available' : 'Network Unavailable'}" />
</mx:HBox>
<mx:TileList id="videoList"
    dataProvider="{ApplicationData.getInstance().videos}"
    width="100%" height="400" columnCount="2"
    horizontalScrollPolicy="off"
    itemRenderer="com.manning.airtube.ui.VideoTileRenderer" />
<mx:Button label="Play Selected Video" click="playVideo();"
    enabled="{videoList.selectedItem != null}" />
</mx:VBox>
```

This new label uses data binding to display the network availability status to the user.

That's all we need to do to update the AirTube application to support basic network status changes.

6.3   *Summary*

In this chapter, we learned about detecting network status changes using the URLMonitor and SocketMonitor classes. We learned that, using these classes, we can detect when a computer has access to specific network resources such as a web page or a particular port on a server. Using these monitor classes, we can create sometimes-connected applications.

In chapter 7, we'll continue with a new topic: working with HTML in AIR. You'll learn how to display HTML, and you'll learn how to integrate with JavaScript functionality in HTML pages loaded into an AIR application.

HTML in AIR

7

Normally, we try to temper our enthusiasm for a particular AIR feature with calm reason. But in the case of HTML in AIR, the feature is just too darn cool for us to bottle up all our excitement. In this chapter, we'll share with you what we know about working with HTML in AIR, and once you've reviewed the facts for yourself, we think you'll share our enthusiasm.

As a Flash or Flex developer, you've undoubtedly placed many an .swf file in an HTML page. Wouldn't it be neat if you could do the inverse: render HTML inside a Flash or Flex application? Using AIR, you can do exactly that, because AIR includes the WebKit (www.webkit.org) web browser engine, the same engine that drives the popular cross-platform browser, Safari. The WebKit engine allows AIR applications to render HTML and execute JavaScript almost exactly as it would in a standard web browser. But what makes this feature even better is that, when the HTML is rendered in the AIR application, it is not only interactive, as HTML in a browser would be, but is also treated as a display object in the AIR application. That means you can do all the things you can do with a display object, including scaling, rotating, blurring, masking, and so forth.

Throughout this chapter, we'll look at important topics relevant to working with HTML in AIR applications. Initially we'll look at the basics, such as how to render and display HTML content in an AIR application. We'll also talk about how to work with the HTML content to do things such as scroll, navigate history, and interact with JavaScript.

7.1   Displaying HTML in AIR

The first thing you need to know when working with HTML is how to load it, render it, and display it in an AIR application. AIR makes all of this remarkably simple. All you have to do is create an instance of a native class called `flash.html.HTMLLoader` and tell it where to find the HTML to render.

If you're creating an AIR application using Flash CS3, you'll only ever work with `HTMLLoader` instances, and you should read the next subsection (section 7.1.1) but can skip section 7.1.3. If you're creating AIR applications using Flex, you'll find that reading both of these subsections will be useful to you. Although Flex allows you to use a component to work with HTML, that component still uses `HTMLLoader` behind the scenes, and the more you understand about the lower-level `HTMLLoader` class, the better.

7.1.1   Using native Flash HTML display objects

The `flash.html.HTMLLoader` class provides practically everything you need for working with HTML in an AIR application. This class is a display object type, meaning you can add instances to the display list. The `HTMLLoader` class also defines functionality that allows you to tell it where to load HTML content, and it then knows how to render the content.

There are two basic ways you can tell an `HTMLLoader` object what HTML to render:

- Use the `load()` method to tell the `HTMLLoader` object to load HTML from a resource such as a page from a server.
- Use the `loadString()` method to pass the `HTMLLoader` object a string of HTML to render.

As you might imagine, it's much more common to load HTML from a resource, so we'll look at how to do that first. The `load()` method requires just one parameter: a `flash.net.URLRequest` object specifying where the `HTMLLoader` object can find the HTML to load. The following example illustrates how simple it is to load and display HTML content. Listing 7.1 loads an HTML page from www.manning.com and renders it in an `HTMLLoader` object.

Listing 7.1   Loading and rendering HTML pages using `HTMLLoader`

```
package com.manning.airinaction.html {

    import flash.display.MovieClip;
    import flash.html.HTMLLoader;
    import flash.net.URLRequest;

    public class Main extends MovieClip {

        private var _htmlLoader:HTMLLoader;

        public function Main() {
            _htmlLoader = new HTMLLoader();
            _htmlLoader.width = stage.stageWidth;
            _htmlLoader.height = stage.stageHeight;
            addChild(_htmlLoader);
            _htmlLoader.load(new URLRequest(
            ➥"http://www.manning.com/lott"));
        }
    }

}
```

The results of the above code are shown in figure 7.1.

As you can see in this example, because the `HTMLLoader` class is a display object type, it has standard display object properties such as width and height, and you can work with those properties as you would any other display object. In this example, we set the width and height of the `HTMLLoader` object, but we could also set things such as the rotation, alpha, and filters (blur, drop shadow, and so on).

As we mentioned earlier, you can also "load" HTML by programmatically assigning strings to an `HTMLLoader`. You can do that using the `loadString()` method, as shown in listing 7.2.

Figure 7.1   Loading an HTML page into an HTMLLoader object using the `load()` method

Listing 7.2   Rendering HTML strings as well

```
package com.manning.airinaction.html {

    import flash.display.MovieClip;
    import flash.html.HTMLLoader;
    import flash.net.URLRequest;

    public class Main extends MovieClip {

        private var _htmlLoader:HTMLLoader;
```

```
        public function Main() {
            _htmlLoader = new HTMLLoader();
            _htmlLoader.width = stage.stageWidth;
            _htmlLoader.height = stage.stageHeight;
            addChild(_htmlLoader);
            _htmlLoader.loadString("<html><body><h1>HTML in AIR</h1>
            ➥</body></html>");
        }
    }

}
```

The result of this code is shown in figure 7.2.

The `loadString()` method is useful when you want to programmatically dictate the HTML that you'd like the AIR application to render. For example, you could create HTML templates that you store in files in the AIR application directory, and you can programmatically load the HTML templates, parse them, assign values to variables within the templates, and then assign the HTML to an `HTMLLoader` object using `loadString()`.

Figure 7.2 Rendering HTML strings using the `loadString()` method

7.1.2 *Loading PDF content*

AIR can use the Adobe Acrobat 8.1 or higher plug-in to render PDF content. If Acrobat Reader 8.1 or higher is installed on the system, loading and rendering a PDF is identical to loading and rendering HTML. All you need to do is specify the PDF URI when requesting the content to load into the `HTMLLoader` instance. However, if the system doesn't have Acrobat Reader 8.1 or higher, the operation won't work. Therefore, AIR provides a way for you to test whether the system is capable of rendering PDF content via the static `HTMLLoader.pdfCapability` property.

The `HTMLLoader.pdfCapability` property returns one of four values. These values map to four constants of the `flash.html.HTMLPDFCapability` class: `STATUS_OK`, `ERROR_INSTALLED_READER_NOT_FOUND`, `ERROR_INSTALLED_READER_TOO_OLD`, `ERROR_PREFERRED_READER_TOO_OLD`. If the value is `STATUS_OK`, then AIR will be able to render the PDF. Otherwise, AIR can't render the PDF, for various reasons such as these: no Acrobat Reader is found, an outdated version is found, or the user has set his preferences to use an older version even if he has 8.1 or higher.

7.1.3 *Using the Flex component*

When you're building Flex-based AIR applications, you'll usually want to use a Flex component in place of a standard display object. For example, for Flex applications, you use a Flex `Text` component to display text instead of using a lower-level `TextField` object directly. The same is true when working with HTML in a Flex application: instead of using an `HTMLLoader` object directly, you'll use a Flex component instead. In this case, the Flex component is called `HTML`.

Just as a `Text` component is a wrapper for a lower-level `TextField` object, the `HTML` component is a wrapper for an `HTMLLoader` object. As such, the `HTML` component enables exactly the same sorts of behavior as an `HTMLLoader` object. The difference is twofold:

- `HTML` components are Flex components and can be added to other Flex components (nested in containers).
- The `HTML` component has a slightly different API than `HTMLLoader`.

When you want to load content into an `HTML` component, you should use the `location` property. Assigning a value to the `location` property causes the component to automatically request, load, and render the content. For example, the code in listing 7.3 loads and renders the same web page as from listing 7.1.

Listing 7.3   The `location` property specifies what HTML to display

```
<?xml version="1.0" encoding="utf-8"?>
<mx:WindowedApplication xmlns:mx="http://www.adobe.com/2006/mxml"
    layout="absolute" width="350">
  <mx:HTML width="100%" height="100%"
      location="http://www.manning.com/lott" />
</mx:WindowedApplication>
```

The result of this code is shown in figure 7.3.

If you're paying careful attention, you might detect a difference between the results of listing 7.1 and 7.3. The difference is that, when we use an HTML component, Flex automatically adds scrollbars to the content for us. Contrast that with using the lower-level `HTML-Loader` class, where we don't get free scrollbars. Don't worry, though. In the next section, we'll talk about how to scroll HTML content. First we have more to discuss about using the HTML component.

You might be asking yourself how you can use the HTML component to render HTML strings in a way that's analogous to using the `loadString()` method of an `HTMLLoader` object. The answer is that the HTML component doesn't directly provide any such functionality. However, the HTML component does provide access to the `HTMLLoader` instance it wraps via

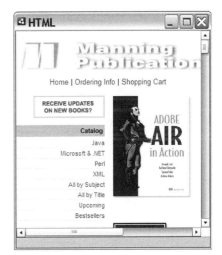

Figure 7.3   Using an HTML component, we can render HTML content in a Flex application.

an htmlLoader property. That means you can use that property to gain a reference to the HTMLLoader object, and you can then call the loadString() method on that object as shown in listing 7.4.

```
<?xml version="1.0" encoding="utf-8"?>
<mx:WindowedApplication xmlns:mx="http://www.adobe.com/2006/mxml"
    layout="absolute" width="350"
    creationComplete="creationCompleteHandler();">
    <mx:Script>
        <![CDATA[

            private function creationCompleteHandler():void {
                html.htmlLoader.loadString("<html><body>
                ➥<h1>HTML in AIR</h1></body></html>");
            }

        ]]>
    </mx:Script>
    <mx:HTML id="html" width="100%" height="100%" />
</mx:WindowedApplication>
```

You can use the HTMLLoader object nested in an HTML component to do anything you'd do with any other HTMLLoader object. That means pretty much anything you learn in this chapter that relates to an HTMLLoader object is also applicable, albeit indirectly, to an HTML component if you access its underlying HTMLLoader object.

You've just had a chance to see how to load and render HTML in an AIR application. You may be thinking to yourself that, while loading and rendering HTML is remarkably simple, there must be a catch. Perhaps, for example, AIR shortchanges you on the ability to control aspects of loading HTML. No, you'd be wrong if you thought that. As we'll see in the next section, AIR allows you to control various aspects of how the AIR application actually loads HTML.

7.2   Controlling how AIR loads HTML

More often than not, you don't need to concern yourself with the details of how an AIR application loads HTML content. Generally, the default settings will work for most HTML content that your application loads. But there are cases when you'll want to slightly alter the way in which the application requests and handles HTML content. For example, you may want to ensure that the application always retrieves content from a server rather than drawing from local cache, or you may want to automate user authentication. In the following sections, we'll look at how you can do these things and more. All of the properties described in the following sections apply to HTMLLoader objects, and you can apply them to HTML components via the internal HTMLLoader object.

7.2.1 Controlling content caching

By default, AIR caches content that applications request via an `HTMLLoader` object (or `HTML` component). That means that, when the user views HTML content in an AIR application, copies of the HTML, images, and more are stored locally; when the AIR application requests any of those resources again, it uses the local cached versions unless they're out of date. Caching content is standard behavior for web browsers, and it can help improve how quickly content loads for users on subsequent visits to the same pages, because the necessary resources are stored locally instead of remotely.

Even though content caching is useful, it's not always the behavior that you want. Sometimes you want to ensure that users are always viewing the content from a server to guarantee they're seeing the latest version. You can control content caching in two ways:

- Tell AIR whether to cache content.
- Tell AIR whether to use previously cached content.

If you'd like to instruct an `HTMLLoader` object not to cache content, you should set the `cacheResponse` property to `false` before calling the `load()` method. The default value of the property is `true`, which means the content for the object will be cached.

If you'd like to instruct an `HTMLLoader` object not to use content that was previously cached, then set the `useCache` property to `false` prior to calling the `load()` method. The default value for the property is `true`, which means the object will read previously cached content if it exists.

7.2.2 Controlling authentication

Sometimes a server requires authentication to grant access to certain content. For example, on many servers, it's possible to use an .htaccess file to challenge a user for credentials when she tries to access a particular directory. In such situations, AIR applications default to displaying a dialog to the user that requests a username and password, allowing the user to authenticate herself. If you'd like to disable that behavior, effectively not allowing the user to authenticate herself, then you can do that using the `authenticate` property of an `HTMLLoader` object. Simply set the `authenticate` property of an `HTMLLoader` object to `false` prior to calling `load()`, and if the server issues a challenge, the AIR application won't display a dialog to the user. Instead the server will return an error.

7.2.3 Specifying a user agent type

An application that requests web content from a server is called a *user agent*. When a user agent makes a request to a server for web content, it sends along information identifying itself. A user agent identifies itself by providing a piece of information called `userAgent`. Some scripts use `userAgent` to determine what content to provide or how to display the content (or whether to display the content at all). For this reason, user agent–spoofing is not uncommon. User agent–spoofing involves a user agent providing false identification in order to appear to be a different type of user agent. For example, one web browser could appear to be another type simply by providing a different value for userAgent.

When you make a request for HTML content using HTMLLoader, you can spoof the user agent as well by setting the userAgent property of the HTMLLoader object. The HTML component also allows you to set the userAgent property directly.

7.2.4   *Managing persistent data*

Some web pages store persistent data in local files managed by the web browser. These files are called *cookies*. Some pages rely on the use of cookies in order to function. By default, AIR stores cookies for pages that you view in an AIR application. But there are various reasons why you might want to disable cookies for HTML content in AIR. One basic reason is that you may want to give the user of your application the option to disable cookies because he might not like the idea of web pages storing information locally on his computer. Whatever the reason, you can explicitly control whether or not AIR stores cookies using the manageCookies property of an HTMLLoader object. The default value is true, and a value of false will disable cookies.

7.2.5   *Setting defaults*

Thus far in this section, we've looked at ways you can affect each individual HTML-Loader object. In most cases, we made reference to the default values that an AIR application uses if you don't explicitly set a property. For example, we said that the default value of the useCache property is true. While that's mostly true, it's not entirely true. That's because you can specify the default values that an AIR application should use for the following properties: authenticate, useCache, cacheResponse, userAgent, and manageCookies. To set the defaults, just assign values to the properties of the same names of the flash.net.URLRequestDefaults class. (All the properties of the class are static.) For example, you can disable caching by default with the following code:

```
URLRequestDefaults.useCache = false;
```

All HTMLLoader objects get their default values from URLRequestDefaults. That means that, if an HTMLLoader object's useCache property is null, it will use the value from URLRequestDefaults. However, you can always override the default values by setting the values of the properties of an HTMLLoader object explicitly.

Now that we've seen how you can control the way in which AIR loads HTML, we'll next look at what you can do with the content once it's loaded. Namely, we'll look at how to control scrolling of content.

7.3   *Scrolling HTML content*

Sometimes HTML content is larger than the area in which you're trying to display it. For example, you may set the height of an HTMLLoader object to 500, but the content might be 1000 pixels. In these cases, you'll most likely want to allow the user to scroll the content. In this section, we'll look at the various issues involving scrolling HTML content in AIR applications.

7.3.1 Scrolling HTML in Flex

As we've seen earlier in this chapter, the Flex `HTML` component automatically adds scrollbars to HTML content when necessary. Therefore, if you want scrollbars to appear when the content is larger than the HTML component, you need do nothing more. If you want to control the scrollbars more explicitly, you can use the `horizontal-ScrollPolicy` and `verticalScrollPolicy` properties. These properties are standard to many Flex components with built-in scrollbars, including `TextArea` and `List`. Possible values for these properties are `auto` (default), `on`, and `off`. When set to `on`, the scrollbars are always visible, even when no scrolling is possible. When set to `off`, the scrollbars are never visible.

NOTE `HTMLLoader` (which underlies the HTML component) automatically allows for vertical scrolling using the scroll wheel on a mouse. Even if you disable scrollbars on an HTML component, the user will still be able to scroll using the scroll wheel.

Because scrolling is built in to the `HTML` component, there isn't much else that you need to know about scrolling if you're working with Flex. If you're interested in understanding the lower-level scrolling mechanisms or if you're building AIR applications using Flash, then continue with the next few sections.

7.3.2 Scrolling HTML content using ActionScript

When you use an `HTMLLoader` object, you don't get built-in scrollbars. But with a small amount of ActionScript, you can scroll content in an `HTMLLoader` object, as we'll see in this section.

The `width` and `height` properties of an `HTMLLoader` object determine the size of the container, but they don't tell you anything about the content of the container. Although the dimensions of the container are important for scrolling, they're only part of what you need to know. You also need to know the dimensions of the content. How can you determine the width and height of the content of an `HTMLLoader` object? AIR makes this nearly as simple as querying the dimensions of the container. All you need to do is read the values of the `contentWidth` and `contentHeight` properties. But there's a catch: you must wait until the content has loaded before you can get an accurate reading for the `contentWidth` and `contentHeight` properties. That raises the question: how can you know when the content has loaded? The answer is that you must wait until the `HTMLLoader` object dispatches a `complete` event. Once the `complete` event is dispatched, you can read the values of `contentWidth` and `contentHeight` to determine the dimensions of the content loaded into the `HTMLLoader` object. If the `contentWidth` is greater than the `width` property, you know that horizontal scrolling is necessary. If the `contentHeight` is greater than the `height` property, you know that vertical scrolling is necessary.

Once you've determined whether scrolling is necessary, the next thing you need to do is actually enable the scrolling behavior. You can programmatically scroll content in an `HTMLLoader` object using the `scrollH` and `scrollV` properties. The `scrollH` property controls horizontal scrolling and the `scrollV` property controls vertical scrolling. A value of `0` in either case means the content is aligned with the container. Positive values cause the content to scroll down and to the right by as many pixels. For example, if you set `scrollH` to `50`, the content will scroll 50 pixels to the right. You can determine the range of scrolling values by using the difference between the dimensions of the content and the container. For example, if you find the difference between `contentWidth` and `width`, that will tell you the maximum value for `scrollH`.

Next we'll look at an example. Listing 7.5. shows the code that adds scrollbars that allow a user to scroll the content of an `HTMLLoader` object.

Listing 7.5   Scrolling content using `scrollH` and `scrollV`

```
package com.manning.airinaction.html {

    import flash.display.MovieClip;
    import flash.html.HTMLLoader;
    import flash.net.URLRequest;
    import fl.controls.ScrollBar;
    import flash.events.Event;

    public class Main extends MovieClip {

        private var _htmlLoader:HTMLLoader;
        private var _scrollBarH:ScrollBar;
        private var _scrollBarV:ScrollBar;             ❶ Create
                                                          vertical
        public function Main() {                          scrollbar
            _scrollBarV = new ScrollBar();        ◁──┘
            _scrollBarV.height = stage.stageHeight - 16;
            _scrollBarV.x = stage.stageWidth - 16;
            _scrollBarV.addEventListener(Event.SCROLL,
                            scrollVerticalHandler);    ❷ Create
            addChild(_scrollBarV);                       horizontal
                                                         scrollbar
            _scrollBarH = new ScrollBar();        ◁──┘
            _scrollBarH.direction = "horizontal";
            _scrollBarH.width = stage.stageWidth - 16;
            _scrollBarH.x = 0;
            _scrollBarH.y = stage.stageHeight - 16;
            _scrollBarH.addEventListener(Event.SCROLL,
                            scrollHorizontalHandler);
            addChild(_scrollBarH);

            _htmlLoader = new HTMLLoader();              Listen for ❸
            _htmlLoader.width = stage.stageWidth - 16;   complete event
            _htmlLoader.height = stage.stageHeight - 16;
            _htmlLoader.addEventListener(Event.COMPLETE, completeHandler);  ◁─┘
            _htmlLoader.addEventListener(Event.SCROLL, scrollHandler);   ◁─┐
            _htmlLoader.load(new URLRequest(
            ➥"http://www.manning.com/lott"));           Listen for
                                                         scroll event ❹
```

```
            addChild(_htmlLoader);
        }

        private function completeHandler(event:Event):void {
            _htmlLoader.scrollH = 0;
            _htmlLoader.scrollV = 0;
            _scrollBarV.setScrollProperties(_htmlLoader.height, 0,
            ➥_htmlLoader.contentHeight - _htmlLoader.height);
            _scrollBarH.setScrollProperties(_htmlLoader.width, 0,
            ➥_htmlLoader.contentWidth - _htmlLoader.width);
        }

        private function scrollVerticalHandler(event:Event):void {
            _htmlLoader.scrollV = _scrollBarV.scrollPosition;
        }

        private function scrollHorizontalHandler(event:Event):void {
            _htmlLoader.scrollH = _scrollBarH.scrollPosition;
        }

        private function scrollHandler(event:Event):void {
            _scrollBarV.scrollPosition = _htmlLoader.scrollV;
        }
    }
}
```

⑤ Set scrollbar properties

Scroll vertically ⑥

Scroll horizontally ⑦

⑧ Update scrollbars

In this example, we use two scrollbars ❶ ❷ to allow the user to scroll vertically and horizontally. As we learned earlier, we need to wait for the complete event ❸ before making scrolling calculations. Once the complete event occurs, we can set the scroll properties of the scrollbars ❺ based on the values of the content dimensions. When the user moves the scrollbars, we can update the scrollV and scrollH properties ❻ ❼. In this example, we also introduce one new item, which is the scroll event. As you can see, we listen for the scroll event ❹ that the HTMLLoader object dispatches. We want to do that because the user might also scroll the content vertically using the mouse scroll wheel. If that occurs, we want to keep the value of the vertical scrollbar in sync ❽. The result of this code is shown in figure 7.4.

Figure 7.4   Adding scrollbars to control the scrolling of HTML content

We've just seen how to programmatically control scrolling. Next we'll see how you can ask AIR to automatically add scrollbars in one specific scenario.

7.3.3   *Creating autoscrolling windows*

There are some times when you want to launch HTML content in a new AIR window. In those cases, it's possible to have AIR launch a new window and add scrollbars automatically all from one method. The `HTMLLoader` class has a static method called `createRootWindow()` that does just this.

The `createRootWindow()` method creates a new `HTMLLoader` object and returns it. It also launches a new AIR window and adds the `HTMLLoader` object to the window. All you need to do then is call the `load()` method of the `HTMLLoader` object in order to load content. The following is an example of how you can use the method:

```
var htmlLoader:HTMLLoader = HTMLLoader.createRootWindow();
htmlLoader.load(new URLRequest("http://www.manning.com/lott"));
```

That code opens www.manning.com/lott in a new AIR window, and it automatically adds scrollbars as necessary.

The `createRootWindow()` method allows you to pass it a few optional parameters as well. The parameters are as follows:

- `visible`—A Boolean value indicating whether the window is initially visible.
- `windowInitOptions`—A `NativeWindowInitOptions` object. See chapter 2 for more information on `NativeWindowInitOptions` objects.
- `scrollBarsVisible`—A Boolean value indicating whether the scrollbars should be visible.
- `bounds`—A `flash.geom.Rectangle` object that allows you to set the x and y coordinates as well as the width and height of the new window.

The following opens a new 250-by-250-pixel window in the upper-left corner of the screen:

```
var htmlLoader:HTMLLoader = HTMLLoader.createRootWindow(true, null,
➥true, new Rectangle(0, 0, 250, 250));
htmlLoader.load(new URLRequest("http://www.manning.com/lott"));
```

Now that we've wrapped up scrolling HTML content, we'll move on to navigating HTML history.

7.4   *Navigating HTML history*

When you use a standard web browser, you're probably used to navigating the history using the Back and Forward buttons. For example, when you click through to a page only to discover it wasn't the page you thought it was, you probably click the browser's Back button to go back to the page you were looking at previously. Up to this point, we haven't seen this sort of functionality in AIR, but that's not because it's impossible. With just a bit of code, you can allow users to navigate their browsing history. All the properties and methods of this section apply equally to both `HTMLLoader` objects and `HTML` components.

`HTMLLoader` and `HTML` both keep track of the user's browsing history using `flash.html.HTMLHistoryItem` objects. `HTMLHistoryItem` objects contain the following properties:

- url—The URL of the page.

- originalUrl—Sometimes pages are redirected, and the value of the url property might be different from the URL to which AIR originally navigated. The originalUrl property reports the value of the URL to which AIR navigated before any redirects. If there were no redirects, originalUrl will have the same value as url.

- title—The title of the page.

- isPost—A Boolean value indicating whether any POST data was submitted to the page.

HTMLLoader and HTML objects have historyLength properties that report the length of the history. That tells you how many HTMLHistoryItem objects they contain. You can use the getHistoryAt() method to request an HTMLHistoryItem with a specific index. Assuming there's at least one history item, calling getHistoryAt() with an index of 0 returns the oldest history item, while calling getHistoryAt() with an index value equal to one less than the value of historyLength returns the most recent history item.

You can also navigate through the history relatively using the historyBack(), historyForward(), and historyGo() methods. The historyBack() method goes to the previous page in history, while the historyForward() method goes to the next page in history. (This is possible only if AIR has already navigated back.) The historyGo() method allows you to navigate in steps other than one. For example, if you want to navigate back two pages in history, you can call historyGo() with a value of -2. Calling historyGo() with negative values goes back, while calling historyGo() with positive values goes forward.

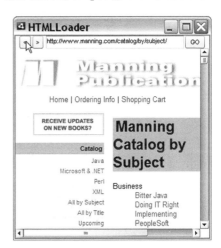

Next we'll build an example that allows a user to navigate the browsing history. Figure 7.5 shows what this application looks like. Note that we're adding Previous and Next buttons as well as an address bar.

Listing 7.6 shows the code that we're using to create this application. Most of the code is the same as listing 7.5, and the new code is shown in bold. Note that, in this example, we're assuming that _next, _previous, and _go are button component instances, that _htmlUrl is a text input component instance, and that all of the components have been added to the stage in Flash.

Figure 7.5 Allowing a user to navigate browsing history

Listing 7.6 Navigating history using historyBack() and historyForward()

```
package com.manning.airinaction.html {

    import flash.display.MovieClip;
    import flash.html.HTMLLoader;
```

```
import flash.net.URLRequest;
import fl.controls.ScrollBar;
import flash.events.Event;
import flash.events.MouseEvent;

public class Main extends MovieClip {

    private var _htmlLoader:HTMLLoader;
    private var _scrollBarH:ScrollBar;
    private var _scrollBarV:ScrollBar;

    public function Main() {
        _scrollBarV = new ScrollBar();
        _scrollBarV.height = stage.stageHeight - 16 - _previous.height;
        _scrollBarV.y = _previous.height;
        _scrollBarV.x = stage.stageWidth - 16;
        _scrollBarV.addEventListener(Event.SCROLL,
                            scrollVerticalHandler);
        addChild(_scrollBarV);

        _scrollBarH = new ScrollBar();
        _scrollBarH.direction = "horizontal";
        _scrollBarH.width = stage.stageWidth - 16;
        _scrollBarH.x = 0;
        _scrollBarH.y = stage.stageHeight - 16;
        _scrollBarH.addEventListener(Event.SCROLL,
                            scrollHorizontalHandler);
        addChild(_scrollBarH);

        _htmlLoader = new HTMLLoader();
        _htmlLoader.width = stage.stageWidth - 16;
        _htmlLoader.height = stage.stageHeight - 16 - _previous.height;
        _htmlLoader.y = _previous.height;
        _htmlLoader.addEventListener(Event.COMPLETE, completeHandler);
        _htmlLoader.addEventListener(Event.SCROLL, scrollHandler);
        addChild(_htmlLoader);

        _previous.addEventListener(MouseEvent.CLICK, previousHandler);
        _next.addEventListener(MouseEvent.CLICK, nextHandler);
        _go.addEventListener(MouseEvent.CLICK, goHandler);
        _htmlUrl.text = "http://www.manning.com/lott";
        goHandler();
    }

    private function completeHandler(event:Event):void {
        _htmlUrl.text = _htmlLoader.location;
        _htmlLoader.scrollH = 0;
        _htmlLoader.scrollV = 0;
        _scrollBarV.enabled = _htmlLoader.contentHeight >
        ➥_htmlLoader.height;
        _scrollBarH.enabled = _htmlLoader.contentWidth >
        ➥_htmlLoader.width;
        _scrollBarV.setScrollProperties(_htmlLoader.height, 0,
        ➥_htmlLoader.contentHeight - _htmlLoader.height);
        _scrollBarH.setScrollProperties(_htmlLoader.width, 0,
        ➥_htmlLoader.contentWidth - _htmlLoader.width);
    }
```

```
            private function scrollVerticalHandler(event:Event):void {
                _htmlLoader.scrollV = _scrollBarV.scrollPosition;
            }

            private function scrollHorizontalHandler(event:Event):void {
                _htmlLoader.scrollH = _scrollBarH.scrollPosition;
            }

            private function scrollHandler(event:Event):void {
                _scrollBarV.scrollPosition = _htmlLoader.scrollV;
            }

            private function goHandler(event:MouseEvent = null):void {
                _htmlLoader.load(new URLRequest(_htmlUrl.text));
            }

            private function previousHandler(event:MouseEvent):void {
                _htmlLoader.historyBack();
            }

            private function nextHandler(event:MouseEvent):void {
                _htmlLoader.historyForward();
            }

        }

    }
```

All that this code does is call the `historyBack()` and `historyForward()` methods when the user clicks on the corresponding buttons. This causes the `HTMLLoader` object to navigate the browsing history.

Now that you're an expert on navigating browsing history, you're probably wondering what new challenges are ahead. Up next, we're going to look at how you can communicate between ActionScript and JavaScript when you load HTML content into an AIR application.

7.5   *Interacting with JavaScript*

AIR isn't content to merely load HTML and render it. Once the content has loaded and rendered, you can still interact with it, and it can interact with the AIR application. That's because the `HTMLLoader` object that loads the HTML exposes the entire HTML document object model (DOM). In the next few sections, we'll look at a variety of ways in which you can cause ActionScript and JavaScript interaction.

7.5.1   *Controlling HTML/JavaScript elements from ActionScript*

When you load HTML content into an `HTMLLoader` object, the entire DOM is available via a `window` property. The `window` property of an `HTMLLoader` object maps directly to the JavaScript `window` property inside an HTML page. That means you can address all the elements of an HTML page using the `HTMLLoader` object's `window` property, just as you would from within an HTML page using the JavaScript `window` property. One caveat when accessing the HTML DOM is that you must wait until the page has loaded before you try to access it.

For the next few examples, we'll use the HTML shown in listing 7.7. For the purpose of our examples, this code is saved in a document called example.html.

Listing 7.7   HTML code saved in example.html

```html
<html>
    <script>

        var pageTitle = "Example";
        var description = "This is an example HTML page";

        function showAlert() {
            alert(description);
        }

    </script>
    <body>
        <p id="p1">
            HTML in AIR
        </p>
        <button onclick="showAlert()">Click</button>
    </body>
</html>
```

As you can see, this HTML code merely does the following:

- Defines two JavaScript variables called `pageTitle` and `description`
- Defines a function called `showAlert()` that displays an alert window with the value of the `description` variable
- Creates a p tag with an `id` of p1
- Creates a button that calls `showAlert()` when clicked

First we'll look at how to retrieve the value of a JavaScript variable from ActionScript. Because the JavaScript variables are created as properties of the `window` object, all we need to do is wait until the `complete` event occurs and then read the value of the corresponding property of the `window` object. In listing 7.8, we read the value of the `pageTitle` property and display it in the window title bar.

Listing 7.8   Reading a JavaScript variable

```actionscript
package com.manning.airinaction.html {

    import flash.display.MovieClip;
    import flash.html.HTMLLoader;
    import flash.net.URLRequest;
    import flash.events.Event;
    import flash.desktop.NativeApplication;

    public class Main extends MovieClip {

        private var _htmlLoader:HTMLLoader;

        public function Main() {
            _htmlLoader = new HTMLLoader();
            _htmlLoader.width = stage.stageWidth;
```

```
        _htmlLoader.height = stage.stageHeight;
        _htmlLoader.addEventListener(Event.COMPLETE, completeHandler);
        _htmlLoader.load(new URLRequest("example.html"));
        addChild(_htmlLoader);
    }

    private function completeHandler(event:Event):void {
        stage.nativeWindow.title = _htmlLoader.window.pageTitle;
    }

}

}
```

You can see that, when the complete event occurs, all we need to do is read the value from _htmlLoader.window.pageTitle to get the value of the pageTitle variable from the HTML page. Figure 7.6 shows the results of this code.

Not only can you read values of JavaScript variables, but you can write them as well. If you test the code in listing 7.8 and click on the button, you'll see an alert window that displays the value of the description variable as it's set in the HTML page. In listing 7.9, we'll write a different value to the variable. Then, when the user clicks on the button, the new value will show up in the alert window.

Figure 7.6 Displaying the value of a JavaScript variable in the window title

Listing 7.9 Writing the value of a JavaScript variable from ActionScript

```
package com.manning.airinaction.html {

    import flash.display.MovieClip;
    import flash.html.HTMLLoader;
    import flash.net.URLRequest;
    import flash.events.Event;
    import flash.desktop.NativeApplication;

    public class Main extends MovieClip {

        private var _htmlLoader:HTMLLoader;

        public function Main() {
            _htmlLoader = new HTMLLoader();
            _htmlLoader.width = stage.stageWidth;
            _htmlLoader.height = stage.stageHeight;
            _htmlLoader.addEventListener(Event.COMPLETE, completeHandler);
            _htmlLoader.load(new URLRequest("example.html"));
            addChild(_htmlLoader);
        }

        private function completeHandler(event:Event):void {
            _htmlLoader.window.description = "This is a new description
```

```
➥from ActionScript";
        }

    }

}
```

As you can see, all we need to do is reference the variable from the `window` object after the `complete` event occurs and assign it a new value. Figure 7.7 shows how the new value gets displayed in the alert window.

Not only can you assign simple data types such as strings and Boolean values, but you can also assign references to more complex data types, including things like functions. In listing 7.10, we assign an ActionScript function to the `showAlert()` function in the HTML page. Therefore, when the user clicks on the button in the HTML page, it calls the ActionScript function instead of the function defined in the HTML page.

Figure 7.7 Displaying a value in an alert that was set from ActionScript

---

Listing 7.10 Assigning reference data types to JavaScript variables

```
package com.manning.airinaction.html {

    import flash.display.MovieClip;
    import flash.html.HTMLLoader;
    import flash.net.URLRequest;
    import flash.events.Event;

    public class Main extends MovieClip {

        private var _htmlLoader:HTMLLoader;

        public function Main() {
            _htmlLoader = new HTMLLoader();
            _htmlLoader.width = stage.stageWidth;
            _htmlLoader.height = stage.stageHeight;
            _htmlLoader.addEventListener(Event.COMPLETE, completeHandler);
            _htmlLoader.load(new URLRequest("example.html"));
            addChild(_htmlLoader);
        }

        private function completeHandler(event:Event):void {
            _htmlLoader.window.showAlert = function():void {
                trace("we've usurped control");
            };
        }

    }

}
```

You can also get references to objects within the document. For example, if you want to reference the p tag in the HTML, you can use _htmlLoader.window.document.getElementById("p1") to gain that reference. Listing 7.11 shows how you can change the text in the p tag.

Listing 7.11 Getting a reference to a document object

```
package com.manning.airinaction.html {

    import flash.display.MovieClip;
    import flash.html.HTMLLoader;
    import flash.net.URLRequest;
    import flash.events.Event;
    import flash.desktop.NativeApplication;

    public class Main extends MovieClip {

        private var _htmlLoader:HTMLLoader;

        public function Main() {
            _htmlLoader = new HTMLLoader();
            _htmlLoader.width = stage.stageWidth;
            _htmlLoader.height = stage.stageHeight;
            _htmlLoader.addEventListener(Event.COMPLETE, completeHandler);
            _htmlLoader.load(new URLRequest("example.html"));
            addChild(_htmlLoader);
        }

        private function completeHandler(event:Event):void {
            _htmlLoader.window.document.getElementById("p1").innerText =
            "Hello from ActionScript";
        }

    }

}
```

When you run the code from listing 7.11, you'll see that the initial text shows at first, but once the content has loaded, the text is replaced by the text specified in ActionScript as shown in figure 7.8.

Now that we've seen how to reference elements of an HTML page from ActionScript, we can take it one step further. In the next section, we'll show how you can handle events from HTML elements in ActionScript.

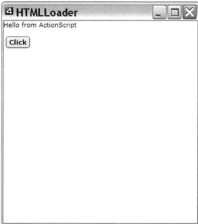

Figure 7.8 Replace text in an HTML page at runtime from ActionScript.

7.5.2 *Handling JavaScript events from ActionScript*

In the previous section, we saw that it's possible to assign an ActionScript function reference to a variable in an HTML page, thus effectively usurping control. In this way, it's possible to call ActionScript functions from JavaScript. But there's much more you can do in regard to handling events than simply usurping existing event handlers. You can also register new event handlers.

There are two ways you can register event listeners: assign a function reference (ActionScript or JavaScript) to the event handler attribute of the HTML object or use the addEventListener() method.

First we'll look at how to assign a function reference to the event handler attribute. If you'd like to call an ActionScript function when the user clicks on the p tag content, you can use code such as listing 7.12.

Listing 7.12   Assigning a function reference to the event handler attribute

```
package com.manning.airinaction.html {

    import flash.display.MovieClip;
    import flash.html.HTMLLoader;
    import flash.net.URLRequest;
    import flash.events.Event;

    public class Main extends MovieClip {

        private var _htmlLoader:HTMLLoader;

        public function Main() {
            _htmlLoader = new HTMLLoader();
            _htmlLoader.width = stage.stageWidth;
            _htmlLoader.height = stage.stageHeight;
            _htmlLoader.addEventListener(Event.COMPLETE, completeHandler);
            _htmlLoader.load(new URLRequest("example.html"));
            addChild(_htmlLoader);
        }

        private function completeHandler(event:Event):void {
            _htmlLoader.window.document.getElementById("p1").onclick =
            ⇒clickHandler;
        }

        private function clickHandler(event:Object):void {
            trace("click");
        }

    }

}
```

While there's nothing wrong with the preceding code, you also have the option of using the standard ActionScript event-dispatching model by registering an event listener using addEventListener(), as shown in listing 7.13.

Listing 7.13   Using `addEventListener()` to register event listeners

```
package com.manning.airinaction.html {

    import flash.display.MovieClip;
    import flash.html.HTMLLoader;
    import flash.net.URLRequest;
    import flash.events.Event;
    import flash.desktop.NativeApplication;

    public class Main extends MovieClip {

        private var _htmlLoader:HTMLLoader;

        public function Main() {
            _htmlLoader = new HTMLLoader();
            _htmlLoader.width = stage.stageWidth;
            _htmlLoader.height = stage.stageHeight;
            _htmlLoader.addEventListener(Event.COMPLETE, completeHandler);
            _htmlLoader.load(new URLRequest("example.html"));
            addChild(_htmlLoader);
        }

        private function completeHandler(event:Event):void {
            _htmlLoader.window.document.getElementById("p1").
            ➥addEventListener("click", clickHandler);
        }

        private function clickHandler(event:Object):void {
            trace("click");
        }

    }

}
```

What you'll notice in both listing 7.12 and 7.13 is that the method that handles the event accepts a parameter of type `Object` rather than type `Event`. The parameter acts much like an `Event` object, and it has `target` and `currentTarget` properties referencing the HTML element that dispatched the event, but the object isn't of type `Event`.

We've learned how to reference JavaScript and HTML elements from ActionScript. Now we'll look at a practical example that shows how to put it all together.

7.5.3   *Building a hybrid application*

You may find yourself wondering why you'd ever want to integrate HTML and JavaScript into one AIR application using what you've learned in the preceding sections. Consider the following scenario: you're building an AIR application that allows the user to fill out questionnaires. Once the AIR application is built, the product owner would like to be able to update the questionnaires using a Ruby on Rails application that runs on a server and generates new questionnaires as HTML files. The AIR application should always load these HTML files. In such a case, it makes a lot of sense to integrate the ActionScript and HTML using the skills you've just learned. In this section, we'll build a simple questionnaire example to illustrate how this might work.

Our simple application in this case will load an HTML page at runtime. The HTML page contains a questionnaire that might contain any number of questions and answers. The AIR application needs to be able to get the responses to the questionnaire when the user clicks on an HTML button. We're going to impose a rule that says that the questionnaire HTML file must name the Submit button with an ID of submit-Button, and the page must have a function called getSurveyResponses() that returns an array of the responses to the questionnaire.

For our example, the HTML file is called questionnaire.html, and listing 7.14 shows what this file looks like.

Listing 7.14   The questionnaire HTML file that displays a survey to the user

```
<html>
   <script>

      function getSurveyResponses() {
         var response;
         var options = document.questionnaire.skyColor;
         for(var i = 0; i < options.length; i++) {
            if(options[i].checked) {
               response = options[i].value;
            }
         }
         var response1 = {question: document.getElementById(
         ➥"question1").innerHTML, answer: response};

         options = document.questionnaire.skySize;
         for(i = 0; i < options.length; i++) {
            if(options[i].checked) {
               response = options[i].value;
            }
         }
         var response2 = {question: document.getElementById(
         ➥"question2").innerHTML, answer: response};

         return [response1, response2];
      }
   </script>
   <body>
      <h1>Questionnaire</h1>
      <form name="questionnaire">
         Please complete the following survey.
         <h2 id="question1">1. What is the color of the sky?</h2>
         <input type="radio" name="skyColor" value="grey">grey
         <input type="radio" name="skyColor" value="blue">blue
         <input type="radio" name="skyColor" value="no color">no color
         <input type="radio" name="skyColor" value="brown">brown

      <h2 id="question2">2. What is the size of the sky?</h2>
         <input type="radio" name="skySize" value="big">big
         <input type="radio" name="skySize" value="really big">
         ➥really big
         <input type="radio" name="skySize" value="not very big">
         ➥not very big
```

```
    <input type="radio" name="skySize" value="smaller than a cow">
    ➥smaller than a cow

    <h2>Click the button to finish
    <button id="submitButton">Submit Answers</button>

  </form>
</body>
</html>
```

Next we create a document class for an ActionScript project that uses an `HTMLLoader` object to load questionnaire.html. We listen for a `click` event on the Submit button, and when the user clicks the button, we'll retrieve the questionnaire responses using the `getSurveyResponses()` function and display them using ActionScript. Listing 7.15 shows the code.

Listing 7.15 The document class for the questionnaire application

```
package com.manning.airinaction.questionnaire {

    import flash.display.MovieClip;
    import flash.events.MouseEvent;
    import flash.html.HTMLLoader;
    import flash.net.URLRequest;
    import flash.events.Event;
    import fl.controls.TextArea;

    public class Main extends MovieClip {

        private var _htmlLoader:HTMLLoader;
        private var _textArea:TextArea;

        public function Main() {
            _htmlLoader = new HTMLLoader();
            _htmlLoader.width = stage.stageWidth;
            _htmlLoader.height = stage.stageHeight;
            _htmlLoader.addEventListener(Event.COMPLETE, completeHandler);
            _htmlLoader.load(new URLRequest("questionnaire.html"));    ◄─┐
            addChild(_htmlLoader);                                       Load
                                                        questionnaire.html ❶
            _textArea = new TextArea();
            _textArea.width = stage.stageWidth;
            _textArea.height = stage.stageHeight;

        }

        private function completeHandler(event:Event):void {
            _htmlLoader.window.document.getElementById("submitButton").
            ➥addEventListener(MouseEvent.CLICK, clickHandler);
        }                                                   Register for
                                                            click event ❷
        private function clickHandler(event:Object):void {
            removeChild(_htmlLoader);
            var responses:Array = _htmlLoader.window.getSurveyResponses();  ◄─┐
            _textArea.text = "";
            var response:Object;                            Get responses ❸
            for(var i:Number = 0; i < responses.length; i++) {
                response = responses[i] as Object;
                _textArea.text += response.question;
```

```
        _textArea.text += "\n\t" + response.answer + "\n\n";
      }
      addChild(_textArea);
    }
  }
}
```

This code is rather straightforward. It uses an `HTMLLoader` object to load an HTML file ❶. When the content has loaded, the code gets a reference to the button inside the HTML content and registers an event listener for the `click` event on that button ❷. When the user clicks on the button, the code calls a JavaScript function ❸ from the HTML content to get the survey responses and display them in a `textArea` component.

Now that we've seen how to control HTML and JavaScript elements from Action-Script, we'll look at how to gain access to ActionScript objects and classes from JavaScript.

7.5.4 *Handling standard JavaScript commands*

Many standard JavaScript commands get issued to the host application, which is typically a web browser. In the case of an AIR application, the host is the AIR application instead. You can configure an AIR application to handle these commands. For example, in a web browser, when the `window.status` property is set, the browser status display changes. In an AIR application, there's no default behavior in response to changes to the `window.status` property from JavaScript.

You can tell AIR to handle the method/property changes shown in table 7.1 by using an object of type `flash.html.HTMLHost`. An `HTMLHost` object has methods and properties that correspond to the JavaScript methods/properties, and those correspondences are also shown in table 7.1.

JavaScript	HTMLHost
`Window.status`	`updateStatus()`
`Window.location`	`updateLocation()`
`Window.document.title`	`updateTitle()`
`Window.open()`	`createWindow()`
`Window.close()`	`windowClose()`
`Window.blur()`	`windowBlur()`
`Window.focus()`	`windowFocus()`
`Window.moveBy()`	`windowRect()`
`Window.moveTo()`	`windowRect()`
`Window.resizeBy()`	`windowRect()`
`Window.resizeTo()`	`windowRect()`

Table 7.1 Correspondences between JavaScript and `HTMLHost`

Here's how it works:

1 Create a custom class that extends HTMLHost.
2 Override the methods as appropriate.
3 Assign an instance of the custom class to the htmlHost property of the HTML-Loader object into which you're loading the HTML content.

Next we'll look at how you can create a subclass of HTMLHost. The HTMLHost constructor allows for an optional Boolean parameter indicating whether the default behaviors should be used. Normally we just implement the same thing for the subclass constructor, as in the following code:

```
package com.manning.airinaction.html {
    import flash.html.HTMLHost;

    public class CustomHTMLHost extends HTMLHost {
        public function CustomHTMLHost(defaultBehavior:Boolean = true) {
            super(defaultBehavior);
        }

    }
}
```

Next we need to override any of the methods for which we want to define custom behavior. The updateStatus(), updateLocation(), and updateTitle() methods all accept one parameter: a string with the new value. We'll implement updateTitle() just to show one of them. There are many ways you could implement the methods of an HTMLHost subclass. In this case, we're just going to set the title of the main window:

```
package com.manning.airinaction.html {
    import flash.html.HTMLHost;
    import flash.desktop.NativeApplication;

    public class CustomHTMLHost extends HTMLHost {
        public function CustomHTMLHost(defaultBehavior:Boolean = true) {
            super(defaultBehavior);
        }

        override public function updateTitle(title:String):void {
            NativeApplication.nativeApplication.openedWindows[0].title =
            ↪title;
        }

    }
}
```

Next we'll implement createWindow(). The createWindow() method gets passed a parameter of type flash.html.HTMLWindowCreateOptions. This object corresponds to the options passed to the window.open() method as the third parameter. Table 7.2 shows the attributes in the window.open() method parameter and the corresponding properties in an HTMLWindowCreateOptions object.

The createWindow() method must return an HTMLLoader object. The create-Window() method doesn't receive information about what data to load into the

Window.open() attribute	HTMLWindowCreateOptions property
Width	width
Height	height
screenX, left	x
screenY, top	y
location	locationBarVisible
Menu	menuBarVisible
scrollbars	scrollBarsVisible
Status	statusBarVisible
toolbar	toolBarVisible
resizable	resizable
fullscreen	fullscreen

Table 7.2   Properties of
HTMLWindowCreateOptions

HTMLLoader object, nor does it need that information. The method merely needs to create an HTMLLoader object and return it. AIR takes care of loading the specified content into the HTMLLoader instance.

Next we'll look at an example of how you might implement createWindow(). In this case, we use the HTMLLoader.createRootWindow() method to create a new window using the dimensions specified in the parameter. Listing 7.16 shows the code.

Listing 7.16   Creating a new scrollable window for HTML content

```
package com.manning.airinaction.html {
    import flash.html.HTMLHost;
    import flash.desktop.NativeApplication;
    import flash.html.HTMLWindowCreateOptions;
    import flash.html.HTMLLoader;
    import flash.geom.Rectangle;

    public class CustomHTMLHost extends HTMLHost {
        public function CustomHTMLHost(defaultBehavior:Boolean = true) {
            super(defaultBehavior);
        }

        override public function updateTitle(title:String):void {
            NativeApplication.nativeApplication.openedWindows[0].title =
            ➥title;
        }

        override public function createWindow(
        ➥options:HTMLWindowCreateOptions):HTMLLoader {
            var bounds:Rectangle = new Rectangle(options.x, options.y,
            ➥options.width, options.height);
```

```
        var loader:HTMLLoader = HTMLLoader.createRootWindow(true,
        ➥null, true, bounds);
        return loader;
    }

  }
}
```

The `windowClose()`, `windowFocus()`, and `windowBlur()` methods all return no value and accept no parameters. In listing 7.17, we'll look at a simple implementation of `windowClose()` that closes the main application window.

```
package com.manning.airinaction.html {
    import flash.html.HTMLHost;
    import flash.desktop.NativeApplication;
    import flash.html.HTMLWindowCreateOptions;
    import flash.html.HTMLLoader;
    import flash.geom.Rectangle;

    public class CustomHTMLHost extends HTMLHost {
        public function CustomHTMLHost(defaultBehavior:Boolean = true) {
            super(defaultBehavior);
        }

        override public function updateTitle(title:String):void {
            NativeApplication.nativeApplication.openedWindows[0].title =
            ➥title;
        }

        override public function
        ➥createWindow(options:HTMLWindowCreateOptions):HTMLLoader {
            var bounds:Rectangle = new Rectangle(options.x, options.y,
            ➥options.width, options.height);
            var loader:HTMLLoader = HTMLLoader.createRootWindow(true,
            ➥null, true, bounds);
            return loader;
        }

        override public function windowClose():void {
            NativeApplication.nativeApplication.openedWindows[0].close();
        }

    }
}
```

You can override the `windowRect` property by overriding a setter method by that name. The `windowRect` property is of type `Rectangle`. Listing 7.18 illustrates how you can use the `windowRect` property to move or resize the main application window.

```
package com.manning.airinaction.html {
    import flash.html.HTMLHost;
    import flash.desktop.NativeApplication;
```

```
import flash.html.HTMLWindowCreateOptions;
import flash.html.HTMLLoader;
import flash.geom.Rectangle;

public class CustomHTMLHost extends HTMLHost {

    override public function set windowRect(value:Rectangle):void {
        NativeApplication.nativeApplication.openedWindows[0].bounds =
        ➥value;
    }

    public function CustomHTMLHost(defaultBehavior:Boolean = true) {
        super(defaultBehavior);
    }

    override public function updateTitle(title:String):void {
        NativeApplication.nativeApplication.openedWindows[0].title =
        ➥title;
    }

    override public function
    ➥createWindow(options:HTMLWindowCreateOptions):HTMLLoader {
        var bounds:Rectangle = new Rectangle(options.x, options.y,
        ➥options.width, options.height);
        var loader:HTMLLoader = HTMLLoader.createRootWindow(true,
        ➥null, true, bounds);
        return loader;
    }

    override public function windowClose():void {
        NativeApplication.nativeApplication.openedWindows[0].close();
    }

  }
}
```

All of this code can be tested by simply loading an HTML page into an HTMLLoader
object that uses an instance of CustomHTMLHost. Listing 7.19 illustrates an example
document class that does this.

Listing 7.19   Using `CustomHTMLHost` in a document class

```
package com.manning.airinaction.html {

    import flash.display.MovieClip;
    import flash.html.HTMLLoader;
    import flash.net.URLRequest;
    import com.manning.airinaction.html.CustomHTMLHost;

    public class Main extends MovieClip {

        private var _htmlLoader:HTMLLoader;

        public function Main() {
            _htmlLoader = new HTMLLoader();
            _htmlLoader.width = stage.stageWidth;
            _htmlLoader.height = stage.stageHeight;
            _htmlLoader.htmlHost = new CustomHTMLHost();
            _htmlLoader.load(new URLRequest("example.html"));
```

```
            addChild(_htmlLoader);
        }
    }
}
```

You can use an HTML file such as is shown in listing 7.20.

Listing 7.20 Using a custom `HTMLHost` implementation

```
<html>
    <body>
        <button onclick="window.document.title='New Title'">Title</button>
        <button onclick="window.open('http://www.manning.com/lott', null,
        ➥'screenX=0, screenY=10, width=500, height=400')">Window</button>
        <button onclick="window.close()">Close</button>
        <button onclick="window.moveTo(0, 0)" />Reset Location</button>
    </body>
</html>
```

Of course, you aren't limited to implementing the `HTMLHost` methods as we've shown in this example. You can implement them in many different ways to achieve many different effects. But the general principles apply no matter how you implement the methods.

NOTE   An `HTMLHost` object (or an instance of a subclass) automatically has a reference to the `HTMLLoader` object that it's assigned to. This reference is stored in a property called `htmlLoader`.

Using `HTMLHost`, you can indirectly call ActionScript methods from JavaScript. In the next section, we'll see how you can reference ActionScript elements more directly from JavaScript.

7.5.5 *Referencing ActionScript elements from JavaScript*

Not only can you reference JavaScript and HTML elements from ActionScript, but you can also reference ActionScript elements from JavaScript. In JavaScript, all of the AIR APIs, including standard Flash Player APIs, are available when the HTML page has been loaded into an AIR application. You can access classes and functions of the runtime from `window.runtime`. For example, if you want to call the global `trace()` method, you can do that using `window.runtime.trace()`. If classes are in packages, you can reference them using the fully qualified class name following the `window.runtime` reference. For example, listing 7.21 shows how to create a new `Shape` object and add it to the stage of the main window.

Listing 7.21 Creating a `Shape` object and adding it to the stage

```
<html>
    <script>

        function loadHandler() {
```

```
            var shape = new window.runtime.flash.display.Shape();
            shape.graphics.lineStyle(0, 0, 0);
            shape.graphics.beginFill(0, 1);
            shape.graphics.drawRect(0, 0, 100, 50);
            shape.graphics.endFill();
            var mainWindow = window.runtime.flash.desktop.
            ➥NativeApplication.nativeApplication.openedWindows[0];
            mainWindow.stage.addChild(shape);
        }

    </script>
    <body onload="loadHandler()">
    </body>
</html>
```

You'll notice that, in the first line of the function, we create a new `Shape` object using `window.runtime.flash.display.Shape` to reference the `Shape` class. Once we've created an object, we can reference all the properties and methods of that instance as we would in ActionScript. In this example, we reference the `graphics` property of the `Shape` object and call the methods of that property. We can also get a reference to the main window using `window.runtime.flash.desktop.NativeApplication.native-Application.openedWindows[0]`.

Not only can you reference standard classes, but you can also reference custom classes. In order to make custom classes available to JavaScript, you must load the HTML page into the same `ApplicationDomain` in which the ActionScript classes are defined. If you're not familiar with the concept of an `ApplicationDomain`, don't be concerned. Most developers haven't had reason to use `ApplicationDomain` before. Basically, an `ApplicationDomain` is a partition within which code is stored. Normally when you load an .swf or HTML content into an AIR application, it gets loaded into a new `ApplicationDomain`, distinct from the `ApplicationDomain` used by the main AIR application. That means that the loaded content doesn't have access to the code contained within the main `ApplicationDomain`. If you want to make the custom ActionScript classes available to JavaScript, you can load the HTML content into the main `ApplicationDomain` by setting the `runtimeApplicationDomain` property of the `HTMLLoader` object to `flash.system.ApplicationDomain.currentDomain`.

We next look at an example of referencing custom classes from JavaScript. We build off the questionnaire example we produced in the previous section. This time we create a custom `Response` type that we use to store the questionnaire response items. Listing 7.22 shows what this class looks like.

Listing 7.22   The custom `Response` class to model questionnaire response items

```
package com.manning.airinaction.questionnaire {

    public class Response {

        private var _question:String;
        private var _answer:String;

        public function get question():String {
```

```
        return _question;
    }

    public function get answer():String {
        return _answer;
    }

    public function Response(question:String, answer:String) {
        _question = question;
        _answer = answer;
    }

    }

}
```

The Response class has two getter methods: question and answer. We next modify the questionnaire.html file to use this custom type to store the responses that are returned by the getSurveyResponses() function. Listing 7.23 shows what the get-SurveyResponses() function looks like, with changes in bold.

Listing 7.23   Using the Response class in JavaScript

```
function getSurveyResponses() {
    var response;
    var options = document.questionnaire.skyColor;
    for(var i = 0; i < options.length; i++) {
        if(options[i].checked) {
            response = options[i].value;
        }
    }
    var response1 = new window.runtime.com.manning.
    ➥airinaction.questionnaire.Response(document.
    ➥getElementById("question1").innerText, response);

    options = document.questionnaire.skySize;
    for(i = 0; i < options.length; i++) {
        if(options[i].checked) {
            response = options[i].value;
        }
    }
    var response2 = new window.runtime.com.manning.
    ➥airinaction.questionnaire.Response(document.
    ➥getElementById("question2").innerText, response);

    return [response1, response2];
}
```

At this point, if we try to run the application, we'll get runtime JavaScript errors that will cause the application to fail silently because the Response class isn't defined at runtime. We next need to modify the document class to add the Response class and load the HTML page in the main ApplicationDomain. Listing 7.24 shows what this class looks like, with changes in bold.

Listing 7.24   Including the new Response class

```
package com.manning.airinaction.questionnaire {

    import flash.display.MovieClip;
    import flash.events.MouseEvent;
    import flash.html.HTMLLoader;
    import flash.net.URLRequest;
    import flash.events.Event;
    import fl.controls.TextArea;
    import flash.system.ApplicationDomain;
    import com.manning.airinaction.questionnaire.Response;

    public class Main extends MovieClip {

        private var _htmlLoader:HTMLLoader;
        private var _textArea:TextArea;

        public function Main() {
            _htmlLoader = new HTMLLoader();
            _htmlLoader.width = stage.stageWidth;
            _htmlLoader.height = stage.stageHeight;
            _htmlLoader.addEventListener(Event.COMPLETE, completeHandler);
            _htmlLoader.runtimeApplicationDomain =
              ApplicationDomain.currentDomain;
            _htmlLoader.load(new URLRequest("questionnaire.html"));
            addChild(_htmlLoader);

            _textArea = new TextArea();
            _textArea.width = stage.stageWidth;
            _textArea.height = stage.stageHeight;

        }

        private function completeHandler(event:Event):void {
            _htmlLoader.window.document.getElementById("submitButton").
              addEventListener(MouseEvent.CLICK, clickHandler);
        }

        private function clickHandler(event):void {
            removeChild(_htmlLoader);
            var responses:Array = _htmlLoader.window.getSurveyResponses();
            _textArea.text = "";
            var response:Object;
            for(var i:Number = 0; i < responses.length; i++) {
                response = responses[i] as Response;
                _textArea.text += response.question;
                _textArea.text += "\n\t" + response.answer + "\n\n";
            }
            addChild(_textArea);
        }
    }

}
```

Now that the Response class is compiled into the AIR application, it's available at runtime. Because the HTML page is getting loaded into the main ApplicationDomain, it can access the Response class, and everything in the application will work.

NOTE Because of security issues that you can read about in the next section, it isn't possible to allow access to custom classes to a file that's loaded outside the application domain. For example, the preceding application won't work if questionnaire.html is loaded from a remote server, because AIR won't allow the remote file access to custom ActionScript classes.

One thing that we haven't yet talked about is the effect of loading HTML from different locations, something we'll look at in the next section.

7.6 *Managing security issues*

Imagine for a moment that you're an expert plumber. You just got hired by MegaCorp to be their chief plumber, which is quite a prestigious job. However, on your first day at work you discover that not only are you responsible for standard plumbing duties, which are all within your realm of expertise, but you're also responsible for security for the entirety of MegaCorp, which has offices in every major city in the world. Sound ridiculous? We think it does. But this scenario isn't entirely dissimilar to the one we find ourselves in first as web developers and then as AIR application developers. While our primary expertise may be application development, we've discovered that we have a second and very serious duty: a responsibility for the security of those applications and their users. Although it may seem unfair (and we think it is), it looks as though it's impossible to completely separate the responsibilities of an application developer from those of an application security engineer. Therefore, although security issues may not currently be part of your expertise, we strongly encourage you to follow along with us through the next few sections as we look at how these issues relate to AIR application development.

AIR opens up a lot of possibilities to HTML and JavaScript content that gets loaded into an AIR application. As you've seen, AIR makes it possible for JavaScript to reference the AIR runtime, accessing all sorts of behaviors that wouldn't normally be available to JavaScript. Therefore, imagine what might happen if you built an AIR application that allowed a user to load any HTML from any location, and one of those pages had malicious JavaScript designed to use the AIR runtime to install a virus on the user's computer. If all HTML pages could get that level of unrestricted access to AIR, you could unwittingly open up the possibility of all sorts of problems for users. For exactly that reason, AIR puts in place a security model to mitigate those sorts of problems.

7.6.1 *Sandboxes*

All HTML content in AIR gets loaded into one of two security sandboxes, each of which has its own rules dictating what the HTML/JavaScript content has access to. These two sandboxes are called the *application sandbox* and the *nonapplication sandbox*. All content loaded from the application directory (the same directory or a subdirectory of the directory in which the application is installed) is automatically placed in the application domain. All other content is placed in the nonapplication domain. That means that all content loaded from a web server is placed in the nonapplication domain.

Each of these sandboxes has a different set of rules for what's permissible. In the application sandbox, restrictions are placed on what can be done dynamically at run-time. The following aren't permitted in the application sandbox:

- The `eval()` statement can't be used for anything other than object literals and constants.
- The `setTimeout()` and `setInterval()` functions can only be used to call function literals, and they won't evaluate strings.
- You can't use `innerHTML` or `outerHTML` to parse script elements.
- You can't use the `javascript` URI scheme.
- You can't import JavaScript files from outside the application domain.

These restrictions are in place as a layer of insurance against loading and running malicious JavaScript code. While these restrictions don't necessarily ensure that no malicious code will ever be loaded, they do create a reasonable level of insurance. This is important because, within the application domain, JavaScript has access to the full AIR API, meaning it can do things like read and write files on the local file system.

On the other hand, files loaded from outside the application domain have none of the restrictions applied to files loaded into the application domain. You may be thinking that it seems terribly unfair to restrict files in the application domain while allowing all the same behaviors to files outside the domain. Before you get too upset about this inequality, let us assure you that there's a tradeoff. You see, files loaded from outside the application domain don't have access to the AIR API. That means that, while a file outside the application domain can run `eval()` statements unhindered, it can't access the local file system.

We're about to tell you how you can work around the limitations of the sandbox restrictions. But before we disclose that information, we want to stress how important it is that you use this technique only when absolutely necessary, and even then you should exercise extreme caution. Err on the side of being too conservative in your use of bridging the sandbox security model. Remember that the sandboxes are in place for a reason, and you shouldn't subvert them without good cause. With that said, in cases when it's absolutely necessary, you can bridge the sandboxes using a technique called *sandbox bridging*.

7.6.2 *Sandbox bridges*

The principle of a sandbox bridge is that an HTML page loaded into an iframe of another HTML page has the ability to communicate with the parent, and the parent can communicate with the child. If the two pages are loaded into different sandboxes (because one is remote and one is in the application directory, for example), they can work together to get around their respective limitations. Typically, the way this works is that you create an HTML file with an iframe that resides in the application directory. This file will be loaded into the application sandbox. This local HTML file loads a nonapplication HTML file (such as a file from a remote server) into the iframe. The nonapplication HTML file is loaded into the nonapplication sandbox. Once the two pages are loaded, they can communicate by defining interfaces that they expose to each other.

You can define interfaces that each page can share with the other using variables called parentSandboxBridge and childSandboxBridge. You can create an object that has properties containing values or references to functions and assign it to a variable called parentSandboxBridge or childSandboxBridge within the HTML content loaded into the iframe. The following example illustrates how this can work. Listing 7.25 shows an HTML page containing an iframe. This HTML page can be saved in the application directory. When it's loaded, it'll have access to the AIR API.

Listing 7.25 Using a local HTML file with an iframe to load remote content

```
<html>
  <script>

    var bridge = new Object();          ❶ Create bridge
    bridge.writeMemo = writeMemo;          object

    function loadHandler() {
      window.document.getElementById("bridgeFrame").    ❷ Assign bridge
      ➥contentWindow.parentSandboxBridge = bridge;          to child
    }

    function writeMemo(subject, message) {
      var file = window.runtime.flash.filesystem.File.
      ➥documentsDirectory.resolvePath("memo.txt");
      var writer = new window.runtime.flash.filesystem.FileStream;
      writer.open(file, "write");
      writer.writeUTFBytes(subject + "\n" + message);
      writer.close();
    }

  </script>
  <body onload="loadHandler()">
    <iframe id="bridgeFrame"
        src="http://www.example.com/texteditor.html"
        width="100%" height="100%"></iframe>
  </body>
</html>
```

As you can see in this example, we create an object to serve as the bridge ❶ and we add a reference to a function. When the page loads, we assign the bridge to a variable called parentSandboxBridge within the content window of the iframe ❷. Now the content in the iframe will be able to call the writeMemo() function using the bridge. Listing 7.26 shows what the code for the content looks like.

Listing 7.26 Calling a function using the bridge

```
<html>
  <body>
    <button onclick="parentSandboxBridge.writeMemo(subject.value,
```

```
          ➥message.value)">Save Memo</button>
        <form>
          Subject <input type="text" id="subject" /><br />
          Message <textarea id="message" /><br />
        </form>
      </body>
    </html>
```

In this case, we're calling parentSandboxBridge.writeMemo() when the user clicks the button. This uses the bridge to allow the frame content, which is loaded into a nonapplication sandbox, to call a function within the parent HTML page, which is in the application sandbox. The result is that we can save a file locally even though the content for the file originates from an HTML page that's outside the application domain.

You can make values and functions accessible to the parent from the child page by using a variable called childSandboxBridge. This works almost identically. From within the content page, you can define an object with properties that contain values or references to functions and then assign that object to a variable called childSandboxBridge. From within the parent page, you can reference the childSandboxBridge from the content window of the iframe once it loads.

7.7   *Adding HTML to AirTube*

Now that we've learned more than we ever imagined about working with HTML in AIR, we can add a new feature to our AirTube application. After what you've just learned, this is going to seem remarkably easy. All we're going to do is allow the user to open the YouTube web page for a video in an AIR window. We'll add a button to the video window that allows the user to launch the HTML page in a window.

The first thing we do is update the HTMLWindow component to display HTML content using an HTML component. To do this, simply open HTMLWindow.mxml and add the code shown in bold in listing 7.27.

Listing 7.27   Showing HTML content in the HTMLWindow component

```
<?xml version="1.0" encoding="utf-8"?>
<mx:Window xmlns:mx="http://www.adobe.com/2006/mxml" layout="absolute"
  width="800" height="800" closing="closingHandler(event);">
  <mx:Script>
    <![CDATA[

      [Bindable]
      private var _url:String;

      public function set url(value:String):void {
        _url = value;
      }

      private function closingHandler(event:Event):void {
        event.preventDefault();
        visible = false;
      }

    ]]>
```

```
    </mx:Script>
    <mx:HTML id="html" location="{_url}" width="100%" height="100%" />
</mx:Window>
```

As you can see, the new code is short. We merely add an HTML component and bind its location attribute to a _url property. We'll next see how we set the URL for the HTML-Window component.

You'll recall that way back in chapter 2 when we initially created the skeleton for HTMLWindow, we also added a method to AirTube.mxml that opens the HTMLWindow instance. That method is called launchHTMLWindow(), and it looks like the following:

```
public function launchHTMLWindow(url:String):void {
    if(_htmlWindow.nativeWindow == null) {
        _htmlWindow.open();
    }
    else {
        _htmlWindow.activate();
    }
}
```

We're going to now update that method by adding one line to it. Listing 7.28 shows the new line of code in bold.

Listing 7.28   Setting the url property of the HTMLWindow instance

```
public function launchHTMLWindow(url:String):void {
    _htmlWindow.url = url;
    if(_htmlWindow.nativeWindow == null) {
        _htmlWindow.open();
    }
    else {
        _htmlWindow.activate();
    }
}
```

Now the only remaining task is to call the launchHTMLWindow() method when the user clicks a button in the VideoWindow. To do that, we need to make changes to the Video-Window component. Listing 7.29 shows what the updated code looks like with changes shown in bold.

Listing 7.29   Adding a button to launch HTML from the video window

```
<?xml version="1.0" encoding="utf-8"?>
<mx:Window xmlns:mx="http://www.adobe.com/2006/mxml" width="400"
    height="400" type="utility" closing="closingHandler(event);"
    creationComplete="creationCompleteHandler();">
    <mx:Script>
        <![CDATA[
            import com.manning.airtube.services.AirTubeService;
            import com.manning.airtube.data.ApplicationData;

            [Bindable]
            private var _applicationData:ApplicationData;
```

```
        private function creationCompleteHandler():void {
            _applicationData = ApplicationData.getInstance();
        }

        private function closingHandler(event:Event):void {
            event.preventDefault();
            visible = false;
        }

        private function saveOffline():void {
            AirTubeService.getInstance().saveToOffline(
            ➥_applicationData.currentVideo);
        }

        private function togglePlayback():void {
            if(videoDisplay.playing) {
                videoDisplay.pause();
                playPauseButton.label = "Play";
            }
            else {
                videoDisplay.play();
                playPauseButton.label = "Pause";
            }
        }

        private function viewOnYouTube():void {
            AirTube.getInstance().launchHTMLWindow(                    ❶ Launch HTML
            ➥_applicationData.currentVideo.video.url);                    window
            videoDisplay.pause();
            playPauseButton.label = "Play";                  ❷ Pause video
        }

    ]]>
</mx:Script>
<mx:VBox>
    <mx:Label text="{_applicationData.currentVideo.video.title}" />
    <mx:VideoDisplay id="videoDisplay"
source="{_applicationData.currentVideo.flvUrl}" width="400" height="300"
/>
    <mx:HBox id="progressContainer" width="100%"
        visible="{_applicationData.downloadProgress > 0}"
        includeInLayout="{progressContainer.visible}">
        <mx:Label text="download progress" />
        <mx:HSlider id="progressIndicator" enabled="false"
         width="100%" minimum="0" maximum="1"
         value="{_applicationData.downloadProgress}" />
    </mx:HBox>
    <mx:HBox>
        <mx:Button id="playPauseButton" label="Pause"
            click="togglePlayback();" />
        <mx:Button id="saveOfflineButton" label="Save Offline"
         visible="{!_applicationData.currentVideo.offline}"
         click="saveOffline();"
         enabled="{!(_applicationData.downloadProgress > 0)}" />
        <mx:Button label="View On YouTube"
            visible="{_applicationData.online}"                  ❸ Add button
            click="viewOnYouTube();" />
```

```
        </mx:HBox>
      </mx:VBox>
    </mx:Window>
```

This new code adds a button ❸ that calls `viewOnYouTube()` when clicked. When the user clicks the button, we first call the `launchHTMLWindow()` method of the application instance ❶, passing it the URL to the YouTube page that's stored in the `AirTubeVideo` object for the current video. And for good measure, we also pause the video ❷.

With the new changes, the application might look something like what you see in figure 7.9.

And with that, you now have a nearly complete AirTube application. All we have left to do with the application is enable the user to double-click on .atv files to launch them in AirTube, which we'll see in the next chapter.

Figure 7.9 Use the new button in the video window to launch the corresponding HTML page.

7.8   *Summary*

In this chapter, you've taken a whirlwind tour of all sorts of details for working with HTML in AIR. We started out by looking at the basics: how can you load and render HTML content within a Flash or Flex-based AIR application. We saw how to do that using the `HTMLLoader` class or the `HTML` component. Next we learned how to control how the AIR application loads and manages HTML content, including things such as caching content and handling authentication challenges from a server. We also looked at the broad topic of ActionScript-JavaScript cross-scripting, and you learned not only how to control JavaScript and HTML elements from ActionScript, but how to target ActionScript elements from JavaScript. Then, before closing the chapter with the additions to the AirTube application, we also looked at security issues related to HTML in AIR.

This chapter marks a real milestone in this book. This is the last chapter dedicated solely to adding new behavior to AIR applications. In the next chapter, we'll focus on tying together everything you've learned thus far and bundling it into a deployable application. Then we'll look at strategies for deploying the application and updating it when necessary.

Distributing and updating AIR applications

8

You've now learned a tremendous amount about Adobe AIR. With what you have learned in the preceding chapters, you've likely already built many applications (such as AirTube), or at least you have ideas for a few great applications. Whatever the current state of those applications, whether complete or still in the idea stages, at some point you're going to face the following questions:

- How can you best distribute the application to users?
- What is the best way for users to install the application?
- How can you make sure users are running the latest version of the application?
- How can you deploy updates?
- What are the various ways in which a user can run an AIR application?

In this chapter, we're going to look at each of these questions in more detail. We'll start by looking at how you can best distribute applications and allow users to install them.

8.1   Distributing applications

All AIR applications must be installed by the user on her system. That means that all users must download the .air file for the application and run it. There are two basic ways in which this can happen. One way is the simple route of providing access for users to directly download the .air file. You can provide instructions such that users know to download the .air file and double-click on it to install it once it's downloaded. This system is absolutely appropriate for intermediate to advanced computer users, because they're not likely to be easily confused. But for users who aren't necessarily familiar with AIR, this simple route may not be the most appropriate. Consider that, in order for this simpler approach to work, the user must already have the AIR runtime installed on her computer. If she doesn't, she may be confused as to why double-clicking the .air file does nothing or has unexpected results.

A second approach to distributing AIR applications requires a little more work on your part but provides a better user experience. This second approach is called *seamless install*, because it automatically detects whether or not the user has the AIR runtime installed and gives her an opportunity to install it if necessary before installing the AIR application. Furthermore, with seamless install, the downloading and running of the .air file is hidden from the user. In this section, we'll take a look at how to use the seamless install feature.

8.1.1   Using the default badge

All seamless installs take place from a web page. The user initiates installation by clicking on what's known as a *badge*. A badge is simply an .swf file that contains the necessary code to run the installation. As we'll see in the next section, you can create your own custom badges. To start, we'll look at how you can work with the default badge that Adobe provides as part of AIR. You can find the default badge files in the sam-ples\badge directory within the AIR SDK (located in the AIK directory within the Flash CS3 installation directory or in the Flex 3 SDK directory). Figure 8.1 shows what the default badge looks like with the sample image provided as part of the AIR SDK.

Download and open the AIR file to begin
the installation.

Figure 8.1   Use a badge such as the default one shown here to allow users to seamlessly install AIR applications.

The primary file you'll need is badge.swf. This is the file that contains all the necessary code for running a seamless install. You can use badge.swf to run an installation of any AIR application because it's designed to allow you to pass it values via FlashVars. The variables that you can pass it in this way are as follows:

- appname—The name of the AIR application this badge should allow users to install. This is the name that the badge will display if the user needs to install the AIR runtime.
- appurl—The absolute URL to the .air file.
- airversion—The version of the AIR runtime required by the application. For AIR 1.0, this value should always be the string 1.0.
- imageurl—The URL of an image file that the badge should load and display.
- buttoncolor—The default color of the button is black, but you can specify a color to use. You can specify the value using a hexadecimal string such as FF00FF.
- messagecolor—The default color of the message that appears below the button is black. You can specify a color to use if you prefer. Use a hexadecimal string such as FF00FF.

Of all these variables, just two are mandatory: appurl and airversion. The rest have default values.

Although you can use the HTML and JavaScript samples provided by Adobe alongside the default badge to embed the badge in an HTML page, we strongly recommend you use SWFObject to embed the .swf in an HTML page and set the FlashVars variables. If you're not already familiar with SWFObject, you can learn more about it and download everything you need from http://code.google.com/p/swfobject/. The following HTML/JavaScript code shows how you can embed badge.swf in an HTML page using SWFObject, specifying appurl, airversion, buttoncolor, and imageurl:

```
<!DOCTYPE html PUBLIC "-//W3C//DTD XHTML 1.0 Strict//EN"
➥"http://www.w3.org/TR/xhtml1/DTD/xhtml1-strict.dtd">
<html xmlns="http://www.w3.org/1999/xhtml" lang="en" xml:lang="en">
  <head>
    <title>AIR Application</title>
    <meta http-equiv="Content-Type" content="text/html;
    ➥charset=iso-8859-1" />

    <script type="text/javascript" src="swfobject.js"></script>

    <script type="text/javascript">
        var flashvars = new Object();
        flashvars.appurl =
        ➥"http://www.example.com/air/applications/example.air";
        flashvars.airversion = "1.0";
        flashvars.buttoncolor = "FF00FF";
        flashvars.imageurl = "image.jpg";
        swfobject.embedSWF("badge.swf", "badgeDiv", "217", "180",
        ➥"9.0.0", null, flashvars);
    </script>

  </head>
```

```
<body>
  <div id="badgeDiv">
    <p>Alternative content</p>
  </div>
</body>
</html>
```

The result of this code might look something like figure 8.2.

That is all that's necessary to enable seamless install for an AIR application. You can deploy the web page and badge.swf to a web site, and users will be able to install your AIR application without any advanced knowledge of AIR. The process is as follows:

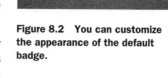

Figure 8.2   You can customize the appearance of the default badge.

1 The user visits the web site and clicks on the badge.

2 The badge detects whether the user has the necessary AIR runtime. If the correct runtime is installed, the user is automatically taken to step 4. Otherwise, he is notified that he needs to install the AIR runtime and is given the opportunity to install the runtime by clicking a button, as shown in figure 8.3.

3 If the user clicks the button to install the runtime, that occurs without the user having to navigate away from the badge. Figure 8.4 shows what this looks like. When the installation is complete, the user is taken automatically to step 4.

4 The .air file is downloaded and run automatically, without requiring interaction from the user until the installer has successfully launched. At that point, the user is taken through a wizard of steps requiring that he accept default values (such as installation location) or specify custom values.

5 Once the user steps through the wizard, the application is successfully installed.

Figure 8.3   The user is given the opportunity to install the AIR runtime if it's not already available on the system.

Figure 8.4   When the user selects to install the runtime, he will see a dialog showing download and installation progress.

We've just seen how to customize and use the default badge. Next we'll look at how you can create an entirely custom badge.

8.1.2 Creating a custom badge

The default badge will work for all AIR applications, and it allows for a degree of customization in appearance, making it useful for many cases. But there will inevitably be times when you want or need to completely customize a badge to the point where you must build the badge from scratch. In this section, we'll look at how badges work so that you can build your own badge if necessary.

All badges must load and rely upon an external .swf file that's hosted by Adobe on its web site. The URL to this .swf file is http://airdownload.adobe.com/air/browserapi/air.swf. This file contains several ActionScript methods that a badge needs to do its job. In order to call these methods, the loading .swf must load the external .swf into the same `ApplicationDomain`. To do this, you must create a `LoaderContext` object specifying the `ApplicationDomain.currentDomain` as the value of its `applicationDomain` property, and you must pass that `LoaderContext` object to the `load()` method of the `Loader` object used to load the external .swf. That may sound rather confusing. It's not confusing in practice though. All you need is something that looks like the following:

```
_loader = new Loader();
var context:LoaderContext = new LoaderContext();
context.applicationDomain = ApplicationDomain.currentDomain;
_loader.contentLoaderInfo.addEventListener(Event.INIT, initHandler);
_loader.load(new URLRequest("http://airdownload.adobe.com/air/
browserapi/air.swf"), context);
```

Once the `init` event occurs, the methods of the external .swf become available, and you can call them from the `content` property of the `Loader` object. Those methods are as follows:

- `getStatus()`—This method simply returns a string value of `available`, `unavailable`, or `installed`. A value of `available` means the AIR runtime is available for the operating system, though it's not currently installed. A value of `unavailable` means the AIR runtime isn't available for the operating system. A value of `installed` means the AIR runtime is currently installed.

- `getApplicationVersion()`—This method returns the version of a specific AIR application that's currently installed on the system. The method requires three parameters: the application ID and publisher ID for the AIR application you want to test for, and a function reference to use as a callback. Because the method works asynchronously, it requires the callback function. When the result is returned, the callback gets called and passed one parameter indicating the version of the application that's currently installed. If no version is currently installed, the version parameter will be null.

NOTE   You likely know how to determine the application ID for an AIR application. As you'll recall, you set the application ID in the descriptor file. But
you may be wondering how you can determine the publisher ID, because
you don't set that in the descriptor file. The publisher ID is created when
you originate an .air file, as `adt` creates a unique publisher ID for a certificate. Therefore, if you use the same certificate for more than one application, each will have the same publisher ID. But how do you retrieve the
publisher ID? You can read it at runtime programmatically using the
`NativeApplication.nativeApplication.publisherID` property.

- `installApplication()`—This method installs an AIR application from an .air
  file. It requires two parameters: the URL to the .air file and the AIR runtime version that is required. (It must be specified as a string.) AIR installers allow users
  to launch the application directly from the installer once they've installed it. If
  you'd like to pass any parameters to the application when it starts, you may pass
  them along as a third parameter to the `installApplication()` method. This
  third parameter can be an array of the values you want to pass to the application
  when it starts.

- `launchApplication()`—This method launches the AIR application (if it's
  installed). You must pass this method at least two parameters: the application ID
  and the publisher ID. You can also specify a third parameter, which is an array of
  values to pass to the application when it launches.

NOTE   In order to launch the application from the browser, the AIR application
must specify a value of `true` for the `allowBrowserInvocation` element in
its descriptor file.

It's not every day that we need to load an external .swf into the same `Application-
Domain`. Nor are we likely to easily remember the methods and their parameters from
the air.swf file. Therefore, one of the most convenient ways to work with these methods is to write a utility class that handles loading the .swf file into the same `Applica-
tionDomain` and provides an API that's inspectable by IDEs such as Flex Builder,
providing the opportunity for code hinting. Listing 8.1 shows how you can write such
a utility class, which we're calling `AirBadgeService`.

> **Listing 8.1   Using a class such as this simplifies working with air.swf**

```
package com.manning.airinaction.utilities {
    import flash.display.Loader;
    import flash.system.LoaderContext;
    import flash.system.ApplicationDomain;
    import flash.events.Event;
    import flash.events.EventDispatcher;
    import flash.net.URLRequest;

    public class AirBadgeService extends EventDispatcher {

        private var _loader:Loader;
```

```
        private var _service:Object;

        public function AirBadgeService() {

            _loader = new Loader();
            var context:LoaderContext = new LoaderContext();
            context.applicationDomain = ApplicationDomain.currentDomain;

            _loader.contentLoaderInfo.addEventListener(Event.INIT,
                                              initHandler);
            _loader.load(new URLRequest(
            ➥"http://airdownload.adobe.com/air/browserapi/air.swf"),
            ➥context);
        }

        private function initHandler(event:Event):void {
            _service = _loader.content;
            dispatchEvent(new Event(Event.COMPLETE));
        }

        public function getStatus():String {
            return _service.getStatus();
        }

        public function getApplicationVersion(applicationId:String,
        ➥publisherId:String, callback:Function):void {
            _service.getApplicationVersion(applicationId,
                                  publisherId,
                                  callback);
        }

        public function installApplication(url:String,
                                  runtimeVersion:String,
                                  parameters:Array = null):void {
            _service.installApplication(url, runtimeVersion, parameters);
        }

        public function launchApplication(applicationId:String,
                                  publisherId:String,
                                  parameters:Array = null):void {
            _service.launchApplication(applicationId,
                                  publisherId,
                                  parameters);
        }

    }
}
```

Now all you need to do is create an instance of AirBadgeService, listen for the complete event, and then call the methods, as in the following example:

```
<?xml version="1.0" encoding="utf-8"?>
<mx:Application xmlns:mx="http://www.adobe.com/2006/mxml" layout="vertical"
    creationComplete="creationCompleteHandler()">
    <mx:Script>
        <![CDATA[
            import com.manning.airinaction.utilities.AirBadgeService;

            private var _badgeService:AirBadgeService;
```

```
        private function creationCompleteHandler():void {
           _badgeService = new AirBadgeService();
           _badgeService.addEventListener(Event.COMPLETE,
                              completeHandler);
        }

        private function completeHandler(event:Event):void {
           textArea.text = "Detecting AIR runtime: " +
        ➥_badgeService.getStatus();
        }

     ]]>
  </mx:Script>
  <mx:TextArea id="textArea" />
</mx:Application>
```

Now you've had a chance to see just how simple it can be to distribute AIR applications. Even though seamless install requires a little work on your part, it's still easy and fast. Next we'll see what AIR provides you to help make sure users are always running the most updated version of an AIR application.

8.2   *Updating applications*

There are two basic strategies for updating applications: passive and active. In the passive approach, an application doesn't take responsibility for detecting newer versions, notifying the user, or helping the user to install updates. In the active approach, the application takes an active role in helping to ensure the user always has the latest version. Taking the passive approach requires no extra work on your part as a developer. If you simply make available new .air files that contain new versions of AIR applications, users can download them and install them on their own. However, the active approach requires a little additional effort on your part, and that is what we'll look at in this section.

In order to implement the active updating approach, your application must take the following steps:

1   Call a service that reports the latest version of the application. This service should be available on the Web in the form of an AMF, REST, SOAP, or similar service that your AIR application can call using standard Flash Player network features.

2   Compare the latest version with the installed version, and determine whether the user needs to update.

3   If the user needs to update, prompt the user to do so.

4   If the user accepts, download the .air file using techniques described in chapter 3.

5   Use a `flash.desktop.Updater` object to run the .air file.

Steps 1 through 4 are all either outside the scope of this book (as they're basic Flash or Flex skills) or are mentioned elsewhere in this book. Only step 5 concerns us right now. We haven't previously mentioned the Updater class, and we'll now go into the details of what it is and how you can use it.

The Updater class has just one responsibility: updating an AIR application. To use an Updater object, you need only create an instance and call the update() method, passing it two parameters: the reference to the .air file (which must be saved locally on the computer) and a string specifying the version of the AIR application. The following is an example that creates a reference to an .air file that resides locally and tells the Updater object to run the update:

```
var airFile:File = File.desktopDirectory.resolvePath(
➥"ExampleApplication_v2.air");
var updater:Updater = new Updater();
updater.update(airFile, "2.0");
```

This code assumes that ExampleApplication_v2.air already exists on the user's desktop, and that in its descriptor file it specifies its version as 2.0. When the updater runs, it takes the following steps:

1. It closes the current version of the AIR application that's running.
2. It verifies that the application ID and the publisher ID of the .air file are the same as the version that was just running.
3. It verifies that the version passed to the update() method is the same as the version specified in the .air file.
4. It installs the updated version (unless any of the previous steps failed).
5. It launches the new version.

If any of the steps fail (for example, the version strings are different), the old version is reopened instead of installing and running the new version.

Next we'll build an example application that is updatable. This application consists of little more than a text area component, a button, and the code to test for whether updating is necessary and to run the update if the user selects the option. Figure 8.5 shows what the application looks like.

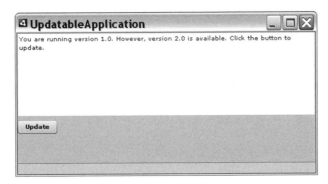

Figure 8.5 The updatable application displays a message to the user and allows him to update the application if a newer version is available.

To build this application, complete the following steps:

1   Create a file called latestversion.txt, and save the following text to the file:

```
2.0,http://www.yourserver.com/UpdatableApplication_v2.air
```

You'll use this file to determine the latest available version of the application. In this case, we're specifying that the latest version is 2.0 and the location of the .air file is UpdatableApplication_v2.air, placed on your server. This assumes that you're replacing www.yourserver.com with a domain name to which you have access. The reason for specifying version 2.0 is that it's greater than the version of the application we'll first create, install, and run.

2   Upload the latestversion.txt file to a web server, and note the URL from which it can be retrieved.

3   Create a new AIR project called UpdatableApplication.

4   Create a descriptor file for the application, as shown in listing 8.2. Note that the version is 1.0.

Listing 8.2   The descriptor file for UpdatableApplication

```
<application xmlns="http://ns.adobe.com/air/application/1.0">
  <id>com.manning.airinaction.UpdatableApplication</id>
  <filename>UpdatableApplication</filename>
  <name>UpdatableApplication</name>
  <version>1.0</version>
  <initialWindow>
    <content>UpdatableApplication.swf</content>
  </initialWindow>
</application>
```

5   Create the application MXML file, name it UpdatableApplication.mxml, and add the code shown in listing 8.3. This code merely sets up the basic structure of the application with a text area component and a button. We'll fill in the rest of the code in subsequent steps.

Listing 8.3   The main application MXML file for the updatable application

```
<?xml version="1.0" encoding="utf-8"?>
<mx:WindowedApplication xmlns:mx="http://www.adobe.com/2006/mxml"
    layout="absolute" creationComplete="creationCompleteHandler()">
    <mx:Script>
        <![CDATA[

            private var _latestVersion:String;
            private var _airFileUrl:String;

            private function creationCompleteHandler():void {
            }

            private function updateApplication():void {
            }

        ]]>
```

```
    </mx:Script>
    <mx:VBox width="100%" height="100%">
        <mx:TextArea id="textArea" width="100%" height="80%" />
        <mx:Button id="updateButton" label="Update"
            enabled="false" click="updateApplication();" />
    </mx:VBox>
</mx:WindowedApplication>
```

When the application starts, we want it to load the latestversion.txt file from the server, parse the data, and determine whether the current version of the application is the same as the latest version. Listing 8.4 shows the code that does this.

Listing 8.4   Loading the data from the server and parsing it

```
<?xml version="1.0" encoding="utf-8"?>
<mx:WindowedApplication xmlns:mx="http://www.adobe.com/2006/mxml"
    layout="absolute" creationComplete="creationCompleteHandler()">
    <mx:Script>
        <![CDATA[

            private var _latestVersion:String;                          Load      ①
            private var _airFileUrl:String;                     latestversion.txt

            private function creationCompleteHandler():void {
                var loader:URLLoader = new URLLoader();
                loader.addEventListener(Event.COMPLETE, completeHandler);
                loader.load(new URLRequest(
                ➥"http://www.yourserver.com/latestversion.txt"));
            }
                                                                  ② Parse
            private function completeHandler(event:Event):void {     version
                var loader:URLLoader = event.target as URLLoader;     string
                _latestVersion = loader.data.split(",")[0];
                var descriptor:XML =
                ➥NativeApplication.nativeApplication.applicationDescriptor;
                var air:Namespace = descriptor.namespaceDeclarations()[0];
                var currentVersion:String = descriptor.air::version;
                if(_latestVersion != currentVersion) {             Test if
                    _airFileUrl = loader.data.split(",")[1];       versions
                    textArea.text = "You are running version " +  ③ are equal
                    ➥currentVersion + ". However, version " +
                    ➥_latestVersion +
                    ➥" is available. Click the button to update.";
                    updateButton.enabled = true;
                }                                                   Parse .air
                else {                                           ④ file URL
                    textArea.text =
                    ➥"You appear to be running the latest version";
                }
            }

            private function updateApplication():void {
            }

        ]]>
    </mx:Script>
```

```
      <mx:VBox width="100%" height="100%">
        <mx:TextArea id="textArea" width="100%" height="80%" />
        <mx:Button id="updateButton" label="Update" enabled="false"
          click="updateApplication();" />
      </mx:VBox>
    </mx:WindowedApplication>
```

With this new code, we load the text from latestversion.txt ❶ and parse the version string from it ❷. We also use `NativeApplication.nativeApplica-tion.applicationDescriptor` to retrieve the version from the descriptor for the current application. If the two versions are different ❸, we parse the URL for the .air file ❹ and enable the Update button.

6 Add the code that allows the user to download the update to the application. Listing 8.5 shows this new code.

Listing 8.5 Downloading the .air file using a `URLStream` object

```
<?xml version="1.0" encoding="utf-8"?>
<mx:WindowedApplication xmlns:mx="http://www.adobe.com/2006/mxml"
    layout="absolute" creationComplete="creationCompleteHandler()">
    <mx:Script>
        <![CDATA[

            private var _latestVersion:String;
            private var _airFileUrl:String;

            private function creationCompleteHandler():void {
                var loader:URLLoader = new URLLoader();
                loader.addEventListener(Event.COMPLETE, completeHandler);
                loader.load(new URLRequest("http://
www.rightactionscript.com/latestversion.txt"));
            }

            private function completeHandler(event:Event):void {
                var loader:URLLoader = event.target as URLLoader;
                _latestVersion = loader.data.split(",")[0];
                var descriptor:XML =
NativeApplication.nativeApplication.applicationDescriptor;
                var air:Namespace = descriptor.namespaceDeclarations()[0];
                var currentVersion:String = descriptor.air::version;
                if(_latestVersion != currentVersion) {
                    _airFileUrl = loader.data.split(",")[1];
                    textArea.text = "You are running version " +
                    ➥currentVersion + ". However, version " + _latestVersion +
                    ➥" is available. Click the button to update.";
                    updateButton.enabled = true;
                }
                else {
                    textArea.text =
                    ➥"You appear to be running the latest version";
                }
            }

            private function updateApplication():void {
                var stream:URLStream = new URLStream();
```

```
        stream.addEventListener(ProgressEvent.PROGRESS,
                            progressHandler);
        stream.addEventListener(Event.COMPLETE,
                            downloadCompleteHandler);
        stream.load(new URLRequest(_airFileUrl));
        textArea.text = "Downloading update";
    }

    private function progressHandler(event:ProgressEvent):void {
    }

    private function downloadCompleteHandler(event:Event):void {
    }

        ]]>
    </mx:Script>
    <mx:VBox width="100%" height="100%">
        <mx:TextArea id="textArea" width="100%" height="80%" />
        <mx:Button id="updateButton" label="Update" enabled="false"
            click="updateApplication();" />
    </mx:VBox>
</mx:WindowedApplication>
```

This code uses a URLStream object to download the .air file. We also add event listeners to handle the progress and complete events.

7 Add the code that handles the progress and complete events. Listing 8.6 shows this code.

Listing 8.6 Displaying progress to the user and running the update when available

```
<?xml version="1.0" encoding="utf-8"?>
<mx:WindowedApplication xmlns:mx="http://www.adobe.com/2006/mxml"
    layout="absolute" creationComplete="creationCompleteHandler()">
    <mx:Script>
        <![CDATA[

        private var _latestVersion:String;
        private var _airFileUrl:String;

        private function creationCompleteHandler():void {
            var loader:URLLoader = new URLLoader();
            loader.addEventListener(Event.COMPLETE, completeHandler);
            loader.load(new URLRequest("http://
www.rightactionscript.com/latestversion.txt"));
        }

        private function completeHandler(event:Event):void {
            var loader:URLLoader = event.target as URLLoader;
            _latestVersion = loader.data.split(",")[0];
            var descriptor:XML =
NativeApplication.nativeApplication.applicationDescriptor;
            var air:Namespace = descriptor.namespaceDeclarations()[0];
            var currentVersion:String = descriptor.air::version;
            if(_latestVersion != currentVersion) {
                _airFileUrl = loader.data.split(",")[1];
                textArea.text = "You are running version " +
```

```
          ➥currentVersion + ". However, version " + _latestVersion +
          ➥" is available. Click the button to update.";
          updateButton.enabled = true;
        }
        else {
          textArea.text =
          ➥"You appear to be running the latest version";
        }
      }

      private function updateApplication():void {
        var stream:URLStream = new URLStream();
        stream.addEventListener(ProgressEvent.PROGRESS,
                      progressHandler);
        stream.addEventListener(Event.COMPLETE,
                      downloadCompleteHandler);
        stream.load(new URLRequest(_airFileUrl));
        textArea.text = "Downloading update";
      }

      private function progressHandler(event:ProgressEvent):void {
        textArea.text = "Downloading update " +
        ➥event.bytesLoaded + " of " + event.bytesTotal + " bytes";
      }

      private function downloadCompleteHandler(event:Event):void {
        textArea.text = "Download complete";
        var urlStream:URLStream = event.target as URLStream;
        var file:File =
        ➥File.applicationStorageDirectory.resolvePath(
        ➥"newVersion.air");
        var fileStream:FileStream = new FileStream();
        fileStream.open(file, FileMode.WRITE);
        var bytes:ByteArray = new ByteArray();
        urlStream.readBytes(bytes);
        fileStream.writeBytes(bytes);
        fileStream.close();
        var updater:Updater = new Updater();
        updater.update(file, _latestVersion);
      }

    ]]>
  </mx:Script>
  <mx:VBox width="100%" height="100%">
    <mx:TextArea id="textArea" width="100%" height="80%" />
    <mx:Button id="updateButton" label="Update" enabled="false"
        click="updateApplication();" />
  </mx:VBox>
</mx:WindowedApplication>
```

This new code displays progress to the user, and when the file is available, we
use a `File` and a `FileStream` object to write it to disk. Then we use an `Updater`
object to update to the latest version.

8 Create the .air file for `UpdatableApplication`, and install the application on
your system. When you run the application, it should notify you that you're

currently running version 1.0, but version 2.0 is available, and it should give you the option to download and install the update. Don't try to update, as we haven't yet created the updated version.

9 Create a new AIR project called UpdatableApplication_v2.

10 Create a descriptor file for this new application, as shown in listing 8.7. You'll notice that this descriptor file is exactly the same as the descriptor file for version 1.0 except that the version string is different. It's important that the ID of the application be the same.

> **Listing 8.7 The descriptor file for UpdatableApplication_v2**

```
<application xmlns="http://ns.adobe.com/air/application/1.0">
  <id>com.manning.airinaction.UpdatableApplication</id>
  <filename>UpdatableApplication</filename>
  <name>UpdatableApplication</name>
  <version>2.0</version>
  <initialWindow>
    <content>UpdatableApplication.swf</content>
  </initialWindow>
</application>
```

11 Create UpdatableApplication_v2.mxml as the application file, and copy the same code from UpdatableApplication.mxml. Although in most cases updates to applications should be different in some way, in this case we're only concerned with verifying that the update actually works, not adding new features.

12 Create the .air file for UpdatableApplication_v2. Use the same certificate that you used to create UpdatableApplication, because the publisher ID must be the same in the new version.

13 Upload the .air file to your web server to the location specified in latestversion.txt.

14 Run the version 1.0 of UpdatableApplication that's already installed on your system, and when prompted, click the Update button. You'll see that the file is downloading, and then you'll see the update run and the new version start.

We've just seen how to build active updating into an AIR application. Even if a user runs an update from outside the application itself (for example, running the update from a badge on a web page), you can still handle the update from the current version that's installed on the system, as we'll see in the next section.

8.3 *Launching AIR applications*

Launching an AIR application may seem a rather remedial topic. You're probably thinking that this surely couldn't be a subject worthy of much mention in a book such as this. After all, isn't launching an AIR application little more than double-clicking on an icon, selecting an option from a menu, or clicking a badge on a web page? Yes, you're correct; launching an AIR application is that simple. What we're more interested in is how you can build an AIR application that can respond based on how it was launched. For example, if a user launches an AIR application by double-clicking on a file of an associated type, you may want the AIR application to automatically open that file or otherwise read the contents of the file. In this section, we'll look at how AIR applications can know how they were launched.

8.3.1 Handling invoke events

When an AIR application launches, the `NativeApplication` (and `WindowedApplication`) dispatches an `invoke` event. When a user launches an application by double-clicking on the application icon, the `invoke` event doesn't contain much information. But in other circumstances the `invoke` event contains additional information that the AIR application can use. Notably, if the user launches an AIR application by double-clicking on a file of an associated type, the `invoke` event contains information about the file that the user clicked: a `File` object pointing to the file. You can use that information as is appropriate. For example, if the user launches an application by double-clicking on a file, it may be appropriate to read the contents of that file into the application when it starts.

The `invoke` event is of type `flash.events.InvokeEvent`, and the additional information, when available, is stored in the object's `arguments` property. The `arguments` property is an array of values. If the user has launched the application by clicking on a file, the file path will be stored in a `File` object as an element of the `arguments` property of the associated `invoke` event. In the next section, we'll see how to use an `invoke` event to open a file in the AirTube application.

8.3.2 Launching AirTube with a file

As you'll recall, way back in chapter 4 we enabled drag-and-drop behavior in AirTube that allowed a user to drag a video into the file system (for example, onto the desktop) and save an .atv file, which is a custom file format to which we save the ID of the video. Now we're going to allow the user to double-click on an .atv file to launch AirTube and open the video file.

1 Open the descriptor file for AirTube and define it as shown in listing 8.8. Notice that we're creating a file type association with files that have the file extension .flv.

Listing 8.8 Setting the file type association for AirTube

```xml
<?xml version="1.0" encoding="UTF-8"?>
<application xmlns="http://ns.adobe.com/air/application/1.0">
   <id>AirTube</id>
   <filename>AirTube</filename>
   <name>AirTube</name>
   <version>1.0</version>
   <initialWindow>
      <content>AirTube.swf</content>
   </initialWindow>
   <fileTypes>
```

```
    <fileType>
        <name>AirTubeVideo</name>
        <extension>atv</extension>
    </fileType>
  </fileTypes>
</application>
```

2 Update AirTubeService.as by adding a public method called getVideoById(). This method searches offline videos by ID. Listing 8.9 shows this method, which you should add to the AirTubeService class.

Listing 8.9 Adding the getVideoById() method to AirTubeService

```
public function getVideoById(id:String):void {
    var sql:SQLStatement = new SQLStatement();
    sql.addEventListener(SQLEvent.RESULT, getOfflineVideosResultHandler);
    sql.sqlConnection = _connection;
    sql.itemClass = Video;
    sql.text = "SELECT * FROM videos WHERE id = @id";
    sql.parameters["@id"] = id;
    sql.execute();
}
```

3 Update the code in AirTube.mxml. First we're going to modify the creation-CompleteHandler() method by adding the code to set AirTube as the default application for .atv files. Listing 8.10 shows this new code.

Listing 8.10 Registering AirTube as the default application for .atv files

```
private function creationCompleteHandler():void {
    _service = AirTubeService.getInstance();
    _service.key = "AhWz9YtBmWM";
    _videoWindow = new VideoWindow();
    _htmlWindow = new HTMLWindow();
    _instance = this;
    registerClassAlias("com.manning.airtube.data.AirTubeVideo",
    ➥AirTubeVideo);
    if(!NativeApplication.nativeApplication.
    ➥isSetAsDefaultApplication("atv")) {
       NativeApplication.nativeApplication.
       ➥setAsDefaultApplication("atv");
    }
}
```

4 Add an invoke attribute to the WindowedApplication tag, telling the AIR application to call a method named invokeHandler() when the invoke event occurs:

```
<mx:WindowedApplication xmlns:mx="http://www.adobe.com/2006/mxml"
   layout="absolute"
   creationComplete="creationCompleteHandler();" width="800"
height="600"
   closing="closingHandler();" invoke="invokeHandler(event);">
```

5 Define `invokeHandler()`. This method accepts an `InvokeEvent` parameter. We determine whether the object's `arguments` property has any elements. If it does, we next determine whether the first element is the path to a file with a file extension of .atv. If it is, we read from the file and call `getVideoById()` to retrieve the video and display it in the results. Note that this assumes that the file is saved locally. Listing 8.11 shows the new `invokeHandler()` method we're adding to the AirTube.mxml.

Listing 8.11 The `invokeHandler()` method in AirTube.mxml

```
private function invokeHandler(event:InvokeEvent):void {
    if(event.arguments.length > 0) {
        var file:File = new File(event.arguments[0]);
        var fileName:Array = file.name.split(".");
        if(fileName[1] != undefined) {
            if(fileName[1] == "atv") {
                var reader:FileStream = new FileStream();
                reader.open(file, FileMode.READ);
                reader.position = 0;
                var id:String = reader.readUTF();
                _service.getVideoById(id);
            }
        }
    }
}
```

6 Export the .air file for AirTube, install it, and run it. Test the new functionality for yourself.

We've now seen how to listen for `invoke` events, and we've even used this to add new behavior to AirTube. Next we'll look at how to handle similar `invoke` events from a browser.

8.3.3 Listening for browser events

We just learned that, when an application starts or when the user triggers the application by double-clicking on a file of an associated file type, an AIR application dispatches an `invoke` event. Similarly, when the user launches an application from the browser, the application dispatches a `browserInvoke` event. Whereas the `invoke` event is of type `InvokeEvent`, `browserInvoke` is of type `flash.events.BrowserInvokeEvent`. These events, like `invoke` events, contain an `arguments` property that's an array of parameters passed to the application. In the case of `browserInvoke` events, the parameters are any values passed along via the third parameter of the `launchApplication()` method.

Unlike `invoke` events, you can't register for `browserInvoke` events directly from a `WindowedApplication`. You must register for events directly from the `NativeApplication` instance, regardless of whether you're building a Flash- or Flex-based application. The following shows how to register for the `browserInvoke` event:

```
NativeApplication.nativeApplication.addEventListener(
➥BrowserInvokeEvent.BROWSER_INVOKE, browserInvokeHandler);
```

Perhaps the easiest way to understand the browserInvoke event is to see it working via an example. We'll next build a simple application that demonstrates how this event works:

1 Create a new AIR project called BrowserInvoke.
2 Create a main application MXML file called BrowserInvoke.mxml, and add the code from listing 8.12 to the file. This code displays the application ID and the publisher ID when it starts. When it receives a browserInvoke event, it displays all the parameters passed to it.

Listing 8.12   The main application file displays the parameters passed to it

```
<?xml version="1.0" encoding="utf-8"?>
<mx:WindowedApplication xmlns:mx="http://www.adobe.com/2006/mxml"
    layout="absolute" creationComplete="creationCompleteHandler()">
    <mx:Script>
        <![CDATA[

            private function creationCompleteHandler():void {
                textArea.text = "application ID: " +
                ➥NativeApplication.nativeApplication.applicationID;
                textArea.text += "\npublisher ID: " +
                ➥NativeApplication.nativeApplication.publisherID;
                NativeApplication.nativeApplication.addEventListener(
                ➥BrowserInvokeEvent.BROWSER_INVOKE, browserInvokeHandler);
            }

            private function browserInvokeHandler(
            ➥event:BrowserInvokeEvent):void {
                textArea.text += "\n* arguments: " +
                ➥event.arguments.length;
                for(var i:Number = 0; i < event.arguments.length; i++) {
                    textArea.text += "\n\t" + event.arguments[i];
                }
            }

        ]]>
    </mx:Script>
    <mx:TextArea width="100%" height="100%" id="textArea" />
</mx:WindowedApplication>
```

3 Create a descriptor file with the value shown in listing 8.13. Note that allow-BrowserInvocation is set to true.

Listing 8.13   Set allowBrowserInvocation to true in the descriptor file

```
<?xml version="1.0" encoding="UTF-8"?>
<application xmlns="http://ns.adobe.com/air/application/1.0">
    <id>com.manning.airinaction.BrowserInvoke</id>
    <filename>BrowserInvoke</filename>
    <name>Initialize</name>
```

```
    <version>1.0</version>
    <initialWindow>
        <content>BrowserInvoke.swf</content>
    </initialWindow>
    <allowBrowserInvocation>true</allowBrowserInvocation>
</application>
```

4 Export the .air file and install it.

5 Run the application and copy the publisher ID. You'll need this in order to launch the application from the browser.

6 Create a new web project called LaunchFromBrowser.

7 Create a main application MXML document called LaunchFromBrowser.mxml and add the code from listing 8.14 to it. This code uses `AirBadgeService` from listing 8.1.

Listing 8.14   Using a web application to launch the AIR application

```
<?xml version="1.0" encoding="utf-8"?>
<mx:Application xmlns:mx="http://www.adobe.com/2006/mxml"
layout="vertical"
    creationComplete="creationCompleteHandler()">
    <mx:Script>
        <![CDATA[
            import com.manning.airinaction.utilities.AirBadgeService;

            private var _badgeService:AirBadgeService;

            private function creationCompleteHandler():void {
                _badgeService = new AirBadgeService();
                _badgeService.addEventListener(Event.COMPLETE,
                                    completeHandler);
            }                                             ❶ If AIR is
                                                            installed
            private function completeHandler(event:Event):void {
                if(_badgeService.getStatus() == "installed") {
                    _badgeService.getApplicationVersion(    Get
                    ➥"com.manning.airinaction.BrowserInvoke",  application
                    ➥" YourPublisherID ", versionHandler);   version
                    launchButton.enabled = true;
                }
            }

            private function versionHandler(version:String):void {
                textArea.text = "version " + version + " installed";
            }

            private function launchApplication():void {
                _badgeService.launchApplication(       ❷ Launch
                ➥"com.manning.airinaction.BrowserInvoke",  application
                ➥"YourPublisherID", ["a", "b", "c", "d"]);
            }

        ]]>
    </mx:Script>
    <mx:TextArea id="textArea" />
```

```
    <mx:Button id="launchButton" label="Launch"
        click="launchApplication();" enabled="false" />
</mx:Application>
```

In this code, we test whether AIR is installed ❶, and if it is, we enable the button allowing the user to launch the application. (We also display the installed version number for good measure.) When the user clicks the button, we call `launchApplication()` ❷ and we pass the application four parameters: a, b, c, and d. Note that you must replace `YourPublisherID` in two places in the code. Use the publisher ID you copied when you ran BrowserInvoke.

8 Close BrowserInvoke if it's still running. Run LaunchFromBrowser in a browser and click the Launch button. You'll see BrowserInvoke launch, and it'll display the four parameters you passed it from the browser.

Now you know not only how to launch an application in the standard way by double-clicking the application icon or selecting a menu item, but also two additional ways to launch applications. You learned how to launch an application using an associated file type, and you just learned how to launch an application from the browser, passing it parameters. With that, you're now an expert on how to launch AIR applications, and we're ready to wrap up the book.

8.4 Summary

In this chapter, we learned how to install, update, and launch AIR applications. You learned that badges are web-based .swf files that allow users to install AIR applications using seamless install, and you learned several ways to create badges. Then you learned how to use the `Updater` class to handle updates to an application. And you also learned how to handle `invoke` events triggered both by the user double-clicking associated file types and by clicking on web-based triggers. You had a chance to apply some of these concepts in a few examples, including the AirTube application.

And with that we rounded out our study of AIR. Believe it or not, we've just reached the end of this book. However, as you no doubt know from your own experience, every ending is really a new beginning. In this case, it may be the end of your introduction to Adobe AIR, but it's just the beginning of the possibilities of what you can build. Please visit this book again whenever you need to review a particular topic, but don't be limited by the contents of this book. We've shown you only the tip of the iceberg. As far as AIR is concerned, you're limited only by your imagination. We wish you all the best in your endeavors.

index